ALL-AMERICAN CITY

ALL-AMERICAN CITY

BLUSTER, BOOM, AND BUST IN WICHITA

CHASE M. BILLINGHAM

UNIVERSITY PRESS OF KANSAS

Published by the University Press of Kansas (Lawrence, Kansas 66045), which was organized by the Kansas Board of Regents and is operated and funded by Emporia State University, Fort Hays State University, Kansas State University, Pittsburg State University, the University of Kansas, and Wichita State University.

British Library Cataloguing-in-Publication Data is available.
EU Authorised Representative Details: Easy Access System Europe Mustamäe tee 50, 10621 Tallinn, Estonia | gpsr.requests@easproject.com

Library of Congress Cataloging-in-Publication Data
Names: Billingham, Chase M. (Chase Michael) author
Title: All-American city : bluster, boom, and bust in Wichita / Chase M. Billingham.
Description: [Lawrence, Kansas] : University Press of Kansas, 2026. | Includes bibliographical references and index.
Identifiers: LCCN 2025031912 (print) | LCCN 2025031913 (ebook) | ISBN 9780700640928 paperback | ISBN 9780700640935 ebook
Subjects: LCSH: Economic development—Kansas—Wichita | Urban policy—Kansas—Wichita | Wichita (Kan.)—Economic conditions—21st century | Wichita (Kan.)—Social conditions—21st century | BISAC: SOCIAL SCIENCE / Sociology / Urban | SOCIAL SCIENCE / Regional Studies
Classification: LCC HC108.W56 B55 2026 (print) | LCC HC108.W56 (ebook) | DDC 330.9781/423—dc23/eng/20260121
LC record available at https://lccn.loc.gov/2025031912
LC ebook record available at https://lccn.loc.gov/2025031913

For Barry Bluestone, a champion of equitable cities, strong data analysis, and sound public policy.

So home, traveler, past the newspaper language factory
under Union Station railroad bridge on Douglas
to the center of the Vortex

—Allen Ginsberg, "Wichita Vortex Sutra," 1966

CONTENTS

FIGURES AND TABLES

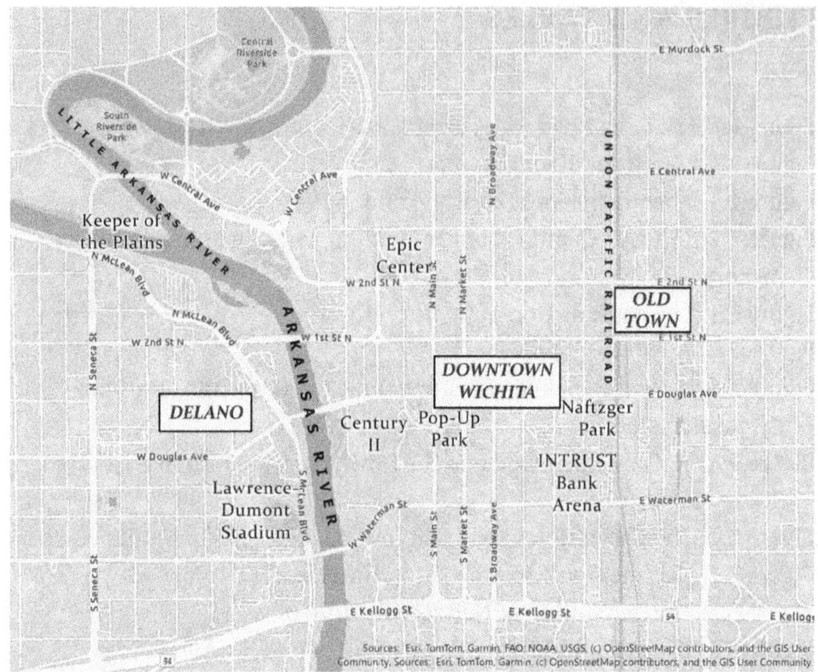

Map portraying key locations in Downtown Wichita. Source: Esri, TomTom, Garmin, FAO, NOAA, USGS, © OpenStreetMap contributors, and the GIS User Community.

PREFACE

When US Figure Skating announced in 2024 that it had selected Wichita as the host city for its upcoming National Championships competition, the small but passionate figure skating community in Kansas's largest city was ecstatic. Smaller regional competitions had come to Wichita in the past but nothing nearly as exciting as nationals. Athletes in the Wichita Figure Skating Club—including my son, Alistair, an aspiring nine-year-old figure skater just beginning to work on his first jumps—would have the chance to meet their idols, learn from them, and watch them on the country's biggest stage. Skating legend Brian Boitano came to Wichita to deliver the announcement, and Alistair was thrilled when Boitano took time out of his interactions with local business leaders to talk with him and give him some pointers on his Salchow and waltz jumps.

The announcement was important not just to admirers of the athleticism, grace, and artistry of the country's top figure skaters. To elected officials, tourism promoters, and the business elite, hosting the championships was a sign that Wichita had risen into a new tier of US cities. Reflecting the culmination of years of efforts to develop relationships with US Figure Skating, the competition would give city leaders the chance to show off Wichita on a national stage. It would inject millions of dollars into the local economy, showcase the cityscape to television viewers, and vindicate their effort two decades earlier to build a new sports arena in the middle of a deteriorated downtown district, along with a separate city-owned training facility nearby known as the Wichita Ice Center.

Athletes, their families, fans, and spectators made their way to Wichita the following January, and the competition lived up to the hype. Elite athletes gave breathtaking performances, and Wichitans relished the chance to see the jumps, hear the distinctive sound of blades carving into ice, and witness the joy of victory and tearful heartbreak of defeat up close. Alistair and several other young figure skaters served as "sweepers" during the competition, collecting the flowers, stuffed animals, and other gifts thrown onto the ice after each performance. They delighted in the opportunity to share the ice with the stars.

For most of the events during the National Championships, attendance was fairly light, and the arena rarely filled to anywhere near capacity. Some attendees complained in online forums that Wichita, with its sparse downtown, limited dining options, and lack of convenient flights for out-of-town visitors, was a letdown compared to previous host cities like Columbus, Ohio. Nevertheless, the weekend was deemed a success overall. Most athletes, coaches, and spectators left the city, but some stayed behind, including a group of youth skaters attending a post-competition training camp at the Wichita Ice Center.

Days later, members of that group—nearly two dozen people, including figure skaters as young as eleven, their parents, and their coaches—were among the sixty-seven victims of the deadliest air disaster in the United States in nearly a quarter century when their aircraft from Wichita collided with a US Army helicopter as it was preparing to land in Washington, DC on January 29, 2025.

News of the tragedy ricocheted across country, with outpourings of grief and pledges to figure out what had gone wrong. The country's figure skating community was rocked by the disaster, their grief aggravated by the fact that it came in such stark contrast to the joy they had just shared together in Wichita.

The city, too, entered a period of mourning. Along with the skaters, several Kansans lost their lives in the collision, and neighbors and communities came together to remember the victims and provide support for their loved ones. Local community leaders expressed heartfelt demonstrations of sorrow. For some of them, however, their grief was directed not just toward the lost lives but also toward the city's lost opportunity to reap the rewards of successfully hosting a marquee athletic event. The fact that the tragedy took the form of an air collision only exacerbated the reputational damage to a city that calls itself the "Air Capital of the World"—a reference to the long history and critical importance of the aircraft manufacturing industry for the region's economy. "This is now unfortunately part of Kansas aviation history," the director of the city's Aviation Museum told the *New York Times*.[1]

Business and government leaders noted that the air disaster was only possible because of the recent success that they had achieved in finally securing a daily direct commercial flight from the nation's capital to the Air Capital, which, despite its nickname, offers few direct connections to major American cities from its commercial airport. That flight "really has helped boost Wichita trade," the museum director emphasized. While claiming the lives of so many innocent individuals, the crash also threatened to undo those hard-won economic gains for the city.

In the Air Capital, the air is the source of the capital. Wichita's unlikely growth into one of the country's largest cities was built upon the rise of its aviation manufacturing sector in the early twentieth century; since that time, the city's fortunes have been intimately tied to the ups and downs of that economic sector. For decades, though, as that industry faltered, local leaders acknowledged that future growth would depend on broadening the region's economic base beyond building airplanes.

Those efforts aimed at diversifying the regional economy have achieved only very modest success, however. In part, that has resulted from unfortunate—and, as in the case of the 2025 air disaster, completely unpredictable—setbacks that have been out of the hands of local leaders. More broadly, though, Wichita's growth aspirations have run up against the fact that dozens of other midsized cities across the country are consistently competing for the same limited set of investments, jobs, visitors, and mobile residents. In their attempts to stand out from the pack, cities rely upon similar economic strategies, replicate each other's economic development tools, and mimic "best practices" drawn from the successes of their competitors. The dilemmas faced by urban leaders who strive to set their cities apart from their peers, while simultaneously imitating those same peers, are not limited to Wichita. Yet the manifestation of those dilemmas in this city's history are so evident that the social and economic history of Wichita can provide lessons for municipal leaders—and their critics—in all American cities.

All-American City tells that story.

INTRODUCTION
CREATING AUTHENTICITY THROUGH MIMICRY

An excited buzz rolled through the auditorium of Newman University, a small Catholic college west of Downtown Wichita, as hundreds waited anxiously in the packed hall for the presentation to begin. The crowd included many of the city's economic and political elite—elected officials from the city and county governments, bank presidents, prominent business executives, and leading figures from the education and nonprofit sectors, among others. Standing on the stage to welcome the evening's presenters were Junetta Everett, the chair of the Wichita Regional Chamber of Commerce, and Jon Rolph, the chair of the Greater Wichita Partnership, a public-private partnership created to promote regional growth. As the presenters approached the dais, audible cheers went up from attendees sporting shirts featuring slogans like "Make Wichita Win" and "Bravely Onward." Something big was about to happen.

It was the evening of January 14, 2020, and the event that had brought so many public- and private-sector leaders out to Newman was the unveiling of the final proposal of the Riverfront Legacy Master Plan, a comprehensive redevelopment project that would completely transform the east bank of the Arkansas River through Downtown Wichita, clearing most of the existing structures within more than fifty acres of urban territory to make way for a new performing arts center, a new convention center, new parks, parking garages, and office space, all situated within a completely redesigned street grid. Alongside those big-ticket items, the plan featured fascinating novelties like a new pedestrian bridge spanning the river, a boat dock, and a public swimming pool carved into the river itself.[1]

Todd Voth, the founder and principal of the Kansas City architectural design firm Populous, received a hero's welcome as he approached the podium following an introduction by Everett. Noting the crowd size and excitement, Voth, in turn, showered praise on the people of Wichita, encouraging them to applaud themselves for their remarkable level of engagement. "We do this all over the country and all over the world," he boasted. "In the community engagement processes that we get into, we have *never* had six hundred people except in Wichita, Kansas. You should give yourself a hand." The crowd gladly obliged, collectively whooping in support of themselves and their city.

Feeding on the excitement in the audience, Voth exclaimed that he, his team, and the city leaders that had hired them wanted to embrace "a bold vision" for Wichita. "We don't want an OK vision; we want a bold vision to take us into the future." He cautioned, though, that realizing that bold vision would require a historically conservative community to undertake massive—and expensive—change. Not everyone would be comfortable with such change, he admitted, but leaning into big and ambitious change was necessary if Wichita wanted something "that distinguishes you from your competition and from other cities."

Distinctive. Unique. Authentic. These would become watchwords in the campaign to revitalize Wichita and to set it apart in the perpetual competition among American urban centers for jobs, investment, population growth, and stature. What would that distinctive, unique, authentic, and bold vision for Wichita's future look like in practice, though? What elements of the Riverfront Legacy Master Plan would help to set Wichita apart from its peers? To provide details, Voth handed the microphone over to his colleague, senior planner Amber Luther, who explained each component of this plan to make Wichita truly distinctive. To illustrate how such a plan to set Wichita apart could be successfully implemented, Luther pointed to the successes that other cities had enjoyed after implementing plans lifted from the same urban design playbook.

"Oklahoma City is probably the one that most directly aligns with what we think you guys should do," she said.

As she spoke, she showed the audience an image of that city's MAPS project, a long-running series of urban redevelopment initiatives featuring a new Populous-designed convention center spilling out onto a series of new parks, just as Wichita's Populous-designed Riverfront Legacy Master Plan would do.[2] From there, she highlighted the success of the Gathering Place, a massive complex of riverfront parks and cultural amenities in Tulsa, then drew attention to the gains in property values that had ensued following the construction of Klyde Warren Park, an inner-city green space surrounded by arts facilities, restaurants, and hotels in Downtown Dallas.[3]

* * *

At the heart of the Riverfront Legacy Master Plan stood an impressive new pedestrian bridge connecting the east and west banks of the Arkansas River, the waterway that courses through the center of the city (Figure I.1). Though arguably superfluous—existing spans sitting less than 1,000 feet in both directions from the proposed new bridge already allowed pedestrians to cross the river easily—this bridge featured prominently in the presentation to the audience at Newman University that night. In a bright, colorful rendering, a diverse collection of imagined visitors traversed the bridge, stopped to admire the river and the Wichita skyline, or posed for pictures. One figure, in particular, stood out in the rendering: a young white man in a blue shirt waving a big blue novelty foam finger adorned with the logo of the city's new Minor League baseball team, the Wichita Wind Surge. This image resonated with the crowd, who were acutely familiar with the new team (which had yet to play its first game in the highly anticipated and recently completed stadium on the west bank of the river). The man with the foam finger, proudly sporting his local pride and looking eagerly in the direction of the stadium, would have fit in well among the audience that evening. Meanwhile, the bridge, while striking in appearance, was not a surprising element of the overall design, as it had previously been floated as a key component of the riverfront stadium development project saga that had gripped the city for the prior two years.[4]

Baseball in Wichita has a long and storied past, and in the twenty-first century, the city's leaders invested their hopes in the potential for that legacy to provide the foundation for newfound prosperity. The first recorded game in Wichita was played in 1874, just four years after the city's incorporation. For years, the young city hosted baseball games at Island Park, a ballpark located on Ackerman Island, situated in the middle of the Arkansas River adjacent to Downtown Wichita. That ballpark burned down in 1933, and soon thereafter, using funds from the Works Progress Administration (WPA) during the New Deal era, the city employed men with shovels and wheelbarrows to systematically dismantle the entire island in order to streamline the river channel. Simultaneously, the WPA sponsored the construction of a new baseball stadium on the west bank of the river, named Lawrence Stadium after Col. Robert Lawrence, an early city pioneer, which opened in 1934. Local journalist and businessman Raymond "Hap" Dumont organized the National Baseball Congress (NBC), a semiprofessional league which would draw teams from across the US to play in its annual

Figure I.1. Arkansas River waterfront and Downtown Wichita skyline. Photo by Chase Billingham.

tournament in Lawrence Stadium (later renamed Lawrence–Dumont Stadium to honor the NBC founder) every year for more than eight decades. Through the NBC, noted players like Satchel Paige and Tom Seaver made their way through Wichita. Over the years, a number of teams—amateur, semiprofessional, and professional—cycled through the city and called Lawrence-Dumont their home. Beginning in 1987, the stadium housed the Wichita Wranglers, the AA Minor League affiliate of the Kansas City Royals, but after the Wranglers moved to Springdale, Arkansas in 2007, Wichita went for over a decade without a Major League Baseball–affiliated team.[5]

By 2017, eighty-three-year-old Lawrence-Dumont was showing its age, and the independent-league baseball team that had occupied the stadium

following the Wranglers' departure, the Wichita Wingnuts, was failing to draw large crowds or generate major excitement along the river corridor. Following a drawn-out process of behind-the-scenes negotiations (which would later draw scrutiny from Minor League Baseball authorities for potential violations of league rules), city officials announced in late 2018 that they had persuaded the New Orleans Baby Cakes to relocate to Wichita. The Baby Cakes, an affiliate of the Miami Marlins organization, played at the AAA level, just one step below the major leagues and higher than the AA affiliation that the Wranglers had previously held. Wichita mayor Jeff Longwell touted that higher level as evidence of the city's prowess and positive growth trajectory, chastising naysayers for believing that "a lower division league was good enough for Wichita" based on a "misperception that we're a quiet little Midwestern town."[6]

To lure the Baby Cakes away from New Orleans, Wichita promised to raze historic Lawrence–Dumont Stadium and construct a new state-of-the-art facility along the west bank of the river, and they terminated the lease of the Wingnuts, which doomed that club's existence. Utilizing the full array of state and local public incentives at their disposal to finance the stadium, city officials boasted that the new facility, and the return of MLB-affiliated baseball, would spark an economic renaissance near the river and throughout the adjacent Delano neighborhood, which had already experienced a modest amount of gentrification and had developed a reputation in recent decades as a burgeoning arts and culture district. It would later emerge that the deal to bring the team to Wichita included provisions to sell prime city-owned riverfront property to the team owners for one dollar per acre to facilitate profitable private business development and the construction of an entertainment district around the stadium. When this information came out in media reports in 2019, it provoked a scandal throughout Wichita, causing many to doubt the soundness of the deal, but Longwell made it clear that the entire arrangement hinged upon the land transfer and that without it, the Baby Cakes would not come to Wichita. (By this point, the city had already torn down Lawrence-Dumont in anticipation of the team's arrival, which had not yet been finalized in a signed contract.) In the face of immense scrutiny and hours of testimony from concerned residents, the Wichita City Council voted to approve the land sale agreements, clearing the way for the city's ambitious vision for the west side of the river (Figure I.2).[7]

Minor league sports franchises have become common components of smaller US cities' economic development aspirations. Despite a wide array of evidence demonstrating that they typically deliver far less economic growth than expected, the larger number of such teams (compared to major league teams), their greater degree of geographic mobility, and the smaller infrastructural footprint (and relatively modest cost) of their stadiums entice many cities to adopt copycat development strategies built around the relocation of a minor league sports franchise. Rather than standing out from their peers, then, the ubiquity of these lower-status teams, and the facilities that serve them, cause smaller cities' economic development plans to increasingly resemble one another.[8]

Wichita struggled with that dilemma in its courtship of the Baby Cakes (renamed the Wind Surge upon moving to Wichita). Throughout the

Figure I.2. Riverfront Stadium. Photo by Chase Billingham.

process, proponents of the stadium project (and the hoped-for accompanying commercial development) rooted their arguments in the idea that the new ballpark would contribute to Wichita's unique identity and help it to stand out from its peers, while *simultaneously* appealing to the need for Wichita to undertake this project in order to maintain the same types of amenities found within those peer cities. At the groundbreaking ceremony for the newly completed Riverfront Stadium in 2019, Kansas Lieutenant Governor David Toland compared the impact of the new Minor League baseball stadium to the impact of the much larger stadium constructed several years earlier for the Washington Nationals Major League Baseball team. "We built a stadium there that has been a catalyst in that city, and what's going to happen here with this stadium is it's going to be yet another catalyst for Wichita." After Toland's remarks likening the benefits in Wichita to those in Washington, DC, Jeff Fluhr, the president of the Greater Wichita Partnership, rose to extol the various ways in which the stadium would, in fact, make Wichita stand out from other cities. "This project is going to make us that great next American river city," Fluhr proclaimed. "Our city is being placed in a new classification of cities," he explained, adding that "it strengthens our quality of uniqueness."[9]

* * *

In both the Riverfront Legacy Master Plan and the Riverfront Stadium initiative—as well as in many other examples discussed throughout this book—business leaders, elected officials, local boosters, and the general public frequently conflated seemingly contradictory impulses: the aspiration, on the one hand, to make the city stand out as a unique, authentic destination, and the obligation to offer a suite of amenities to visitors, residents, and businesses similar or identical to those that could be found in other places believed to be competitors in a zero-sum contest for lucrative, but elusive, urban prizes. The simultaneous appeals to authenticity and mimicry may seem absurd, particularly in a city like Wichita, which has repeatedly struggled in recent decades to successfully implement bold visions of urban revitalization.

In recent decades there has been a trend toward imitation and homogeneity in the urban built environment and in the range of residential, commercial, retail, and leisure amenities offered to residents and visitors. Cities across the country—indeed, across the world—which had previously enjoyed their own local flavors, regional cuisines, unique accents, and quirky customs increasingly look and feel the same.[10] We can see that, of course, in the proliferation of chain stores and restaurants, the ubiquitous Starbucks cafes scattered across the urban and suburban landscape, and the requisite craft breweries and gastropubs decorated with very similar chic motifs in city after city.[11] Lifestyle amenities aimed at satisfying the presumed tastes of the young professional classes abound in places large and small. These amenities are promoted by visitors' bureaus with strikingly similar campaigns and messages, offering identical products to residents and tourists alike with the promise of their uniqueness. The visitors' guide for Abilene, Texas, for instance, encourages tourists to experience that city's "coffee craze" by exploring its "coffee hot spots."[12] Dubuque, Iowa, is "a place unlike any other," its visitors' guide boasts, "a unique mash-up of old & new, quirky & quaint, traditional & unconventional." Among some of the "essentials" that visitors to Dubuque "have to try" are cheeseburgers, coffee, and t-shirts.[13] Meanwhile, the visitors' guide for Bakersfield, California, touts that city's "unique creative culture" on its cover; above a photo of a cheeseburger, it invites guests to sample its "unique dining experiences."[14]

In this way, Wichita is far from unique among cities in its tendency to embrace similarity, even while touting distinctiveness. Economic development agencies in cities as diverse as Rockford, Illinois, Mesa, Arizona, New Bedford, Massachusetts, and Amarillo, Texas, offer potential developers and investors similar sets of incentive packages, utilizing mechanisms such as tax increment financing, enterprise zones, opportunity zones, small business loans, and entrepreneurship incubators designed to encourage new business investment. While drawing from copycat toolkits to chase business investment, those same economic development agencies are constantly looking over their shoulders to assess how they are performing in relation to peer cities chasing those same business investments.

Rankings—even those of dubious origin—factor heavily in that competitive pursuit. Economic development leaders in Toledo, Ohio, have touted their city's ranking by CoworkingCafe, an online repository of coworking sites, as the twentieth (out of forty-six) fastest-growing city with a population between 250,000 and 500,000. Still, they continue to chase other cities higher up in the rankings. "Is there room to improve? Yes," acknowledged a vice president at the Toledo Port Authority, reacting to the city's ranking on that list. "But we're right behind Cleveland at 19. It's good to be there in the top 20. We're pretty consistent across a lot of different categories, and we're above university towns like Madison, Wisconsin, and major port cities like Long Beach, California." Meanwhile, in Nebraska, economic development leaders working to incubate a "Silicon Prairie" in the Plains expressed excitement when both Lincoln and Omaha moved up (to twenty and eighteen, respectively) in StartupCity's rankings of the best metro areas in the Midwest to start a new technology business. For their part, Wichita leaders conducted a months-long publicity campaign in 2025 to tout the fact that the Milken Institute, an economic think tank, had ranked Wichita as the forty-third "Best Performing" large city in the United States over the previous year. Taking these and many other cases into consideration, it is clear that Wichita's story is reflective of common trends found across the American urban landscape. This book is designed to use Wichita's story as a window through which to examine the delicate balance between sameness and distinction that characterizes many cities' economic development strategies.[15]

One example of how cities frame ubiquitous offerings as esoteric markers of authenticity can be found in the realm of transportation, where inner-city vitality is promoted through the deployment (often facilitated by partnerships between public transit agencies and private companies) of nontraditional "last-mile" modes of transit like rental bicycles and scooters, which are generally characterized by their convenience of use, relatively low cost, and tendency to get discarded by users and thieves alike in rivers, lakes, and ditches. While highly common, these conveyances often sport localized branding and feature heavily in promotional campaigns from local chambers of commerce and convention and visitors' bureaus. In Duluth, Leaf Rides, a company begun by students at the local branch of the University of Minnesota, provides scooters throughout the city center, billing itself as "a community focused micro mobility rental service, intent on providing the most convenient, fun to use and environmentally friendly means of transportation in the twin ports area" of Duluth and neighboring Superior, Wisconsin. The scooter service in Chattanooga—dubbed ChattaScooter—touts its status as a "better way to explore the city." While major nationwide scooter rental companies, such as Lime, Bird, and Veo, coordinate directly with city governments to distribute and regulate scooter usage, Scoot Spokane departs from this model in that it reflects a partnership between Lime and Visit Spokane, the region's convention and visitors' bureau, through which Visit Spokane provides riders with recommended itineraries and maps designed, according to the agency's CEO, to help "visitors see Spokane from a totally different view."[16]

What drives this urge among places to tout their uniqueness, to stake claims in "authenticity," and to pursue place-based branding campaigns? In cities as varied in size, geographic location, and economic specialization as New York City, New Orleans, Chester, Pennsylvania, and Troy, New York, scholars have located the source of these efforts in strategic responses to deindustrialization, globalization, suburban flight, and other recent demographic and economic phenomena that upended the sources of urban prosperity in the early to mid-twentieth century.[17] Still, though the specific branding strategies that cities adopt and the economic imperatives underlying them have evolved over time, boosterism and self-promotion are by no means new phenomena for cities in the United States. Indeed, boosterism played a major role in the initial emergence of Wichita as an urban center in the 1870s, and it has remained a central pursuit of business and government leaders in the city through the present day.

Charting a Path Forward

The pressures inflicted by global economic competition, the growing polarization of metropolitan fortunes within the international marketplace, and the incontestable triumph of entrepreneurialism in urban governance—in recent decades these forces have synergized into a tightening snare, severely hindering the maneuverability of urban leaders. Especially for less powerful cities, there is no escape from the impulse to compete; as John Logan and Harvey Molotch observed decades ago in their landmark statement on metropolitan political economy, *Urban Fortunes*, the incessant pursuit of jobs, outside investment, and "economic development" opportunities drives the thinking of the elected officials and bureaucratic staffs that occupy the offices of city halls from coast to coast.[18] Caught in the snare, they have little hope of escape from the competition. Still, they struggle—as if their cities' lives depend on it—against their constraints, devising plans that they believe are clever and original but most of which have been used before by their peers, all of whom are caught indelibly in their own snares. Cities must compete, but relatively few will emerge unscathed from the struggle to become the triumphal success stories. What happens to the rest? How does the drive to generate authenticity through mimicry affect them, and what are the results for economic development, inequality, and the shape of the built environment?

Logan and Molotch famously likened the contemporary capitalist city to a "growth machine," in which the perpetual pursuit of economic growth motivates the activities of public- and private-sector leaders, who, in spite of whatever other political differences may divide them, come together to champion economic expansion, forming powerful "growth coalitions" to advance that cause. In the years since *Urban Fortunes* was published, the growth machine perspective has been elaborated, refined, and challenged, but most commonly it has been applied in order to understand the causes and consequences of economic growth and development in cities around the world. However, our understanding of the urban growth machine has been limited by the fact that, for the most part, applications of growth machine theory have been affected by selection on the dependent variable. In other words, places in which growth coalitions are studied tend to be the places in which robust growth is occurring. But what about places in which growth is more sluggish or nonexistent altogether? How useful is the growth machine perspective for understanding those cities? Do growth coalitions exist there at all?[19]

This book is designed to address those questions, using Wichita's experience at the end of the twentieth century and beginning of the twenty-first century as a case study to examine patterns affecting midsized cities in the US. Utilizing historical data drawn from archival research, government documents, and contemporary media accounts, in-depth interviews conducted with local public- and private-sector leaders, and ethnographic observations highlighting social, economic, and physical change in the urban core, this study brings together the results of over a decade of research on the sociopolitical history of modern Wichita. By examining more than a half century's worth of successes, stagnations, and utter failures in Wichita, and situating them within the context of urban social theory, my aim is to illustrate the manifestations of the competitive pressures on cities in the contemporary capitalist era. That story will unfold over the course of the following six chapters.

Chapter 1 grounds the recent story of Wichita in the history of the city's origins and early economic growth, as well as in the theoretical frameworks that help to structure my analysis. I examine the long history of boosterism and the important role it played in urban growth during the westward expansion of the United States, drawing upon the activities of the powerful newspaper editor Marshall Murdock to illustrate how this tendency played out in this growing city in south central Kansas. Cities' attempts to compete against one another are nothing new, as I show, and I draw upon classical and contemporary urban social and cultural analysis to situate and contextualize Wichita's early competitive and boosterist spirit, linking it to the contemporary competitive and boosterist campaigns that form the focus of the following chapters.

In chapter 2, I return to the place where this introduction began: the banks of the Arkansas River, the site of so much optimism, exuberance, and repeated disappointment regarding the potential for explosive growth in Downtown Wichita. Recounting the years-long saga surrounding a grand redevelopment vision put forward in the late 1980s by an eccentric billionaire, I document the process through which the entire city came together to refashion Wichita in a bold and distinctive manner, and I trace the emergence of the political fissures that ultimately halted implementation of his ambitious plan. Among the most important impediments to realizing this sweeping redevelopment vision was the discovery of a massive plume of groundwater contamination leaching beneath the entirety of Downtown Wichita, which imperiled investment in the core and prompted local officials to propose a genuinely unique local solution designed to clean up the pollution and rescue the economic viability of the city center. Juxtaposing the riverfront redevelopment plan against the groundwater crisis, I demonstrate how tenuous Wichita's local leaders have believed the city's economic development potential to be, and I examine how they have struggled to balance a desire to make it a unique, distinctive urban place against the impulse to pursue copycat strategies in their development schemes.

Chapter 3 focuses on the problem that economic development boosters have consistently found to be the hardest and most intractable obstacle to realizing gentrification in Downtown Wichita: the persistent presence of unwanted human beings. Beginning with an overview of efforts during the mid-century era of urban renewal to clear the single-room-occupancy hotels, shelters, missions, bars, flophouses, and other establishments that made up Wichita's "skid row," I highlight key moments from the second half of the twentieth century and the beginning of the twenty-first century to remove low-income men and the institutions serving their needs from an area on the outskirts of Downtown Wichita seen as ripe for upscaling. Aiming to mimic the successful "festival marketplace" developments sprouting up in larger cities in the 1970s and 1980s, public- and private-sector officials worked diligently for decades to oust homeless people from the area to make room for a new destination hub of nightlife and entertainment. Despite these strategies, the desired high-end development arrived slowly, unevenly, and sporadically, leaving Wichita with a nightlife district that remains underwhelming relative to comparable districts in competitor cities. To remedy that lack of success, further efforts to marginalize unwanted groups have continued apace over the past several decades, including additional efforts to criminalize and evict the homeless, as well as plans to restrict the activities of social service agencies, Christian missionaries, unruly teenagers, and Black Lives Matter protesters.

How can places that persistently fall behind in the incessant intercity competitive struggle continue to justify the immense public expense that booster and tourism-generation campaigns entail, and how can they demonstrate the efficacy of prior efforts? Addressing this question is the focus of the book's fourth chapter. Detailing what I refer to as "Potemkin City" strategies, which mask economic vulnerabilities using bold displays of vibrancy, this chapter examines Wichita's embrace of several such approaches in recent decades. These public relations–fueled efforts projected economic vitality even as the region's economic foundation—rooted primarily in its most important industry, the aircraft manufacturing sector—showed repeated signs of weakness. I devote considerable attention in this chapter to one particularly noteworthy, and highly destructive, saga in the city's recent experiences with economic development and boosterism, documenting the arrival to Wichita of a group of out-of-state developers who were lauded by the press and public officials when they bought up large swaths of underutilized downtown land with the promise to rejuvenate the entire urban core, only to see those plans unravel when the instability of their financing became revealed. The collapse of their Wichita empire in a web of fraud charges and bankruptcies set back downtown development for years.

In early 2020, American cities, including Wichita, seemed to be in robust financial shape after several years of strong economic growth as the country shook off the last doldrums of the Great Recession. But the arrival of the coronavirus pandemic immediately halted much of that economic progress, caused catastrophic damage to the culture, convention, and entertainment industries that lay at the heart of the twenty-first century entrepreneurial urban economy, and disrupted many major flows of municipal revenue, thereby throwing cities' finances into turmoil. In Wichita, the problems caused by the pandemic were magnified by the disease's impact on the city's primary source of economic activity, the aircraft manufacturing industry, which suffered as the pandemic slowed air travel to a trickle for months. Meanwhile, the city's largest employer was beset by its own (largely self-inflicted) operational crisis, which, when combined with the COVID-induced economic dislocations, wreaked havoc on the regional economy. Chapter 5 examines this compound collection of crises, noting how some of the problems that Wichita faced were like those experienced in peer cities, while others were completely unique, and it evaluates how these challenges further hindered the implementation of the ambitious Riverfront Legacy Master Plan discussed at the beginning of this introduction.

Finally, in the book's conclusion, I draw together all of the empirical findings, link them back to the theoretical frameworks that have structured my thinking about Wichita's past and present, and examine what the future holds for this simultaneously typical and unique American city. In doing so, I lay the groundwork for a series of public policy recommendations designed to encourage greater independence and greater equity in urban economic policy for American cities as they embark on the path to the post-pandemic age.

CATALYZING GROWTH IN COW TOWN

1

A Renewed Focus on Small-City Urbanism

Approximately one in six Americans lives within a city of 100,000–500,000 residents (substantially higher than the proportion residing in cities with more than 500,000 people), yet urban social science has historically focused most of its attention on the largest and most influential metropolitan spaces.[1] Understanding the dynamics of small-city urbanism, and identifying the ways in which political and economic dynamics in small and medium-sized cities resemble or differ from those found in larger regions, is more important than ever as affordability pressures in major cities, combined with the opportunities presented by the expansion of remote work, are poised to draw an even greater share of the population to smaller metropolitan regions in the years to come.[2]

Over the past decade, there has been an encouraging trend in urban studies of newfound attention to developments in the country's smaller regions (though little of that research has been situated within the urban regions of the Great Plains). Recognizing the importance of smaller places for the contemporary metropolitan ecosystem, scholars have issued multiple calls for expanded research in this area. Sociologist Deirdre Oakley exhorted urbanists to examine small and midsized cities, calling it "a new frontier in urban sociology." Richard Ocejo, Ervin Kosta, and Alexis Mann echoed this sentiment, instructing urban scholars to "step back from uncritical acceptance of large size as the arbiter of urbanity" in their introduction to a special issue dedicated to "Centering Small Cities" in *City & Community*, the leading journal for urban sociological research in the United States. In a concurring statement, Japonica Brown-Saracino has explained how concentrating too heavily on the largest and busiest cities can blind social scientists to the diversity of urban life, leading to "substantial gaps in our knowledge of place and related processes and dynamics."[3]

Not content to simply note the absence of robust research on the topic, these and many other scholars have embraced the need to augment the empirical literature on small-city urbanism. Brown-Saracino's nuanced examination of community, sexuality, and urban life in four smaller cities provided a provocative challenge to prevailing theories in urban sociology about the impact of place on personality and identity. For his part, Ocejo has made major contributions to the sociological understanding of gentrification by investigating its manifestations in the small postindustrial city of Newburgh, New York. Like other metropolitan phenomena, Ocejo notes, gentrification in small cities "is unfolding differently than it does in big cities, which provide the model cases for urban theory."[4]

This is important, because the refinement of urban theory requires the analysis of comparative data across a wide range of metropolitan locations. The growth in empirical research into small-city urbanism, then, has greatly bolstered our ability to generalize and theorize. Cuberes and Ramsawak's comparative research into variable rates of growth across small cities in New England; Nevarez and Simons's work on the diffusion of big-city tendencies into smaller cities (which they term "Brooklynization"); and Mele's incisive dissection of the racialized politics of small-city revitalization in Chester, Pennsylvania—these and many other case studies identify the unique struggles that small and midsized regions face, while also pointing out the links that they have to their larger peers. This work is complemented by studies that attempt to draw out general patterns across smaller cities, such as Norman's useful research on the economic and demographic trajectories of dozens of small cities across the US, Tumber's environmentally driven look into the politics of green urban redevelopment in twenty-five cities across the country, and the diverse essays on small-city postindustrial transformations contained in Connolly's *After the Factory*.[5]

This book is designed to contribute to that expanding literature on small-city urbanism. The influential critical geographer Jamie Peck has called for the deployment of a "conjunctural" approach to urban studies. This approach involves "a mode of analysis that works deliberately across levels of abstraction in dialogue with evolving midlevel formulations and connective concepts," and, in practice, it privileges local case studies as links in a theoretical chain that highlights and illustrates the manifestations of the entrepreneurial turn in urban governance. My aim in the chapters that follow is to forge one link in that "conjunctural" chain, telling the story of a city that for decades has lagged behind its peers in terms of population growth, economic ascent, and "creative" vitality, despite consistently viewing its fortunes in relation to those of its peers and chasing the same elusive jobs by using the same lifestyle-based development strategies as those same peers. In order to fully understand the contemporary story of urban economic development strategies in Wichita, though, it is important to begin with the city's origins to demonstrate just how thoroughly bombastic boosterism has infused the city's culture since it first emerged on the banks of the Arkansas River in the late nineteenth century.[6]

Booms and Busts Along Wichita's Path from Cow Town to Air Capital

Evidence of competition among municipalities for investment, infrastructure, and population growth can be found dating back to the earliest days of the country's colonial history. Booster rhetoric grew more bombastic and outlandish in the late nineteenth and early twentieth centuries as westward expansion introduced a plethora of new burghs dotting the landscape of the central US and as railroad construction pitted one place against another for a coveted stop upon the rail corridors linking these new developments to the established metropolises of the East.[7] The sloganeering of the boosters—lampooned most pointedly by Sinclair Lewis in the character of George Babbitt, who boasted of his fictional hometown of Zenith that it offered "the finest example of American life and prosperity to be found anywhere"—commonly outpaced the actual levels of economic progress and quality-of-life amenities available in these burgeoning cities.[8]

Kansas, whose mid-nineteenth-century growth was spurred by the arrival of abolitionist Free State migrants, was no stranger to the booster impulse.[9] This trend was driven most vociferously by the synergistic energies of business elites, local government leaders, and newspaper editors (who were, not infrequently, the same people). As geographer James Shortridge has explained, "The local newspapermen headed this group and wrote exaggerated claims that sounded nearly identical to those made in neighboring communities."[10]

Newspapers played an outsize role in hyping their surrounding communities everywhere, but on this front few could match the rhetorical flourish of Colonel Marshall Murdock, the editor of *The Wichita Eagle*. Persuaded by James Mead, one of the city's founders, to relocate his printing press from Burlingame, Kansas, Murdock moved to Wichita and established the *Eagle* in 1872, just two years after the new city was incorporated. He and his paper soon gained a reputation for hyperbole, combining a penchant for dubious exaggerations with a fondness for alliteration in the service of boosting Wichita's reputation throughout Kansas and across the nation. Coining nicknames for the city that persist to this day—"The Magic City," "The Mascot of the Meridian," and, most famously, "The Peerless Princess of the Plains"—Murdock's *Eagle* bolstered the young city's reputation for rapid growth, exuberance, and friendliness toward business investment that helped to fuel an early speculative boom.[11]

"Wichita was born booming!" Murdock proclaimed, inflating the city's growth while minimizing the lesser booms of its competitors. "The chemistry of each individual boom," he explained, "no doubt differs with the locality, to properly analyze which would employ the trained powers of an expert, but—Wichita's boom is a self evident fact!"[12] And Murdock's description may well have been a fair characterization of the sui generis nature of Wichita's boom in the 1870s (Figure 1.1). While reporting on and cheering on Wichita's early boom, Murdock's jubilant rhetoric played no small part in bringing about the speculative real estate activity that he so eagerly hoped to see.[13]

The settlement of central and western Kansas in the mid- to late 1800s coincided with the growth and proliferation of railroad travel; whereas location along a navigable waterway had previously been key to the development of a commercial hub, the railroad soon came to be seen as the sine qua non of growth. As in other states, the promoters of new towns in the Sunflower State competed and schemed mightily against one another to influence the decisions of the powerful railroad companies regarding where to lay new track. Wichita's major early regional competitor was the

Figure 1.1. Wichita business booster train. Source: Courtesy of the Wichita-Sedgwick County Historical Museum. Used by permission.

city of Newton, located twenty miles to the north. Though already established as a strategic location along the cattle trail, Newton lacked a substantial reliable source of water to support a growing urban region.[14]

By comparison, the new settlement of Wichita sat alongside the Arkansas River, and it provided a convenient location for the Santa Fe railroad to cross that river on its pathway toward the Colorado border. Through a series of deals and machinations among the new city's leaders, Wichita became a destination for this line, which, in combination with the town's location alongside the profitable Chisolm Trail cattle pathway, created the promise of economic success. Even as the cattle trade shifted elsewhere within a few years, Wichita's stature had been established, and it grew more stable with the arrival of new rail lines, especially a branch of the expanding St. Louis and San Francisco Railroad (the "Frisco"), which made Wichita a junction point when the new track crossed the already built Santa Fe and later a third line built by the Missouri Pacific. The arrival of all of these railroads, of course, would have been unachievable without massive local subsidy in the form of bonds approved by a vote of local residents and without the exuberant boosterism of Murdock and others, who beckoned the railroad companies and exhorted the voters to approve the bonds. "No Kansas town ever won," Murdock later reminisced, "except through running the gauntlet of relentless rivalry."[15]

Wichita's initial boom was short-lived, however. The 1880s marked a period of uneven growth, punctuated by notable signs of progress like the opening of a federal courthouse, the construction of a municipal water system, the electrification of downtown streetlamps, the erection of new bridges and buildings, and the expansion of new neighborhoods to accommodate a swelling population. Quickly, though, the growth ceased in the face of rapidly rising fears among investors that speculation had outpaced real economic progress. A prolonged economic slump followed through much of the 1890s, characterized by population decline and rising vacancies in the overbuilt city, made worse by natural disasters.[16]

Prosperity returned to Wichita in the first decades of the twentieth century thanks primarily to industrialization within a city that had originally made its name as a cow town, agricultural center, and rail hub. The Coleman Company, which would grow through the twentieth century to become one of the premier manufacturers of lamps, stoves, and camping equipment, and one of the region's largest employers for decades, was established in 1901, helping to jolt Wichita's industrial prowess. But something even bigger was yet to come.[17]

Clyde Cessna, who by the mid-1910s had several years of experience building airplanes, was summoned to Wichita in 1916 to work for a local automobile manufacturer named J. J. Jones, and Cessna soon designed and built the first airplanes manufactured in the city in Jones's automobile factory. Airplane companies quickly blossomed across the city. The Laird Airplane Company, staffed by future aircraft tycoons Walter Beech and

Lloyd Stearman, launched the "Swallow" aircraft in 1920. Cessna joined them a few years later to form a new enterprise, the Travel Air Manufacturing Company, with Cessna at the helm. He departed in 1927 to create the Cessna Aircraft Company, leaving Beech in charge of Travel Air, which would go on to become Beechcraft. Meanwhile Stearman went on with business partners to form the Stearman Airplane Company, which, through a series of mergers and reshufflings, would eventually become a division of the Boeing Company.[18]

With the establishment of these and many other firms building planes and their constituent parts, aircraft manufacturing became the primary vehicle of economic growth for the Wichita region, especially following the American mobilization for combat in World War II. The city's strategic location in the middle of the country insulated it from potential enemy attack, making it a useful site for military aircraft manufacturing. Cessna and Beechcraft began taking large orders for aircraft from the US military, and Stearman rapidly expanded its workforce to accommodate the demand for new bombers at its South Wichita plant, which would come to be known as Boeing Plant II. The Boeing plant ran continuously, three shifts per day, producing over one thousand B-29 bombers and thousands of smaller aircraft. By the end of the war, it was estimated that Wichita's aircraft companies had built more than 22,000 military planes for the war effort, employing over 50,000 people.[19]

War mobilization brought tens of thousands of workers to the region, requiring a vast expansion of housing and municipal services and supporting a wide range of secondary commercial and industrial ventures. This included thousands of African Americans, who came to Wichita to work for the Air Force or to staff the growing aircraft manufacturing plants. As in cities across the United States, the confluence of racist housing policies, housing market discrimination, and home lending practices led African American migrants to concentrate in segregated neighborhoods, particularly in the northeastern neighborhoods of Wichita characterized primarily by modest, low-cost single-family homes. This area would develop into the heart of Wichita's Black community in the mid-twentieth century, a distinction it continues to hold to this day.[20]

Following the end of World War II, the city's population declined temporarily then increased again as the country once more mobilized for war, this time in Korea. The US Air Force, which had held a presence at the

Wichita Municipal Airport for decades, expanded the airport in 1951 and established the Wichita Air Force Base (renamed McConnell Air Force Base three years later) at the site.[21]

The boosterism that Marshall Murdock and his collaborators pioneered in the city's early cow town days was reborn as business leaders worked to promote Wichita's new leading industry in the early twentieth century.[22] Where Murdock had famously conferred the title of "Peerless Princess of the Plains" in the nineteenth century, Wichita's twentieth-century business leaders came together and settled on a new moniker: "The Air Capital of America." As a promotional chamber of commerce article proclaimed:

> No city in the world has experienced such growth in things of aviation interest; certainly no city is more air-minded, and we are repeatedly informed by passing aviators that Wichita, because of her central location, her level land and the fact that fogs, the bane of the aviator, are almost unknown, is the best airplane district in the nation. . . . Within the last few years Wichita has breathed, eaten, and dreamed aviation. Aviation is the topic of discussion in the club, across the breakfast table, on the street, and in the office. No matter how great a bore a man may be, if he will talk aviation he is always welcome.[23]

The "Air Capital of America" label stuck, quickly growing in geographic scope and boastfulness to position Wichita as the "Air Capital of the World." Visitors flying into Wichita would find the slogan emblazoned on the façade of the city's airport (Figure 1.2). Booster campaigns regularly featured the slogan, and to this day it remains the most widely used and recognized nickname for the city.[24]

In contrast to Murdock's bombastic claims, designed to provoke desired growth at least as much as to describe existing growth, the "Air Capital" identity reflected an important reality about Wichita's distinctiveness in the mid-twentieth century. Wichita was, indeed, by far the leading producer of airplanes in the country. In the second half of the century, small-plane manufacturing—at Cessna, Beech, Learjet, and other companies—would turn Wichita into the "Detroit of the Small Plane Age." And even as other corporate successes, such as Pizza Hut and Koch Industries, contributed to Wichita's rising reputation as an entrepreneurial hub, its identity remained firmly connected to the aviation industry in a way that has held true to the present day.[25] In 2022 (even after several decades of faltering

Figure 1.2. "The Air Capital" hangar building, Wichita Municipal Airport. Source: Edgar B. Smith Photographs, Chamber of Commerce Photograph Collection. Courtesy of Local History Section, Wichita Public Library. Used by permission.

employment levels), among all counties across the United States, Sedgwick County, Kansas, ranked second in its concentration of aerospace manufacturing employment, trailing only Snohomish County, Washington, the site of Boeing's headquarters.[26]

Of course, being so closely tied to one industry meant that Wichita's fortunes rose and fell with the fortunes of the aircraft industry, and the region's prosperity was highly reliant upon the corporate moves of its major manufacturing firms, especially Boeing.[27] Already by the late 1980s, employment in aircraft manufacturing in the Wichita metropolitan area had plateaued just under 40,000 people. Contractions during the 1990s shrank that workforce dramatically, falling nearly 25 percent through the middle of the decade before rebounding rapidly in the second half of the decade and reaching a new peak above 47,000 in early 1999. Job losses began again as the national economy entered a recession in early 2001, then accelerated following the airplane-facilitated terrorist attacks of September 11, 2001, which devastated the aviation industry.

By 2004, Wichita's aircraft employment had dropped to its lowest level in decades. Between 2005 and 2010, sustained national economic growth restored many of those manufacturing jobs. This growth continued even as the country entered the Great Recession in 2007 and 2008.[28] That recession-era employment growth would not last, though, and in the latest iteration of Wichita's history of booms and busts, a series of massive aircraft industry layoffs would devastate the local economy as the recession deepened.

In early 2009, Cessna announced that it would cut over 4,000 jobs at its Wichita location. Boeing and Beechcraft followed suit with major reductions as well.[29] By 2010, nearly all of the aircraft manufacturing jobs that had been added to the metropolitan area during the economic expansion of the 2000s had vanished, and things would only get worse from there. On January 5, 2012, after eighty-five years in Wichita, Boeing announced that it would leave the city altogether. The 2,160 jobs eliminated by Boeing's departure represented a relatively modest workforce reduction compared to some of the other recession-era layoffs, but they took a profound psychological toll on the city, whose identity had for decades been bound up with the mid-century triumphs achieved on Boeing's production line.[30]

Aircraft employment continued to fall through most of the 2010s, and though the industry remained a central part of the regional economy, elected officials, economic development proponents, and analysts grew increasingly concerned that Wichita may need to look beyond aviation to ensure regional prosperity into the future. For decades, the city had boasted of its unique and distinctive character—the Air Capital of the World—a designation that truly set it apart from other places and provided a singular status and identity. However, tying the city's fortunes so closely to that one industry posed a fundamental risk of widespread economic impacts ensuing from any potential downturn in that sector.[31]

This was a story that was all too familiar to residents of manufacturing cities across the US. In the wake of widespread deindustrialization in the late twentieth century, revitalizing the urban core and retooling for a new postindustrial economy have been major priorities for older industrial cities nationwide. From Manchester, New Hampshire, to Greenville, South Carolina, former mills and factories have been repurposed into office space, loft apartments and condominiums, and venues for visual and performing arts. Some metropolitan regions have succeeded in shaking off past industrial decline. In Boston, for instance, the shift from an economy rooted in manufacturing to one built on education, medical research, and finance helped to usher in what Bluestone and Stevenson called the "Boston Renaissance." Many other cities, however, have struggled to move beyond the industrial past. At the extreme end, cities like Youngstown, Flint, and Detroit have had to think innovatively about downsizing in order to account for vast amounts of vacancy and blight, potentially clearing the way for new, cleaner economic investments in the future.[32]

Although deindustrialization did not cause nearly as much economic fallout in Wichita and the aircraft industry remains at the heart of the regional economy, calls to "diversify the economy" have grown in frequency and volume. These alarms, sounded by leaders in the public sector and private sector alike, have stemmed primarily from the fear that a steep downturn in that industry could imperil the region's economy in ways reminiscent of the hardest-hit manufacturing cities in the US rustbelt. And so while the "Air Capital" nickname has remained in widespread use as a marker of civic pride, the urge to "diversify the economy" is a forward-looking priority aimed at guiding Wichita toward a postindustrial future. To that end, regional economic development strategies have increasingly involved local leaders looking over their shoulders to figure out how other midsized cities in the US are strategizing to promote development and generate new kinds of metropolitan prosperity.[33]

The Creep of Sameness Across Urban Space

Replication, imitation, and mimicry across places are not new phenomena. Patterns of urban structure and culture have long filtered outward from the largest, most influential, and most dynamic cities and regions toward the metropolitan hinterland. Early seminal statements in the burgeoning field of urban sociology provided similar observations. In his classic essay on "the metropolis and mental life," for instance, German sociologist Georg Simmel linked the origins of the money economy, the distinctly modern and complex division of labor, and the quintessentially urban "blasé attitude" to the largest industrializing cities, but he noted that, as modernity progresses, these same trends take root in smaller and less sophisticated locales as well.[34] Similarly, Louis Wirth's essay on "urbanism as a way of life," one of the theoretical cornerstones of American urban sociology, directly linked urbanism—"that complex of traits which makes up the characteristic mode of life in cities"—to modernization itself, a process begun in, though not limited to, life within the great cities.[35] Herbert Gans noted this important caveat within Wirth's analysis, finding that his predecessor's article "deals with urban-industrial society, rather than with the city," and he extended that same theoretical process to consider how ecological factors and environments affect the development of various styles of life in similar ways within both the inner city and suburban settlements of modern American metropolitan areas.[36]

Theoretical statements regarding the growth of urban areas, too, have consistently stressed replication and predictability across locations. Ernest Burgess's classic "concentric zone" model of urban growth—among the most famous diagrams in the history of American sociology—purported to illustrate quintessential patterns of city expansion found throughout the United States in the early twentieth century (though it quickly came under criticism for its obvious reflection of the specific shape of growth in the city of Chicago).[37] In their effort to refine the ideas of Burgess and other scholars who had attempted to model patterns of urban growth, Harris and Ullman produced a more nuanced typology of places situated within networks and flows of resources and capital, yet they continued to emphasize commonalities across places, stressing that cities "develop in definite patterns in response to economic and social needs."[38]

Later efforts to systematize the social scientific understanding of cities further emphasized similarity, generalizability across cases, and mathematical formulae for deriving patterns in urban trends like population size, population density, and geographic trade areas served by urban production centers.[39] Even the theoretical salvo by the "Los Angeles School" of American urban theorists—though rooted in Marxist and post-structural theories and stressing notions of difference and uneven development in the urban built environment—nonetheless strove to identify new paradigms of growth, generalizing from the decentered pastiche of sprawling development in southern California to make sweeping claims about broad trends affecting places far removed from Los Angeles.[40] Summarizing the school's contributions to the reconceptualization of urban development, geographer Michael Dear asserted confidently: "*For it is no longer the center that organizes the urban hinterlands, but the hinterlands that determine what remains of the center*. The imperatives toward decentralization (including suburbanization) have become the principal dynamic in contemporary cities; and the 21st century's emerging world cities (including L.A.) are ground-zero loci in a communications-driven globalizing political economy."[41] Even through the lens of postmodernist perspectives stressing fragmentation, then, we see the emergence of regularities across the urban landscape.

Conformity, consistency, imitation—these are longstanding traits in the metropolitan built environment.[42] Among urban sociologists, geographers, architectural critics, and other students of cities, lamenting the homogenization of place, castigating the disappearance of esoteric or quirky urban landscapes, and warning about the impending loss of authenticity, localized uniqueness, and racial and economic diversity have become popular pastimes. In an increasingly mechanized modern world hurtling toward cultural sterilization and nuclear calamity, Lewis Mumford alleged that the suburb served as a major vehicle of contemporary degradation, despoiling both the creative exuberance of the urban and the virgin magnificence of the wilderness, replacing both with "a dreary substitute, devoid of form and even more devoid of the original suburban values."[43] Such suspicion of the suburb and its role in the flattening of modern American culture gained widespread endorsement.[44]

Just as suburbanization became a major concern among urbanists lamenting the loss of "authentic places," so has a newer—and, in many ways, inverse—phenomenon: gentrification. Over the past half century, perhaps no issue has galvanized urban scholars, activists, and critics as profoundly as the gentrification of previously undervalued urban spaces.[45] The long-running and frequently acrimonious arguments in the pages of academic journals over the meaning and usefulness of the term, the causes of the process, the geographic scale at which it ought to be studied, the adverse consequences that it can provoke (most importantly, the displacement of previous residential and commercial occupants), and—overhanging all of these—whether it represents a force for good or bad in the neighborhoods and cities it affects sometimes seem as if they will never be exhausted, much less resolved.[46] This is due in large part to the steady diffusion of the concept beyond the confines of the lecture hall and the protest march and into popular discourse. Many of the "gentrification debates," as Brown-Saracino has called them, which had already been continuously rehashed in the academic literature, have been rekindled in newly developed spaces—magazines, television, blogs, and podcasts, to name a few—in recent decades.[47] Along with class-based concerns about upscaling, displacement, and uneven development, many critics of gentrification charge that the process does aesthetic harm to cities. As suburban-style national and global chain franchises supplant unique boutique shops and eateries, critics have noted a sort of suburbanization of the inner city, with commercial ventures catering to the bland tastes of newcomers and contributing to the loss of esoteric character in city neighborhoods. Reflecting on the rapid pace of change across neighborhoods in New York City, urban sociologist Sharon Zukin, the preeminent observer and critic of contemporary cities, has lamented the process of "people, streets, neighborhoods, and public spaces being upscaled, redeveloped, and homogenized to the point of losing their distinctive identity."[48]

Critiques of the creeping homogeneity of gentrified urban space focus frequently on the physical appearance of the streetscape and especially the architectural trends that tend to characterize new residential and commercial structures in these neighborhoods. Architect and urban critic Kenneth Frampton located the origins of the progressive homogeneity of urban places in the rise of modern rationalization in design, the prioritization of maximizing land value and rents, and the rise of the enveloping "mass culture" that had been the subject of so much consternation among the critical theorists of the Frankfurt School. In place of the suffocating "universalism" of late-twentieth century urban patterns, he advocated for the adoption of a "critical regionalism" that would take account of localized topography, climate, and culture to create new, and newly distinctive, places.[49] Since the publication of his noted architectural cri de coeur, though, the troubling trends of homogenization have simply continued and expanded, as "the economic momentum and market integration produced by globalism" facilitated the growth of "a kind of homogenized design" that has "rendered similar many global cities and tourist outposts," according to architect and writer Li Wen.[50]

Noting and criticizing the ubiquity of specific design elements has become more commonplace, not just among architectural critics and social scientists but among popular writers, journalists, and bloggers. The headline of a 2018 article in the online urban design website *Curbed* asked, "Why do all new apartment buildings look the same?" The answers could be found, the article asserted, in a range of structural impediments to regional creativity in design and construction, including the high and rising costs of land, labor, and materials, which push developers to prioritize low-grade, mass-produced materials and formulaic, repetitive floorplans; restrictive zoning codes, which severely limit where multifamily housing complexes can be built; and precise building codes, which incentivize builders to utilize structures of similar height constructed of similar materials with similar façade designs (for example, the ubiquitous "stick-built five-over-one" apartment complex).[51] Similar observations of the problem of bland construction, along with similar diagnoses of its structural causes, appeared in respected national news outlets like *Bloomberg* and *The New York Times* as well as in self-published explainers by architects and urban commentators, and comparable complaints have emerged regularly on the local level in cities large and small.[52]

The outward symptoms of homogenization are thus evident to many observers of the contemporary urban landscape. Less obvious are the structural mechanisms that facilitate trends toward homogeneity among cities. Here, and in the analyses that will follow throughout the book, I will focus on three interrelated developments that work together to encourage patterns of repetition, replication, and sameness across cities. First, declining federal investment in cities in the late twentieth and early twenty-first centuries has led many cities to adopt austerity measures while embracing debt, catering increasingly to the imperatives of the major bond rating agencies and deploying a range of new debt financing tools, especially tax increment financing, which ties the creation of new municipal infrastructure to the profitability of new private development.[53]

Second, the standardization of financing tools at cities' disposal has been facilitated by the growth of a new class of budget experts, analysts, and consultants receiving standardized training. This cadre of finance professionals has helped to exploit fears about the top-down federal spending policies that characterized the mid-century urban renewal regime in order to encourage municipalities to instead embrace private property tax incentives as a major urban development strategy.[54] The influence of third-party vendors to provide tourism and convention services to cities, as well, has led to the promotion of tourism marketing campaigns that bear striking resemblance to one another from city to city, as described in the introduction, and it has driven the emphasis on new facility construction designed to meet the standardized needs of the convention industry. (This was among the most compelling reasons behind the alleged obsolescence of Wichita's Century II Performing Arts & Convention Center, whose proposed demolition as part of the Riverfront Legacy Master Plan unleashed a torrent of public opposition, as I detail in chapter 5.)

Third, the growing reliance upon "public-private partnerships" has dovetailed with shifts in urban governance and in the relationships between municipal leaders and the beneficiaries of public investment. Sociologist Nicole Marwell and her coauthors have argued that city leaders, moving away from a quid pro quo "patronage dynamic," are more likely to pursue symbiotic "partnership" relationships with nonprofit organizations, whose needs dictate the formation of much urban policy, especially since much governmental urban investment has increasingly come in the form of grants targeted toward nonprofits.[55] These patterns can be observed not just in the largest metropolitan areas—the "global cities"—but also in smaller metropolitan regions in the interior of the country. As sociologist Josh Pacewicz has explained, major national policy shifts, including financial deregulation, antiunion policies that weakened labor unions and thereby disempowered traditional power centers affiliated with labor, and Reagan-era cuts to federal urban funding allocations (which prompted cities to adopt the "entrepreneurial" approach to urban development that has characterized the past several decades) have combined to lead local public- and private-sector leaders to downplay divisive partisan rhetoric and work instead in partnership toward the promotion of place, economic development, and marketing. Pacewicz observed the manifestation of these patterns in the governance dynamics of "River City," the small Rust Belt city where he conducted his research.[56]

"Some time ago, I woke up in a hotel room unable to determine where I was in the world," the writer Darran Anderson declared at the opening of an expansive essay examining architectural homogenization and lauding contemporary efforts to implement Frampton's "critical regionalism" around the world.[57] In my view, though, truly embracing "critical regionalism" means moving beyond a specific focus on design and construction and instead taking a more critical approach to understanding how—and for whom—the contemporary city is built; this entails problematizing gentrification, entrenched inequality, climate change, and other major social and economic issues that affect, and are affected by, the spatial. Attending to the links between all these contemporary problems requires identifying their mutual origins within the contemporary critical political economy of the city. It is through this robust critical theoretical tradition that we can most clearly view the pressures that contemporary urban leaders face and most effectively frame a discussion of recent struggles to promote growth in the Wichita metropolitan region.

The Authentic Image Meets the Replicated Reality

Paradoxically, the creeping homogeneity of cities lamented by urban theorists, social scientists, and architectural critics has coincided with the rising urgency with which cities feel the need to differentiate themselves in order to gain advantage in the pervasive game of regional competition. While cities had long jockeyed for growth and investment (as evidenced by the nineteenth-century wrangling over railroad routes outlined above), the pressure to compete had taken on new and exaggerated forms by the middle of the twentieth century. In a searing 1967 critique, Harvey Molotch challenged the land use model developed by the human ecology tradition that had long dominated urban studies in the United States, which posited that urban form reflected the working out of competition over scarce space and resources among a variety of urban actors.[58] Increasingly, he asserted, it is *places* that compete for people and businesses, not the other way around, and understanding those competitive processes is central to developing a thorough model of contemporary patterns in urban economic development. Uncovering the mechanisms of that competitive struggle became a key component of critical urban theories in the ensuing decades, including in the development of Molotch's own highly influential concept of the "city as a growth machine."[59]

Cities' embrace of the entrepreneurial spirit of contemporary capitalism was most clearly laid out by the geographer David Harvey in his pivotal essay on "the transformation in urban governance in late capitalism," which he characterized as a transition "from managerialism to entrepreneurialism." Departing from their traditional mandate to provide reliable municipal services to their residents, Harvey argued, cities have utilized novel financial vehicles, collaborations with the private sector, and strategies to subsidize private profit making in their quest to fuel bold urban growth ambitions. This process frequently involves public absorption of investment risks in order to promote new investment, in large part through the provision of new consumption amenities, such as retail and dining destinations, along with festivals and large-scale cultural events. The ways in which city governments (as well as governments at various other geographic scales) participate in the entrepreneurial game—through the emphasis on a "good business climate"; the provision of relocation incentives, tax abatements, and other subsidies to big businesses as recruitment lures; and the proliferation of tax increment financing and other novel debt finance strategies that link the construction of new public infrastructure to the expectation of new property value escalation—necessarily pit individual cities against one another. The result can be a race to the bottom, as the sacrifices required to offer generous incentives put a strain on competitors' municipal revenues and, by consequence, cities' abilities to sustain their "managerial" functions, maintain public infrastructure, and provide basic services.[60]

Those sacrifices may well be worth it, however, if the forgone revenues work to augment business investment, incubate high-wage job development, and persuade highly educated and highly skilled new residents (those people often blithely referred to as "talent") to relocate. Indeed, the dire prognostications of critical urbanists notwithstanding, the pivot to entrepreneurialism in urban governance has not been ridiculed among all scholars studying urban development. In fact, it is celebrated by many of the most influential urbanists of our time.

No scholar has had a more significant impact upon the trajectory of urban economic development strategy in cities across the United States in the past quarter century than the urban theorist and planner Richard Florida. His most influential book, *The Rise of the Creative Class*, made waves among planners and municipal leaders by confidently asserting that structural changes to the class structure in postindustrial economies would have monumental impacts upon the fortunes of places.[61] According to Florida, the increasing economic dominance of "the Creative Class"—a broad and rather amorphous group comprising white-collar professionals, intellectuals, artists, and others who engage in "creative" labor—presaged a new sorting of cities; those places best able to cater to, recruit, and retain larger segments of the society's affluent "creatives" would flourish, while those who failed to attract this group (by not embracing Florida's "*3Ts* of economic development: *technology*, *talent*, and *tolerance*") would languish, with dire consequences for the broader economic prosperity of their geographic regions:

> The 3Ts explain why cities such as Baltimore, St. Louis, and Pittsburgh fail to grow despite their deep reservoirs of technology and world-class universities: they are unwilling to be sufficiently tolerant and open to attract and retain top creative talent. The interdependence of the 3Ts also explains why cities such as Miami and New Orleans do not make the grade even though they are lifestyle meccas: they lack the required technology base. The most successful places—the San Francisco Bay area, Boston, Washington, DC, Austin, and Seattle—put all 3Ts together. They are truly creative places.[62]

Celebration of the winners in this competitive game of talent retention, and the desire to emulate those winners, has driven urban economic development strategies in American cities throughout the twenty-first century, especially among those cities that have typically come out on the losing end of the creative entrepreneurial game. How can we attract the Creative Class to our city? How can we become the next Austin? Can the industrial grittiness of the past be repurposed into a cool, high-tech future? These are the questions that keep many small-city mayors up at night.[63]

They are also the questions that have driven the work of economic development boosters and chambers of commerce for many decades, and the answers have frequently been found in a suite of consumption amenities targeted toward the tastes of Creative Class professionals.[64] Noted urban economist Edward Glaeser asserts that contemporary metropolitan growth depends on satisfying the consumption tastes of the mobile global elite: "Historically, most people were far too poor to let their tastes in entertainment guide where they chose to live, and cities were hardly pleasure zones. Yet as people have become richer, they have increasingly chosen cities based on lifestyle—and the consumer city was born."[65] The pivot away from cities as places of production and toward cities as places of creative consumption underlies the Creative Class hypothesis, and it similarly drives Glaeser's conclusion that "successful cities, old or young, attract smart entrepreneurial people, in part, by being urban theme parks."[66]

Of course, becoming an "urban theme park" that "creative" professionals want to visit is more easily accomplished in some cities than others. The processes of globalization—including the growth of multinational corporations, the increasing pace of flows of capital, and monumental breakthroughs in communication technology from the mid-twentieth century to the present day—have fundamentally altered the role that cities play in the world economy, and importantly, these changes have exacerbated geographic stratification. A select few metropolises have become true "global cities," the command-and-control centers that house an overwhelming proportion of global corporate headquarters and serve also as sites of cutting-edge culture, cuisine, entertainment, and commerce.[67] But most cities cannot be global cities, though all cities (and all people) are affected to a greater or lesser degree by globalization. Instead, smaller, less dynamic, and less "creative" places tend to get relegated to the economic hinterland, providing subordinate roles (for example, housing call centers, back offices, warehouses, and data storage facilities) in service to the more dynamic and more global cities.[68]

These dynamics pose real obstacles to growth, development, and prosperity in the country's midsized cities, particularly older industrial cities located far from the coasts. Though small and medium-sized cities are geographically, demographically, and economically diverse, on average they tended to grow at slower rates than their bigger peers in the late twentieth and early twenty-first centuries. These places struggle with the decidedly urban social problems facing larger regions, including crime, violence, housing insecurity, and poverty, yet on average they have been slower and less successful in their attempts to shed their industrial past and generate new growth and prosperity in the postindustrial economy.

All-American City tells the story of one such city. The chapters that follow will draw upon historical data to focus specifically on economic growth and stagnation in the Wichita metropolitan region. Readers from that region are likely to take a particular interest in the historical events recounted, and they may recall—or even have had personal experiences with—the people, places, and developments described. They will likely find much that they did not previously know, and past events that they do recall will receive a critical sociological framing that I believe will help them to think in a different way about their own history.

The book is not just for them, though. Despite the local focus of the data, the urban themes that I explore to contextualize Wichita's modern social and economic history will resonate with residents of midsized and slower-growing metropolitan areas across the United States. As I have argued throughout this chapter, replicating strategies undertaken by other cities, utilizing economic development plans drawn from the same limited municipal toolbox, and relying heavily on organizational "best practices" all serve as mechanisms that make the experience of place feel eerily similar in contemporary cities across the urban landscape. *All-American City* is Wichita's story, but in many ways it is the story of Erie, and Fresno, and Pawtucket, and Wichita Falls, too. And just as economic development professionals make use of other cities' examples when devising their own growth strategies, my hope is that urban analysts and critics, too, can find productive insights and resources from the examples provided by peers who study other metropolitan contexts.

In that spirit, my evaluation of urban economic trends will now turn back to the historical example of this specific case. By the 1980s, Wichita's struggles to compete against peer cities for investment were becoming increasingly evident. Catching up, city leaders surmised, would require vision, planning, and a lot of money. First, though, it would require a leader to step up and carry the city into the future.

SELLING A DREAM OF WICHITA'S FUTURE

2

The Unlikely Metropolis

When you look at a map of Wichita, Kansas, it is not immediately clear that there ought to be a city here in the first place. Isolated, remote, separated by more than 150 miles from any other substantial metropolitan settlement, Wichita appears in an aerial image of the landscape as simply the largest of a series of evenly spaced gray oblong blips against the green, yellow, and beige background of the unforgiving Kansas prairie. The lived experience of entering and leaving the city makes that geographic isolation impossible to ignore. Unlike driving through the sprawling megalopolises of the East and West Coasts and the Great Lakes, where one metropolitan area's suburbs bleed into the suburbs of the next city in a nearly unending chain of development, driving into Wichita by highway from any direction requires first traveling for hours across remote plains, with little breaking up the monotony of the landscape but wind turbines, hand-painted antiabortion billboards, and cows. Meanwhile, first-time visitors arriving by air—especially if their plane approaches from the southwest—are often surprised to learn there is a city at all, as they will have seen nothing but farmland through their entire descent until touching down. Wichita has few significant suburbs to speak of, and when you exit the city, you know it for sure.

Despite a metropolitan population exceeding half a million people in the twenty-first century, that remoteness lingers as a persistent experience for those living in Wichita; it is a feeling that has endured since the area's first development by white settlers in the mid-nineteenth century. The climate—dictated largely by the vicissitudes of the seemingly ceaseless wind—has tried the patience of residents for decades, carrying temperatures that reach the 110s in the summer and the -10s in the winter, punctuated in the spring and fall by the looming threat of baseball-sized hailstones, tornadoes, and calamitous inundations of rain, coupled with long stretches of drought and the constant allergenic terrors of dust, pollen, and ragweed.[1]

These climatic challenges are not new; the perils posed by weather, terrain, and distance have been obstacles to Wichita's survival since before Wichita existed. Indeed, to the extent that the city has flourished, it has arguably been in spite of its geographical assets. The settlers of the plains endured what Willa Cather later described as the "stimulating extremes of climate: burning summer when the world lies green and billowy beneath a brilliant sky, when one is fairly stifled in vegetation, in the colour and smell of strong weeds and heavy harvests; blustery winters with little snow, when the whole country is stripped bare and grey as sheet iron."[2] After all, as historian Craig Miner asserts, "It was people—their drives and ambitions—that made Wichita what it became, not its geography."[3] But why? Who were these people, and why is there a city here at all?[4]

The Arkansas: A River City's Underutilized River

Cutting through the topographical monotony of central Kansas is the Arkansas River, which flows as a powerful tributary of the Mississippi when it reaches eastern Oklahoma and Arkansas, but which meanders as a minor (sometimes completely dry) stream from its headwaters in Colorado through the sparsely populated expanse of western Kansas. At the site that would become Wichita, the Arkansas (named "Ne Shutsa," or "Red Water," by the Osage Nation) is met by its own tributary, the Little Arkansas (which the Osage called "Ne Shutsa Sinka," or "Younger Red Water"). These rivers, sustaining the countless bison that roamed the Kansas prairie, regularly attracted generations of Indigenous hunting expeditions and became the sites of Indigenous settlements. They also captivated European and white American explorers, who passed down tales of gold found in the riverbed, setting off a series of frustrating and ultimately fruitless expeditions.[5]

The region was the site of perpetual conflict among warring Native tribes, westward expanding settlers, and the Union and Confederate armies. The Wichita, who had moved southward toward present-day Oklahoma from the Arkansas River valley in the eighteenth century following attacks by the Apache and Spanish colonizers, returned in the 1860s after further conflicts with the Comanche and Union soldiers, eventually settling on the banks of the Little Arkansas. It was there that hunter and trader James R. Mead, too, set up a cabin, becoming well acquainted with the Wichita and other local tribes. Other white settlers—traders, hunters, soldiers, and frontiersmen—followed, and a small village, informally named after the Wichita, began to emerge near the confluence of the rivers, with easy access to clean water and bountiful bison hunting prospects. Despite their loyalty to the Union cause, the Wichita received inadequate support and supplies from the government in Washington, and amidst continued internecine conflicts over food and land, the Office of Indian Affairs orchestrated a catastrophic relocation effort to return the Wichita to Indian Territory (present-day Oklahoma); dozens died, and all suffered during the long and harsh march southward.

The white traders—Mead, as well as newcomers like William Greiffenstein and William Mathewson—thrived, however, and they began to talk of forming a city at the site named for the Native people who had been driven off the land. A series of treaties negotiated between the United States and the tribes in the 1860s essentially ceded the land of Kansas to white settlers, who previously had been forbidden from owning it, while forcing the tribes to move south to Indian Territory. This new freedom for the white Americans made the idea of a settled city at the confluence of the rivers possible, and just days after the last Natives had been driven out, the new City of Wichita was incorporated on July 21, 1870.[6]

And so the Arkansas and Little Arkansas served as the lifeblood of Wichita while the young city expanded, bridged the water to connect to the Wild West town of Delano on the west bank, and continued to grow into the boomtown that Marshall Murdock and his compatriots began hyping in the 1870s.

Although the junction of the rivers, more than any other specific cause, was the major reason for the original establishment of Wichita at that location, the rivers never served a central strategic purpose for the city's economic development aspirations. As Miner has explained, "The city's exact position seems unimportant. The junction of the Big and Little Arkansas rivers, was not particularly important, though there were attempts through the 1870s to make the Big Arkansas navigable. Only a few steamboats and rafts ever reached Wichita, and never with enough predictability to be of any economic advantage whatever."[7] Except during the earliest years of settlement, Wichitans never utilized the Big or Little Arkansas Rivers for their drinking water supply. Most households had private wells into the early twentieth century, when the groundwater in the Equus Beds Aquifer north of the city was tapped to provide a more reliable public water supply. Later, the completion of the Cheney Reservoir west of the city in 1964 provided additional water supply to the growing metropolitan region.[8]

In the first half of the twentieth century, light industry and warehousing did congregate near the river in Downtown Wichita, in part to make use of the waterway as a location to dump industrial waste and in part because the city was still so small that nearly all activities were sited in rather close proximity to the area where James Mead had first settled in the 1860s.[9] But with its relatively low volume, the river did not serve as a significant source of industrial power, and due to its lack of navigability that far north, the city never developed a port. Industrial facilities spread to other parts of the city, with many manufacturing, warehousing, refining, and grain storage facilities hugging the railroad corridor that ran from north to south along the eastern edge of downtown. As Wichita's economy became increasingly dominated by the aircraft manufacturing industry, its major factories expanded to the outskirts to take advantage of the abundant open land needed for huge hangars and sprawling runways.[10]

By the middle of the twentieth century, the downtown industrial area adjacent to the river had deteriorated, as had the Forum, the central civic auditorium that had played host to political rallies, livestock shows, concerts, rodeos, and other major events since 1911. Like cities across the US struggling with mid-century blight, Wichita took advantage of an infusion of federal Urban Renewal dollars to clear and redevelop the whole area. The run-down industrial structures were all swept away, as was the Forum, and a new facility combining the roles of civic center, performing arts center, and convention center took its place. Completed in time to ring in Wichita's one hundredth birthday, the wide, low-slung, blue-domed structure was named Century II, as city leaders hoped that it would usher in a prosperous, dynamic, and progressive second century for the Air Capital.

Figure 2.1. The construction of Century II. Source: Chamber of Commerce Photograph Collection. Courtesy of Local History Section, Wichita Public Library. Used by permission.

Over the next half century, Century II would become a Wichita icon, the most noteworthy and recognizable structure on the city's skyline and a key part of civic life (Figure 2.1). Remarkably, however, despite its location adjacent to the banks of the Arkansas, the Century II complex did not engage in any meaningful way with the riverfront. Instead, visitors entered the facility from the north and east, and new parks and plazas led down to the water's edge while the riverfront itself was left undeveloped, preserved for recreation and public use. When an expanded convention center was constructed adjacent to the round Century II building in 1986, the portion of the new structure facing the river was designated as the loading dock.[11]

This was in contrast to a widespread trend of waterfront-based redevelopment efforts that occurred in cities nationwide during the second half of the twentieth century. Led by prominent developers like the Rouse Company, deteriorated waterfront territory in many American urban centers came to be seen as prime space for themed "festival marketplace" redevelopment projects. "Preferring the density of historic areas to wide-open shopping malls," urban historian M. Christine Boyer has explained, "the Rouse Company rejected large-scaled, single-use structures like department stores in favor of small retail shops lining pedestrian passageways and open-air shopping promenades in a carefully regulated yet varied visual environment." Historic urban waterfronts provided scenic backdrops for these types of shopping promenades in locations like New York's South Street Seaport, Boston's Faneuil Hall Marketplace, and Baltimore's Harborplace. In cities away from the coasts, riverfronts became sites of tourism-oriented redevelopment activities. In New Orleans, for instance, the Moonwalk promenade along the Mississippi River contributed to the nearby restoration of the French Quarter as a major attraction to visitors. The evolution of Pittsburgh's reputation—from a dirty, smoky industrial city into a cleaner hub of business and technology—depended fundamentally on a radical rethinking of its riverfront landscape, which transformed from an industrial dumping ground into a pedestrian-oriented corridor of parks, trails, and leisure amenities. In Wichita, though, mid-century redevelopment turned its back, for the most part, on the city's downtown riverfront.[12]

Urban renewal did dramatically change the city center in the mid-twentieth century. It cleared away many of the dense clusters of small warehouses and run-down industrial structures while opening up the area with broad plazas, notable modern civic structures like Century II, and an abundance of new parking lots and other amenities for a more autocentric culture. As I explain in chapter 3, new redevelopment and gentrification began to percolate along the eastern edge of Downtown Wichita in the 1970s as the city, business groups, and young professionals worked to create an "Old Town" entertainment district within a downtrodden industrial area surrounding the railroad corridor. Despite these efforts, retail, business, and cultural amenities continued to relocate to the fringe, facilitated by highway construction and suburban sprawl; the urban core languished. Though some excitement did begin to emerge in the developing Old Town area, Downtown Wichita itself remained dull, uninspiring, and largely empty—especially near the riverfront, where the city had been born a century earlier.[13]

As the final decades of the twentieth century approached, Wichita's riverfront remained sparsely developed. Pedestrians retained easy access to the water along grass-covered riverbanks, and automobile drivers on McLean Boulevard, which ran parallel to the Arkansas along its west bank, enjoyed unobstructed views of Century II and the city skyline as they approached the downtown core. While many Wichitans treasured this low-key pattern of urban underdevelopment, city leaders and economic boosters saw an untapped possibility for a reimagined downtown riverfront that could promote newfound urban vibrancy and profitability.

Jack DeBoer: Prophet and Salesman

Leading the charge to reimagine Wichita's waterfront and usher in the vibrant city of the future was Jack DeBoer. With a bombastic personality, an irascible temper, a reputation for exuberance, and a personalized license plate on his car that read "CAN DO," DeBoer was a larger-than-life salesman and civic booster.[14] Born and raised in Kalamazoo, Michigan, he had begun developing apartment complexes after a stint in the military. It was aviation, a personal passion since boyhood, that initially brought him to Wichita in the 1960s. As he would later recount in a 2018 interview: "I was building apartments around the country. Came to Wichita, and because I like airplanes—Wichita was the Air Capital—I met a lot of people who knew about airplanes, and Wichita's got the best, friendliest, most honest people that I'd ever met. So we moved. Fifty years, we've been here."[15] DeBoer quickly made a name for himself locally as a leading developer of apartment complexes and gained national prominence—and immense wealth—by pioneering the concept of the "extended stay" hotel. His Residence Inn franchise began as one Downtown Wichita hotel before spreading nationwide. The Marriott Corporation purchased the company in 1987, and DeBoer went on to found a number of profitable extended-stay hotel chains, including Summerfield Suites, Candlewood Suites, and Value Place. These franchises, and their subsequent purchases by major hotel corporations, generated a great fortune for DeBoer, allowing him to garner major influence and acclaim in the 1970s and 1980s Wichita business community.[16]

Though DeBoer's name would become synonymous with riverfront reinvention in Wichita, he did not originate the idea of centering the riverfront in a grand redevelopment plan. Indeed, such a plan had already been in the works under the auspices of the Wichita/Sedgwick County Partnership for Growth (otherwise known as WI/SE). This public-private partnership, aimed at promoting regional economic development, engaged the Dallas-based architecture and planning firm RTKL in February 1988 to produce "a major downtown revitalization planning study" to examine strategies to reverse the trend of suburbanization that had "drained the vitality of downtown."[17] The "RTKL Plan," as this proposal came to be known, envisioned a "pedestrian-friendly" core district anchored on the west by a revitalized river corridor called "The Water Walk" and on the east by a strengthened Old Town situated among redeveloped warehouses near the railroad tracks. RTKL estimated that realizing this vision would require $13.5 million in public investment, which would catalyze an estimated $74 million in private investment over the course of five years. This was, the planners acknowledged, a rather modest plan that was "achievable," and the RTKL planners argued that the various components of the proposal could be accomplished in a piecemeal fashion as funds became available.[18]

The RTKL plan entailed revitalization throughout Downtown Wichita, but its primary focus rested upon the river corridor. Unveiling the initial plan to the public in May 1988, RTKL principal John Gosling admonished the city for underutilizing the Arkansas: "Look, Wichita," he said. "You've got this river corridor, it's distinctive and you understand it's an asset. But why don't you capitalize on it and make it much more of a part of the urban experience of living or working downtown?" Immediately, tensions over the riverfront's use value and its potential exchange value were laid bare, as Wichita City Manager Chris Cherches expressed reservations about overexploiting the undeveloped riverfront land in the manner proposed by RTKL. As *The Wichita Eagle-Beacon* reported, Cherches "wanted to see the city acquire all of the land along the river corridor so that the public would always have access to the river banks, even though the city might lease the land adjacent to that for development."[19] The city's parks director, Frank Smith, went even further, advocating for the total preservation of the west bank of the Arkansas as permanent, undeveloped parkland.[20]

Despite enthusiasm among elected officials and the boosters at WI/SE for the RTKL plan, no serious action was taken to implement it following the filing of the final report in early 1989. By the middle of that year, even an attempt to put into motion one minor component of the proposal—the conversion of one downtown street into a tree-lined pedestrian retail corridor—was met with a tepid response and little financial backing from the private sector. Frustrated with the sluggish pace of progress, downtown business owners approached the Downtown Action Corporation (DAC), a branch of WI/SE that had been established in late 1988 (on a recommendation by RTKL) to catalyze the downtown revitalization plan. While the retail corridor idea received verbal endorsement from the DAC board, DAC itself had no major resources of its own to get the ball moving on the RTKL plan. This message to the impatient business owners came directly from the chairman of the DAC board—none other than Jack DeBoer.[21]

Upon taking the helm at DAC, DeBoer had said modestly, "My goal is not to put my own personal stamp on downtown. It is to achieve a consensus."[22] That humility was short-lived, however. As months dragged on with little tangible action taken to implement the RTKL plan, DeBoer, with DAC under his control, increasingly took matters into his own hands. By the fall of 1989, Wichita was buzzing with talk that a grander plan to revitalize the entire urban core was afoot and that the plan, while incorporating elements of RTKL's proposal, would mostly be the brainchild of DeBoer himself. Indeed, the name RTKL quickly faded from public discourse in Wichita, and the plan came to be known simply as "the DeBoer plan."

Even before DeBoer unveiled his design, Bill Hancock, the chairman of the Sedgwick County Commission, proclaimed that it was "much larger than the RTKL plan" in scope, and a Denver-based collaborator whom DeBoer had worked with on his plan predicted that it would "blow your socks off when you see it." Though the details remained sketchy, commentators suggested that the DeBoer plan included mass clearance of dilapidated structures and the development of fanciful new features on both sides of the riverbank to attract visitors to Downtown Wichita. Early ideas of what might be incorporated into this plan included an ice rink, a floating amphitheater, and other cultural and leisure amenities.[23]

Part of the enthusiasm surrounding DeBoer's plan reflected sheer exhaustion regarding the prolonged dereliction and abandonment of Downtown Wichita. "By God, we've got to get something started. We're all studied out. Right, wrong or indifferent, somebody's got to get things moving," said Sedgwick County Commissioner Dave Bayouth. County Manager Kim Dewey, though, noting the fickleness with which previous plans for Downtown Wichita had come and gone, cautioned reservation in considering this bold new agenda. "What I'm concerned about is we keep changing our focus. We can't seem to stick with something before we're off again in another direction," Dewey asserted. This would prove to be a wise foresight.[24]

Many Cooks in the Redevelopment Kitchen

As anticipation built for the release of the DeBoer plan, architect David Burk, DAC executive director Nat Griffin, and banker Drayton Alldritt put forward a separate plan to open a farmers market in the burgeoning "Old Town" area within the city's former industrial district east of downtown—this was another idea that had been featured in the RTKL proposal. As chairman of DAC, DeBoer—Burk's mentor and occasional business partner—supported the farmers market plan. But when Burk and his team approached the Sedgwick County Commission asking for support, the commissioners demurred, wanting to know how the plan would fit into DeBoer's still unreleased master plan for downtown and sensing little public support for the farmers market as a standalone project. Explaining how the market would dovetail with the DeBoer plan was a challenge for Burk, however, because at that point the details of DeBoer's plan were still murky. At a DAC meeting in January 1990, DeBoer pledged to present a detailed plan within two months. By late February, though, the plan had not yet been revealed.[25]

For their part, WI/SE, which (through DAC) had been promoting downtown growth as one of its key initiatives for more than two years with little tangible result, was laying the groundwork for a series of ambitious proposals. These included the Burk-led farmers market plan and the grand—but still vague—DeBoer revitalization plan, which would likely carry a price tag in the hundreds of millions of dollars and likely require substantial public subsidy. Though the details of DeBoer's plan were still unknown, it was widely expected that a key element of it would be a high-end hotel along the east bank of the river. Businessman Phil Ruffin, who owned a high-rise Marriott hotel on the city's east side, doubted that a downtown hotel could be economically viable. "If it would work, we would have built downtown ourselves," he said, noting that any riverfront hotel would be unsustainable without massive public subsidy.[26]

With taxpayers likely to bear much of the cost, debate ensued about whether the DeBoer plan—which had still not yet been unveiled—should be put up for a public vote. "Let people vote it up or down. If they don't want to do it, let's quit wasting their time and money," said County Commissioner Bud Hentzen. His colleague, Commissioner Dave Bayouth, facing reelection that year, was skeptical about the idea of a public vote, stating bluntly, "'I don't want a $200 million bond election during my campaign."[27]

While the county government debated a public vote, the separate city government moved forward. The riverfront hotel idea gained movement in early 1990, as the Wichita City Council approved a contract with a Denver architecture firm to draft plans for a new high-rise structure that could attract a top-name flag like Marriott or Hilton. The project would likely involve millions of dollars in public spending on infrastructure projects, including widening a bridge across the Arkansas River and reorienting city streets. Even before construction crews broke ground on the hotel, it was expected that taxpayers would have to support the facility's operating losses. But WI/SE President Tim Witsman, acknowledging Downtown Wichita's failures while simultaneously projecting the perpetual optimism of the city's boosters, stated, "I have faced a great deal of public skepticism because of previous efforts that failed. This agreement demonstrates that something is happening."[28]

DeBoer Keeps Wichita Waiting

Despite having promised in January 1990 to deliver his plan within two months, DeBoer dragged his feet, pushing back the announced date for his unveiling until May. When that date came around, the announcement consisted of nothing more than the same vague set of ideas that he had already presented in private to WI/SE and DAC members. "I view this as a preliminary proposal, an initial step. I can't be more specific right now," said Nat Griffin, DAC's executive director. In broad strokes, DeBoer explained that the proposal would involve new amenities like an ice rink on the west bank of the Arkansas, dredging and expanding the river to facilitate pleasure boating and leisure activities on the water, and a new downtown arena. A new local public Urban Renewal–like agency would oversee all of this redevelopment, thereby centralizing action and avoiding unreliable piecemeal private development. The massive plan would require huge amounts of tax dollars—$320 million, according to DeBoer's initial estimate. This reality provoked much skepticism in conservative and tax-averse Wichita. "It's hilarious. I don't know where the money will come from. God, maybe," remarked one anonymous elected official.

The idea of a new downtown arena in particular raised concerns among some members of the Sedgwick County Commission, as the county government had just funded the construction of a new arena, the Kansas

Coliseum, on the northern outskirts of the city a few years earlier. The Coliseum, which hosted professional indoor soccer, rodeos, concerts, and other events, would suffer greatly from the competition created by a new downtown arena, commissioners worried. DeBoer and the board of WI/SE assured them that the downtown arena would be built only if research demonstrated that it would not have an adverse financial impact on the Coliseum.[29]

An arena, a more heavily activated river, an ice rink—these seemed like promising additions to Downtown Wichita for current residents, but they would not be likely to attract and wow visitors. Ever the salesman, DeBoer knew that he needed something iconic to symbolize the entire endeavor and help to sell a grandiose vision to the community. From its earliest iterations, then, the keystone of the whole project was a proposed three-hundred-foot-tall replica of *The Keeper of the Plains* statue.

Since its construction and installation in 1974 at the confluence of the Arkansas and Little Arkansas Rivers just northwest of Downtown Wichita, the forty-four-foot-tall *Keeper* statue, crafted by noted Native American artist Blackbear Bosin, had arguably been the city's most celebrated and identifiable landmark (Figure 2.2). Depicting an Indigenous man with arms upraised to the sky, the statue's symbolic placement at the juncture of the rivers paid homage to the Indigenous settlements and trading grounds that predated James Mead's arrival, and it drew attention to the rivers' significance in Wichita's history and cultural life. It remains a beloved cultural treasure in Wichita to this day, serving as the most widely used and recognized symbol for the city and region.[30]

Less than two decades after its initial erection, the *Keeper* had already cemented itself as a treasured Wichita landmark. DeBoer's plan would get rid of the original *Keeper* and replace it with a replica over six times as tall—indeed, the statue would approach the height of the Epic Center, the city's tallest skyscraper. In DeBoer's vision, this imposing new sculpture would rival the Statue of Liberty and the Gateway Arch in both stature and symbolic importance. The idea for an enlarged *Keeper* statue was popular both with Blackbear Bosin's widow and with the artist's friend and advisor Truman Ware, who at the time was board chair of the Mid-America All Indian Center, a museum dedicated to Indigenous history and culture situated adjacent to the *Keeper* statue along the rivers. Also excited about the idea was Richard Mitchell, the museum's director. "It is a gorgeous and priceless

Figure 2.2. *The Keeper of the Plains*. Photo by Chase Billingham.

work of art. Compared with the Keeper, the St. Louis arch would look like half a McDonald's sign," said Mitchell. The presumed need to compete with other cities through the creation of a distinctive landmark coursed through comments like these in support of the colossal *Keeper*. Meanwhile, some local Indigenous artists worried that the enlarged *Keeper* would unnecessarily commercialize Bosin's artistic vision.[31]

The giant *Keeper*, DeBoer hoped, would someday advertise Wichita to the world. In the meantime, the vision of the statue came to symbolize the DeBoer plan itself, even as the public continued to wait to hear the plan's visionary relay the rest of his project's details. Finally, after months of anticipation, the DeBoer plan finally got a full public unveiling in late May 1990 at a forum presented at Century II. DeBoer, with the enthusiasm of a revivalist preacher, worked hard to sell the public on his vision, whose price tag by this point had risen to an estimated $375 million. "It ain't that expensive," he asserted, exhorting city and county leaders to find the money, while simultaneously cautioning them not to raise property taxes to do so and not to hold a referendum to gauge public support for the idea. In his view, half of the money should come from city and county governments, while the other half should come from private donors and investors. At the unveiling, he personally pledged $1 million toward the project, and he aimed to raise over $50 million in private donations before the end of the year to demonstrate the robustness of the business community's support for the project.[32]

During the unveiling ceremony, DeBoer filled in more of the details: In addition to the arena, the ice rink, and the giant *Keeper*, there would be a new children's museum, an amphitheater, and a trolley system, along with new restaurants and hotels. DeBoer was adamant, however, that the entire project must happen in a comprehensive, not piecemeal, fashion. "We have to do it all at once. We can't do it in pieces. We're shooting craps here. We're stepping up to the big table, Wichita," he proclaimed. In a maudlin appeal to the crowd, DeBoer added one more symbolic change to initial ideas for the project: The height of the new *Keeper of the Plains* would be reduced to 299 feet—one foot shorter, he said, than the Statue of Liberty—because "we're Americans first."[33]

In making his pitch, DeBoer lambasted Wichita's habit of making plan after plan after plan for its downtown core without ever implementing anything. Indeed, many of the individual elements included in his comprehensive vision had been pitched before, and many could be found in the since-disregarded RTKL plan delivered just one year prior. What set him apart was his gumption and his willingness to get it done. "We spent too much energy figuring out where we were going to do something. We studied until the cows came home where something is going to be built. Who gives a damn, as long as it's part of the plan? Let's get it built," DeBoer said. Endorsements came in from public- and private-sector leaders, including the chairman of the Cessna Aircraft Corporation and the chairman of Fidelity Bank. Officials in state government examined the possibility of consolidating state agencies and over 1,000 state employees in a new building in Downtown Wichita—another idea originating in the RTKL proposal—in conjunction with DeBoer's plan.[34]

DeBoer and his supporters soon hit the road, holding public forums to promote the project and devoting millions of dollars to advertising. Confident that this extravagant redevelopment would attract many out-of-state tourists to Wichita, DeBoer felt that advertising was critical to draw those tourists to see what the city had accomplished. "You bet your life they'll come here," he said. "And when they come here . . . by golly, they're going to plan another weekend and they're going to come back the next time."[35]

Very quickly, though, the plan's aspirations were deflated, as members of the Wichita City Council expressed skepticism about committing tens of millions of public dollars toward the initiative. Only begrudgingly did they approve a motion ordering City Manager Chris Cherches to study whether it would be worthwhile to hire a consultant to investigate the proposal in depth. The skepticism of local elected officials was just a minor challenge to DeBoer, however, when compared to the existential crisis that was soon to grip all of Downtown Wichita and hamper all redevelopment efforts for decades.

Pollution Surprise: Groundwater Contamination Imperils Downtown Wichita

In 1986, the Kansas Department of Health and Environment (KDHE) discovered substantial pollution in the soil near an industrial firm about three miles south of Downtown Wichita. As further tests were conducted over the following years, it became clear that the city's pollution problem was not confined to this property. The scale of the problem that Wichita was dealing with began to emerge in 1990, just as the city was mobilizing to execute the DeBoer redevelopment plan. While many small sites of contamination had been identified for remediation, a major plume of groundwater pollution was found underneath the massive factory of the Coleman Company, the Wichita-based manufacturer of lamps and camping equipment (Figure 2.3). Unlike the original contamination that had been discovered south of downtown in 1986, the Coleman factory was located mere blocks from the heart of Downtown Wichita, and the leaching contaminants had infiltrated the groundwater that lay beneath most of the city's central business district and were spreading slowly southward, affecting an area roughly one mile wide and four and a half miles long. Immediately, business owners, downtown boosters, developers, and city leaders grew concerned, claiming that downtown real estate would be rendered unsellable and effectively worthless due to the pollution. This would cause banks to halt lending in the city's core, the already sluggish economic activity in the central business district would stagnate even further, and any significant redevelopment proposal would be doomed.[36]

Figure 2.3. Coleman Company factory, Downtown Wichita, awaiting demolition. Source: Courtesy of Keith Wondra. Used by permission. ©2011 KW Photography.

These fears intensified when KDHE revealed that the area of contamination—including all of Downtown Wichita—might be designated a Superfund site by the federal Environmental Protection Agency (EPA). The Coleman location was just one of hundreds of industrial spaces that had potentially contributed to the area's groundwater contamination; many, if not most, of the establishments that had contributed to the pollution were either no longer in business or had changed hands, further complicating the determination of blame and responsibility for cleanup.[37]

This was precisely the kind of situation that Superfund was designed to deal with. By sidestepping the tedious and contentious process of identifying individual responsibility, the EPA could step in and manage a centralized and efficient cleanup process. The idea of a Superfund declaration for Downtown Wichita, however, was a nonstarter for municipal and financial leaders in Wichita. There was of course the issue of the stigma associated with the Superfund designation itself. City officials feared that the stigma attached to that label could doom redevelopment efforts in the already moribund urban core. Equally troubling, though, was the issue of liability.

Superfund gave the EPA expansive power to collect the cost of cleanup from current property owners, regardless of whether they contributed to the pollution. The potential for such liability for ostensibly innocent parties could make potential buyers and investors wary of all downtown property. "You buy the property, you buy the cleanup. That's a fact, Jack," said a local attorney representing a downtown property owner.[38]

Because of the contamination, and because of the threat of Superfund liability, banks essentially stopped lending altogether in Downtown Wichita. Real estate transactions could not proceed, property owners worried that their property values would plummet, and—perhaps most importantly, in the eyes of local leaders—the entire DeBoer plan would become unsustainable without financing. They needed a solution, and they needed it immediately. While they discussed a few alternatives, the solution that the city (led by Cherches) came up with was to use tax increment financing (TIF) in a way that it had never been used before to finance the cleanup.

TIF is a municipal finance tool that has been in use across the country for decades, primarily as a means for financing urban redevelopment efforts in blighted areas. Normally, governments utilize TIF by issuing bonds to fund some sort of capital project in order to make a run-down area of the city more attractive and appealing to potential investors—in other words, to make the land more profitable. The logic behind TIF is that that public investment will spur private investment. As private developers come in and redevelop the area, property values will go up, generating additional property tax revenue. That additional revenue—the tax increment between what the area would have yielded in tax revenue if not for the public investment and the amount that it does yield after the redevelopment—is diverted away from the normal property tax stream and is used to pay off the bonds.[39]

The Wichita groundwater TIF plan would work differently, and it was sometimes referred to not as TIF per se but as a "tax decrement financing" plan. The assumption underlying Cherches's TIF plan was that, as a result of the contamination, all property values in this large affected area had automatically dropped by a big margin (40 percent, they often argued). But, because the city stepped in to fund the cleanup, the cause of that potential decline in values had been eliminated, and property values, they assumed, immediately rebounded to their prior level. That difference—between what people's property values had been and what the city presumed they *might* have dropped to because of the pollution—became the "increment" from which property tax revenue was diverted from its normal uses (to fund local schools and city and county services) and instead used to finance the cleanup operation.[40]

This was the first time that TIF would be employed in Wichita; it was not very well understood, and this proposal was unlike just about any TIF that had been previously attempted anywhere else. Implementing it would require getting approval from the city, the county, the local school district, and the state legislature, all of whom would be affected by this change in tax revenue. And so this idea of a novel mechanism for financing an urban environmental cleanup effort had to be sold to taxpayers, to local taxing authorities, and to the state.

Selling the idea required several important rhetorical strategies aimed at persuading various constituencies. First, it was necessary to persuade the public that if the city did not act quickly, the EPA would step in and take over, turning all of Downtown Wichita into a Superfund site. This had to be resisted, city leaders argued, because the use of Superfund would entail significant delays to the cleanup, would end up costing more money, would result in litigation, and would make innocent parties liable for paying for the cleanup. Perhaps more than anything else, the "Superfund" label would generate enormous stigma that would hinder the city's attempts to rejuvenate and rebrand its downtown core. Superfund was consistently portrayed as a looming federal threat to local control, an argument that resonated with many conservative, limited-government advocates in the city and state. Acting decisively and agreeing to pay for the cleanup with local money, TIF proponents argued, would allow them to avoid those federal delays, lawsuits, cost overruns, and stigma.[41]

Second, facing widespread concerns that a TIF district would place the burden for cleanup on the taxpayers of Wichita instead of on the businesses that caused the pollution (especially Coleman), selling the TIF plan required the city to declare that they would first seek repayment from the responsible polluting parties. Taxpayers would only be on the hook for the amount that the city was unable to collect from the guilty parties. In practice, though, this meant that the city got tied up in litigation for years trying to recover the costs of pollution remediation, and the city lost in court on most of its cases. As such, despite assurances that polluters would pay and that TIF proceeds would essentially just be a backup funding mechanism, Wichita taxpayers in reality ended up paying for the bulk of the cleanup, and those cost estimates ballooned over time. Original estimates for the cleanup cost were around $20–$30 million; by the expiration of the groundwater cleanup TIF district, the estimates had risen to $80–$90 million.

Third, it was necessary to place the emphasis on the environmental goals of the cleanup project, when in fact much of the driving force for the initiative was economic, not environmental, in nature. There certainly was contaminated groundwater underneath much of Downtown Wichita, but this was not an immediate public health or environmental crisis. The pollution did not pose a threat to the drinking water within the contaminated area. Except for a few private wells, the groundwater in this area was not used and did not threaten residents' health. The major and immediate threat was economic: Public- and private-sector leaders' major concern was that Superfund would trigger liability concerns and potentially harm property values. Stepping in quickly with the TIF district was therefore not primarily about environmental urgency but economic strategy. Still, the environmental threat was very useful in helping Wichita to sell the TIF plan, and city leaders used it effectively. "Wichita is in the middle of a community-wide campaign to revitalize its downtown," Cherches wrote. "The discovery of groundwater contamination marked the end of these development plans unless local policy could be devised to counter the dampening effects of environmental liability associated with Superfund."[42]

Looming over these worries was the economic stagnation of Downtown Wichita, and what ultimately hung in the balance was the grand DeBoer redevelopment plan and the 299-foot-tall *Keeper of the Plains* statue. If lending and credit seized up entirely in the city core, in Cherches's estimation, it would scuttle the potential for nearly $400 million in downtown revitalization. When Cherches put into place the "tax decrement" strategy to fund groundwater remediation, thus preventing a Superfund declaration in Downtown Wichita and freeing up lending in the core, DeBoer was ecstatic, claiming that he "sent Chris [Cherches] a note and said, 'God bless you. How can I help?'"[43]

Skeptics, Cynics, and Other Speedbumps

As local officials confronted the groundwater crisis, DeBoer's ambitious yet vague redevelopment scheme appeared more and more fanciful. DeBoer reacted harshly to the skepticism of public officials, stating bluntly to

DAC members that "we cannot afford to have our governing bodies fiddle around with a whole lot of questions while they try to avoid making the hard decisions." Impatient, DeBoer organized a series of public forums to be held at Century II, at Wichita State University, and at a city park community center to pitch the plan directly to city residents. "I'm going to say a lot of stuff the political types don't say," he promised.

Following through on his pledge, he directly challenged skeptics in the audience at the Century II forum. "Have you seen *Field of Dreams*?" he asked them. "Build it! They will come," he pledged, echoing a famous catchphrase from that film. He went on to warn and cajole, telling the crowd that they could risk having "the future of our city directed by a negative minority. Get involved!" Still, he provided no firm data to support the claim that there would be steady demand for a new 18,000-seat arena, nor what its main purpose would be. "I think it's premature to talk about the specifics of how it would be used," he stated. This represented precisely the type of wishful and unsupported promise that had characterized past downtown plans and had provoked so much angst among the elected officials whom DeBoer expected to pick up the tab.[44]

When a poll conducted by a local television station yielded 234 people in favor of DeBoer's plan, 457 against, and over 1,300 respondents undecided, DeBoer spun the numbers confidently, proclaiming that "all of [the undecided respondents] would have been positive." In this way, unpersuaded members of the public joined reticent politicians on DeBoer's list of unenlightened obstructionists. His lack of any firm financials and his inability to guarantee residents that their property taxes would not go up (despite optimistic projections on that front from Cherches) frustrated attendees at a public forum, serving to undermine DeBoer's credibility with the public. "It's an investment," he assured them vaguely. "It will pay off." At least once, he had to fend off hecklers.[45]

While Cherches may have held out hope that city property taxes would not be forced to rise to pay for the sweeping riverfront overhaul, at the county level, public officials were less confident. County Commissioner Bud Hentzen held his own news conference in June 1990, making clear that county property tax collections would have to rise to support the county's portion of the public investment in DeBoer's project. Though he stipulated that he supported the idea of the project in theory, Hentzen simultaneously admonished promoters of the project, stating bluntly that "we should be telling people the truth right now up front." County Commission Chairman Mark Schroeder concurred with Hentzen's conclusion, and County Commissioner Billy McCray went further, calling DeBoer's idea a "fantasy" that would end up harming and burdening the region's poor, senior citizens, racial and ethnic minorities, and working families. McCray refused to support what he believed would be a necessary tax increase to make it possible, despite DeBoer's pledge that no tax increases would be required.[46]

At city hall, the Wichita City Council did ultimately approve up to $300,000 to study the feasibility of the plan, despite an impending crunch in municipal finances. Lower-than-expected revenues and recent court judgments against the city caused Cherches to recommend a property tax rate increase and higher water and sewer fees on residents to balance the budget in 1991 and 1992. A poll commissioned by WI/SE showed that a majority of county residents favored the downtown plan, but only a small percentage were in favor of raising property taxes to finance it.[47]

Some evidence emerged to suggest, as DeBoer and his supporters had promised, that a major public investment in this grand redevelopment scheme could produce positive multiplier effects by stoking new private investment downtown. One example of this encouraging trend came from the Coleman Company, which was in the process of seeking a new location for its corporate headquarters even as it worked to evade liability for the groundwater pollution generated by its former downtown manufacturing facility. Coleman considered the possibility of leasing space in the recently constructed Epic Center, the tallest office tower in Kansas, which was still only about 50 percent occupied. But they also announced that as a component of the DeBoer downtown plan, they might consider building an entirely new downtown headquarters structure. The Wichita branch of the Boy Scouts of America, too, committed to building a new downtown headquarters on the condition that the city get to work executing DeBoer's entire plan.[48]

The first real test of the viability of the downtown revitalization campaign came as Dave Burk and his business partners moved forward with their farmers market plan and sought subsidies and tax incentives from city and county government. The city agreed to move forward with negotiations with Burk, and local business leaders encouraged the project as a first step in realizing DeBoer's vision. "I think this can be an excellent demonstration of our overall commitment to the downtown revitalization plan," said Marvin Wynn, the chief operating officer at WI/SE, directly tying the farmers market project to the DeBoer plan in his testimony before the city council. The city government's approval put pressure on the county government, which soon approved money for infrastructure improvements to support Burk's plan to transform an old warehouse into the farmers market building and revitalize other nearby buildings for retail and dining. But County Commission Chair Mark Schroeder was not pleased with the awkward position that the city and the developers had put the county in. "If we don't support it, we're the devils of Wichita," he lamented, adding that he was still waiting for more information regarding how this project would fit into DeBoer's overall vision and how much it would cost the county.[49]

The revitalization proposal had become so closely identified with DeBoer that its fortunes, in many ways, rose and fell with the public's perception of its originator. The initial public enthusiasm for the vision owed much to DeBoer's gusto and skill as a salesman. Soon, though, the close association of the project with the outspoken, hard-driving, and often irascible DeBoer came to be seen as a potential liability, and he made the strategic decision to step back from his public-facing leadership role. "I don't want people to support this because I'm some kind of silver-tongued devil," he insisted. "I want them to support it because it makes sense." To that end, he enlisted local leaders in business and banking to take more prominent roles and lead committees charged with elaborating the details of the plan. The need for leadership intensified when DAC Executive Director Nat Griffin left Wichita to take another job, and the push to create a powerful new public Urban Renewal–like agency to oversee redevelopment activities gained steam.[50]

As plans evolved for the proposed new riverfront hotel, public- and private-sector leaders flew to Denver to meet with Ross Investments, the development company behind the hotel proposal. Though he had suggested that he would take a backseat role going forward, Jack DeBoer joined them. DeBoer's role in the negotiations was "nebulous," according to *The Wichita Eagle*. He had thrust himself into the process by his adamant claims that, although the hotel was necessary for Downtown Wichita, it would fail in the absence of the adoption of the comprehensive redevelopment package he had proposed. The city council had yet to endorse the totality of DeBoer's plan, however, making DeBoer's presence during the hotel negotiations in Denver all the more awkward. DeBoer also strongly and very publicly opposed the use of public incentives or giveaways to developers, substantially weakening the city's negotiating position in its conversations with Ross.[51]

Nevertheless, representatives from Ross unveiled their plans to Wichita the following month, proudly predicting that the new 314-room riverfront hotel would be so successful that it would simultaneously boost occupancy at the city's other hotels by attracting new visitors to the city. DeBoer, while impressed by the design, continued to preach to the public about how the city should offer no incentives to the developer, adding that "build[ing] that hotel free-standing, without this entire plan, is foolhardy, is folly." The city must, he insisted, adopt all elements of his vision as one comprehensive package. "Until we can make this whole plan come together, I'm opposed to doing anything," he declared. This, of course, put city officials negotiating with Ross in a difficult position, as they badly wanted to secure the hotel deal but did not want to alienate De Boer in the process. For their part, the hotel developers brushed off DeBoer, stating curtly, "We appreciate Jack's opinion. We disagree with it in a number of areas."[52]

Finding the Money

By November 1990, Cherches and members of the city council were confidently boasting that they could fund their portion of the public commitment to the DeBoer downtown plan without raising property taxes. Instead, they would utilize tax increment financing (despite the fact that the Gilbert-Mosley TIF overlay district covering all of Downtown Wichita to fund groundwater remediation was already in the works). On the county side, Schroeder and other county commissioners were incredulous about the city's ability to pay its share without tax hikes, and they asserted that such a pledge from the county government would be impossible. In addition, the county commission would not commit to any public funding until DeBoer had secured his promised private donations, yet by November private fundraising had not even begun.[53]

The stakes were high. "This is one of the most important decisions I think elected officials have been called upon to make in the 120-year history of this city," said Wichita Mayor Bob Knight. The city government decided to roll the dice, though, committing in November to about $113 million in investment, to be funded with TIF, new sales taxes on food, rental cars, and hotel rooms, and a redirection of previously planned capital expenditures. When Council Member Sheldon Kamen proposed putting the city's financial commitment to a referendum the following month, Mayor Knight led the charge against the motion, rallying his colleagues to get behind DeBoer; Kamen's referendum motion failed.[54]

Still, city leaders' pledge not to raise property taxes was clearly untenable, since they were also demanding that the county government put up a third of the public financing for the project, and county leaders were firm in their claims that that would be impossible without a county-level property tax increase. Property owners paid only one property tax bill, with separate mill levies established by the county government and the various cities and school districts that residents inhabited, and most taxpayers did not look closely enough at their tax bills to be able to clearly distinguish which governing entity had caused their tax rates to go up. So even if the City of Wichita bragged to residents that they had not raised their property taxes, those residents might not see the situation the same way if the city's demands on the county caused the county commission to increase its share of property owners' tax bills. "The plan does in effect call for an increase in property taxes," said Schroeder. The proposal for new sales taxes also drew concern from state legislators, who would be required to approve such new taxes.[55]

To make the project feasible, public officials expected DeBoer and WI/SE to come up with over $50 million in private financial commitments by the following February. As February rolled around though, DeBoer and his allies still had not begun their fundraising effort. "Obviously not only are we not going to have the money in the bank by February 15, we are not going to be anywhere near having the full pledges committed by then," conceded prominent local advertising executive Al Higdon, whom DeBoer had charged with helping to lead the fundraising effort. Still, even as the sluggish pace of private fundraising promised to cause further delays in the project, Higdon and DeBoer remained confident that they could smooth things over with the city.[56]

The City Election and Its Impact

Downtown revitalization was a key issue in the county commission election in the fall of 1990, and, as plans dragged on with little progress, it remained the central question when elections for mayor and city council were held the following spring. Knight, the incumbent mayor, had tied his fortunes tightly to the DeBoer plan; his main opponent, attorney Jim Lawing, was generally supportive of the plan, but he exploited public reticence about the cost to challenge Knight politically. Jack DeBoer watched nonchalantly as he became a key focus of debates that could determine who would run the city government—and, by consequence, have authority over his ambitious agenda—in the future. "I don't understand city politics at all. To me, it's just about as interesting as watching hair grow," he said. DeBoer did contribute the maximum allowable amount to Knight's reelection campaign, however, and he also contributed to the electoral opponent of Council Member Sheldon Kamen, the most outspoken skeptic of DeBoer's vision on the council.[57]

Cracks in the edifice of the fabulous and comprehensive downtown proposal became increasingly clear as the months dragged on. By March 1991, support for the massive *Keeper of the Plains* was waning among the local Native American community, neighborhood activists, and anti-tax skeptics, and Knight acknowledged that the giant replica of the statue would probably never be built. According to Higdon, the *Keeper* statue—and the entire proposal—suffered from a public "malaise" attributable to the lack of action and the sluggish pace of fundraising. Meanwhile, DeBoer had retreated from his bombastic public appearances, and he had taken to communicating to the public via letters sent directly to Knight, which the mayor would read aloud during city council meetings.[58]

In his own reelection campaign, Council Member Greg Ferris asserted about DeBoer's plan that "nobody's for it," and he suggested that the various components of the project should be considered one at a time, rather than in a comprehensive simultaneous manner. The people of his district, according to Ferris, "are for reasonable development [but] not for some $375 million pie in the sky." Members of a local anti-tax group that called itself the Wichita Symposium for Economic Responsibility (WISER) challenged Knight and DeBoer to a public debate on the proposal, which they declined. To stoke public opposition to the plan, WISER also erected a billboard downtown portraying a destitute taxpayer wearing a barrel. As candidates canvassed neighborhoods, residents told them that taxes were their biggest concern. City staff reported that Wichita faced a substantial budget shortfall over the coming years and—even leaving aside the expenditures necessary for the DeBoer development plan or the groundwater remediation effort—the city would likely require either a tax increase or a cutback on city services.[59]

Mayor Knight won reelection in the spring campaign, but also reelected that year were Council Members Sheldon Kamen and Greg Ferris, the council's two most vocal DeBoer skeptics; both Kamen and Ferris defeated opponents who had strongly supported the DeBoer plan. Kamen interpreted his victory as an endorsement of a more "prudent approach" to downtown redevelopment. Knight himself interpreted the results in a similar manner, admitting that "it has gone to the point now where I believe the [DeBoer] subject is uncertain at best." Going forward, the idea of a comprehensive all-or-nothing package was unsustainable; all downtown projects would have to be considered individually.[60]

The Standoff

After months of silence, DeBoer reemerged shortly after the election to receive the "Uncommon Citizen Award" from the Wichita Area Chamber of Commerce. He used his acceptance speech to excoriate the naysayers whose skepticism had prevailed at the polls, tying his emphasis on an all-encompassing redevelopment effort to a broader theoretical understanding of entrepreneurialism in urban governance. "We have to remember that the '90s are not going to be a continuation of filling out forms for yet another giveaway or handout from the federal government," he declared. Rather, "We must compete with the world and that will take uncommon leadership." City and county officials did not take kindly to DeBoer's public lambasting, returning fire at DeBoer and accusing him and Higdon of failing to raise the private support for the project that they had promised. "They haven't done a thing. They've done zero, zip," said Ferris. Realizing the precarious situation facing the downtown plan, DeBoer and the WI/SE directors met and issued an ultimatum to local politicians. They needed to be totally committed to his plan, DeBoer proclaimed: "If they're not, let's quit talking about it."[61]

Those public officials would not give DeBoer the commitment that he wanted. County Commissioner Billy McCray told *The Wichita Eagle* that public support for DeBoer's vision was "so soft it's like melted butter." The state government had rejected Wichita's proposal to levy meals and rental car taxes to support the plan, leaving the city with fewer resources to commit to the initiative, and business leaders were failing to raise significant amounts of private funding. With support flagging, DeBoer suggested that the city council, which had voted to endorse his plan the previous year, vote once again to reiterate its confidence in him and his proposal. The county government, too, grew weary of DeBoer and WI/SE, urging boosters to make some progress on the stagnant riverfront hotel project before they would commit any public resources to the grand riverfront scheme. What ensued was a standoff between public and private forces, which, in the words of City Council Member Jim Ward, amounted to "a game of chicken." Soon, Higdon was stating publicly that DeBoer's vision would have to be cut nearly in half to be feasible, but he did so without consulting DeBoer, who was not on board with that idea.[62]

Meanwhile, retailers continued to flee Downtown Wichita or close down altogether, and it appeared that the area was even further in peril than it had been when DeBoer had first unveiled his plan nearly two years earlier. But the city center was not the only area of Wichita suffering from underinvestment, and members of the city council, growing weary of an all-encompassing approach to downtown redevelopment, began to assert that attention to the core must be balanced with investment in outlying neighborhoods. Council Member Stan Reeser, who represented the deteriorating lower-income and racially diverse south side of the city (which was also beset by widespread groundwater contamination), was particularly adamant on this point. This drew another angry rebuke from DeBoer, who shouted during a televised forum that he was "sick and tired of spending my time listening to the negative, do-nothing minority" before calling out the members of WISER for "spreading this crap."[63]

The Showdown

The tense standoff led to an ultimate showdown in the city council in late June 1991. Knight intended to grant DeBoer his wish of a second vote of commitment, even as he made concessions toward the possibility of scaling back the plan's ambitions. Yet following a rollicking four-hour debate, all that was accomplished was another vague pledge from the council to the notion of downtown revitalization and an abstract schedule for considering various individual items over the following months. During the meeting, the business leaders who had pledged to have raised over $50 million by February conceded that they had managed to secure less than $5 million. Witnessing the lack of progress on display, members of the county commission who attended the city meeting came away with little motivation to invest the county's money in the project.[64]

With the proposed new meals and rental car taxes off the table after the state government spiked the idea, city staff, who had assured the city council the previous year that they could commit $113 million in public funds toward downtown redevelopment without raising property tax rates, came back to the council with a revised estimate: $76 million. The city council planned a series of special nighttime meetings through July and August to consider individual aspects of the redevelopment effort—a clear affront to DeBoer's insistence that his proposal was an all-or-nothing deal. The first of these meetings was largely successful, as city leaders approved plans to build a new central bus depot, renovate a run-down and unprofitable hotel, improve parking options in the burgeoning Old Town district, and study the possibility of renovating a former department store building to house state government offices. Though these were big expenditures for major projects that could potentially have some impact on the vitality of Downtown Wichita, they were mostly unconnected to the grandiose plans for leisure and entertainment amenities that made up the core of the DeBoer proposal. City officials chose these items to vote on first because they were the least controversial; their quick approval, they hoped, could potentially help build momentum for the more ambitious aspects of the DeBoer plan. Reflecting on this modest set of downtown accomplishments, Council Member Frank Ojile remarked, "We're off, and walking."[65]

By the second of the special evening meetings, though, momentum began to sputter. The city council timidly endorsed the general idea of building the new riverfront hotel but remained divided on the prospect of public subsidies for the project. Council members were generally unanimous in their support for abstract proposals for downtown rejuvenation, yet when it came time to commit to specific tangible items, such as a controversial conversion of Main Street in the heart of the central business district from a one-way to a two-way street, consensus proved elusive.[66]

The dissension on display among city leaders over those rather modest initiatives paled in comparison to what would emerge when core components of the DeBoer plan appeared for votes. In late July, the council unanimously rejected the idea—pushed by DeBoer himself—of constructing a new restaurant in Riverside Park, fronting on the river near downtown. Since the earliest incarnations of the DeBoer plan, residents of the quiet Riverside neighborhood adjacent to the park expressed grave reservations about the new development that was proposed for their neighborhood. DeBoer had seen the riverfront restaurant as a keystone of his vision for the city center. Another key DeBoer idea, the construction of a system of locks along the Arkansas River to facilitate boat travel, was also unanimously rejected. On a third key element of the DeBoer plan, closing off the very busy riverfront thruway of McLean Boulevard to all vehicle traffic, the council punted, deferring a decision on that controversial question until later in the summer.[67]

A proposal to establish a $40 million endowment to support riverfront museums also generated controversy. Would this endowment supplement the public subsidies that Wichita already provided to those museums or replace those subsidies, thus helping, in the hopes of Ferris, to "get the city out of the museum business" once and for all? WI/SE chairman Marvin Wynn admitted that "I don't think there is a clear understanding on that." As they had on the McLean Boulevard issue, the council deferred on the museum endowment.[68]

These votes spelled trouble for the viability of DeBoer's vision, but more than all the others, one vote essentially sealed the fate of this proposal that had gripped Wichita for two full years. In August, the city council unanimously and unequivocally rejected the emblem of DeBoer's entire vision, the 299-foot-tall *Keeper of the Plains*, which Ferris denounced as "frivolous."[69]

The following week, they balked at a proposal to build the 18,000-seat arena on the west bank of the river following protests from residents whose houses would have to be destroyed to make way for the venue. They did vote, however, to build a new ice rink, which had been discussed for years and had been co-opted into the DeBoer plan. The council endorsed the idea of establishing a system of buses mocked up to look like antique trolleys, but they opposed the idea of spending a recommended $275,000 in city money on annual operating expenses for the trolleys. Thus, the conversation in Wichita had shifted downward over a period of two years from DeBoer's fiery calls for $375 million in new downtown spending to the city council's wariness over finding $275,000 to run a few gussied-up buses through the core. They also rejected a proposal to spend $4.5 million on a downtown marketing campaign.[70]

Few components of the downtown plan divided the community as strongly as the recommendation to close McLean Boulevard to vehicle traffic. The busy riverfront road was used by many area commuters to get to jobs in the city center, and drivers enjoyed the unimpeded views of the Arkansas that driving along McLean afforded (Figure 2.4). In August, supporters and opponents of the plan to close McLean reached a compromise, agreeing to keep the road but reroute it slightly westward, away from the river, in order to allow more room for riverfront development. Even this compromise, however, provoked some dissent among council members who worried that riverfront development would impede drivers' views of the river.[71]

Finally, in early September, the city council did commit to $75 million in spending on downtown revitalization, and they urged the county government to pitch in another $25 million. Though just a small fraction of what DeBoer had sought at the beginning of this initiative nearly two years earlier, this financial pledge marked progress in the minds of many downtown boosters. Leaders at WI/SE claimed that this public-sector commitment would help to get private-sector leaders off the sidelines and finally make good on their pledges of philanthropic support for downtown development. However, the financial commitments that the city council approved were directly contingent on private-sector matching, so despite the council's vote, public spending would remain unlikely in the absence of private fundraising. "The private side has got to come forward, or roughly half of what the city has committed to is going to go away," said Ferris.[72]

The private side did not, in fact, come forward in response to the city's largesse. Instead, just the opposite happened. Claiming that they were unconvinced the city had put up enough money to make a real impact on the project, business leaders stopped their fundraising campaign altogether a month later. With no arena, no restaurant in the park, and no 299-foot-tall statue, the business community wondered what, exactly, they were committing to. Al Higdon, who had expressed optimism in September when the city council approved its $75 million, struck a much different tone in October, asking rhetorically, "Is it the right $75 million, or even close to it, to have the right effect on economic development?" Business owner Hale Ritchie, a leading voice at WI/SE, had also celebrated the council vote in

Figure 2.4. McLean Boulevard and the Downtown Wichita riverfront, 2002. Source: Leslie R. Broadstreet. Courtesy of Wichita State University Libraries, Special Collections and University Archives. Used by permission.

September, but he changed his tune in October, claiming that the council "voted to do $75 million worth of stuff, but it wasn't the same stuff that was in the plan to begin with."

For his part, Ferris became exhausted with the business community's dodging. "They're great cheerleaders," he said, "but when it comes time to put up or shut up, they are not really true players. They've never carried, in my estimation, the share that they ask us to carry." One of the major sources of consternation, it turned out, was the council's earlier compromise over McLean Boulevard. While Knight had seen this move as a great facilitator of progress in the city center, DeBoer was nonplussed, as he had demanded that the road be shut down to cars entirely. By moving the road westward, the city had actually designed it to run across parcels where DeBoer had wanted to put up an amusement park and an apartment complex. Though DeBoer himself continued to avoid speaking to the public, Fidelity Bank President Marvin Bastian, a leader of the private fundraising drive, said of DeBoer, "I think he is filled with disgust."[73]

WI/SE Regroups

By early 1992, WI/SE had a new leader, former Boeing executive Lionel Alford. Despite his reputation for working hard and getting things done, Alford did not exude confidence about the potential for significant fund-raising toward the downtown campaign that his organization had spear-headed three years earlier. "The fund-raising drive has started, but it's sputtering. So it's got to have a jump start," Alford said of the fund drive that WI/SE had pledged to have completely wrapped up twelve months prior. He made a new commitment, saying that by April 1992, WI/SE would come up with a plan for how to raise the money. Despite this further delay, Knight continued to project enthusiasm. When Kansas Governor Joan Finney announced that some state government offices would move into a former department store building in Downtown Wichita, Knight called it "nothing less than a defining moment for our core area," even though it had little to do with the DeBoer plan for a rejuvenated core that Knight had championed.[74]

As Alford's new April deadline approached, it became more and more clear that the business community would not come close to achieving even their more modest goal of $40 million in private commitments. Meanwhile, it appeared that the plan for the riverfront hotel was crumbling, too; the developers demanded at least $8 million in public subsidy, but the city could not pay it. "We are not going to come up with $8 million of taxpayer money for a hotel," Knight acknowledged with resignation, adding, "We don't have it." Just two months into the job, and with his own self-imposed deadline coming up quickly, Alford was fed up, threatening to quit as WI/SE chairman in the face of inaction. His exasperation elevating, he gave the WI/SE board an ultimatum: "I have to have a plan that you agreed we're gonna do, or you'll have somebody else try it, OK?"[75]

WI/SE did not give Alford the victory he wanted, and they did not meet his April deadline. Instead, in a May meeting they proudly announced a new coordinated strategy to start fundraising in June, taking a new tack toward catalyzing downtown growth. In that same meeting, they officially disbanded the Downtown Action Corporation, the group Jack DeBoer had led when he unveiled the bold vision that had sparked the previous three years of effort. After eliminating DAC, Alford asked DeBoer to sit on a new committee that would replace it, called the Core Area Advisory Committee.

Again, the private sector did not meet their self-imposed deadline. By the fall of 1992, WI/SE had clearly lowered its aspirations, declaring that developments like the opening of small antique stores and a barber shop downtown were signals of a rebounding core. Rather than securing the massive upfront private endowment required to initiate large-scale revitalization, WI/SE's president hedged, stating that "most of the private money will come at the back end, after some of these things are here and it's clear that downtown is alive and well and it's a good place to invest."[76]

Betting on the Arkansas

Talks with Ross Investment Group, the developer pushing the hotel along the river, fell apart, and Ross withdrew from negotiations in April 1992. Still, the City of Wichita did not give up on its hopes for a high-rise riverfront hotel. Very quickly, new figures moved in to seize on the city's hotel enthusiasm with new proposals. One proposal came from Phil Ruffin, the businessman who had earlier dismissed the idea of a major hotel on the river as unworkable without massive subsidy. Ruffin proposed a scaled-down hotel near the highway, which, though more modest in scope, would nevertheless also involve rerouting the Arkansas River to build a horseshoe-shaped island in the middle of Downtown Wichita. This idea did not excite the city council.[77]

The other proposal, which did catch the council's attention, came from a brash twenty-nine-year-old real estate developer named George Laham, who, in collaboration with the Wyandotte Nation, put forward a plan for a $100 million hotel and casino complex. Gambling had never been mentioned as a component of a rejuvenated Downtown Wichita, and it flew in the face of the family-friendly environment comprising the amusement park, ice rink, children's museum, and aquatic activities that DeBoer had envisioned. Its backers promised, however, that the inclusion of casino gambling would allow the hotel to be built with no taxpayer subsidy. The cost-free element of the casino proposal was particularly appealing to Ferris, whose cynicism regarding DeBoer's plan was rooted in a commitment to fiscal conservatism.[78]

Laham's idea involved the City of Wichita selling riverfront property to the Wyandotte Nation for the casino portion of the project, thereby giving the tribe sovereignty over the land and allowing for casino gambling without requiring much bureaucratic interference from the city or state. With the endorsement of six out of its seven members, the Wichita City Council, just months after ending talks with Ross, began negotiating with Laham and his partners. The one early opponent of the project on the city council was the most powerful voice, Mayor Bob Knight, who worried that the city's socially conservative culture would look unfavorably upon such an idea. "I don't like gambling being sold as a strategy where the city gets something for nothing. That's just not true," Knight said. Though a poll showed two-thirds of Wichitans supporting the casino proposal, many religious leaders, as well as Lionel Alford and other key business leaders, came out against it, as did US Senators Nancy Kassebaum and Bob Dole along with Congressman Dan Glickman.[79]

Despite this opposition, the city council voted in August to move forward with Laham's proposal, dubbed "Riverport Plaza." Disregarding this endorsement by Wichita's elected leaders, the business community continued to act as if the casino would never be constructed. "I happen to be very skeptical as to whether the casino will ever materialize," said Don Slawson, the chair of the WI/SE Core Areas Advisory Committee. WI/SE would conduct its own study of Laham's proposal, Slawson added, as well as other alternative plans that the council had rejected. Also opposed to the downtown casino were the owners of the Wichita Greyhound Park, who feared that casino gambling would lead to financial ruin for their racetrack, which had opened just three years earlier in the northern suburb of Park City. Bending to WI/SE's obstruction, Knight called for a referendum asking voters whether they wanted casino gambling in Downtown Wichita, even though the city council had already decided to move forward in negotiations with Laham just one week earlier. Laham and his partners had no patience for this type of delay, warning that proceeding with such a referendum would provoke them to look for an alternate location for their casino. The city council did not go along with Knight's call for a referendum, but casino opponents, led by local religious and business leaders, mobilized to try to gain enough signatures on a petition to force the referendum.[80]

Riverport Plaza faced another obstacle, as other Native American tribes voiced objections to the State of Kansas allowing the Wyandotte, who were located in Oklahoma, to get priority in the chance to expand casino gambling in Kansas. Some observers with expertise in the business of Native American casino operations saw Wichita's plan as farfetched, since most profitable casinos had been built on existing reservation land; Laham's proposal would require ceding large amounts of prime, centrally located city-owned land to an out-of-state tribe, which would require approval from the US Department of the Interior.[81]

Even in the face of this widespread opposition from the business elite, religious moralists, federal elected officials, and other Native American tribes, the Wichita City Council moved in November to formalize the deal with Laham and his partners, working to finalize negotiations before opponents could gather the requisite number of signatures to trigger the referendum. Casino opponents cried foul, but Greg Ferris, the leading proponent on the city council for Riverport Plaza, retorted that time was of the essence if they wanted to keep Laham from walking away from the table. "If we don't do it Tuesday, we're not going to do it, ever," Ferris warned. In advance of the vote, however, Stand Up for Wichita, the organization formed to represent casino opponents, sought an injunction against the council's action in Sedgwick County District Court. On the same day, Council Member Frank Ojile reversed his support for Riverport Plaza. The hotel and casino, which had enjoyed majority support on the Wichita City Council just months earlier, now appeared doomed.[82]

The district court judge rejected the casino opponents' request for an injunction. Regardless, rather than finalizing the contract as they had planned, the council voted to delay action on the project. Such a delay imperiled the entire plan, as state and federal officials were working on legislation to limit the allowable sites for Native American casinos, and Kansas Governor Joan Finney threatened that she would not approve the deal if the Wyandotte did not have possession of the riverfront land before the beginning of the new year. The city council, with one seat vacant after Knight abruptly resigned to become Kansas secretary of commerce, was split, 3–3, in their support for Laham's plan after Ojile's reversal. The project's fate hinged on the selection of an interim council member to fill the vacant seat.[83]

Jerry Aday, the director of Wichita's Mid-American All-Indian Center Museum and a Riverport supporter, was selected to join the city council. This encouraging appointment notwithstanding, Laham and his partners had grown exhausted with Wichita; Laham's attorney and spokesman, David Elkouri, lamented that the council seemed to have very little power over the city that they nominally oversaw. "There are any number of non-elected officials who seem to have a lot of decision-making power around here, and that's contributed to a hostile environment in this city," Elkouri said. Ferris seemed resigned to the fate of the casino that he had championed, stating, "I would be very, very surprised if it even comes up again."[84]

Nevertheless, casino opponents continued to gather signatures on their petition. Elkouri blasted his opponents, including the prominent business leaders who had previously championed the DeBoer plan but had failed to generate the requisite private financing. "They have not put any money where their mouths are as far as downtown is concerned," Elkouri charged. The looming potential for a long, ugly, and expensive election fight eventually convinced Laham to abandon the project. By January 1993, the dream of Riverport Plaza was dead.

City leaders had thus given up the hotel deal with Ross, drastically scaled back the DeBoer downtown overhaul, and now lost the casino. The future of growth in Wichita's core looked bleak. On top of it all, Boeing, the city's largest employer, announced a wave of layoffs at its Wichita manufacturing facility. Lionel Alford acknowledged these foreboding prospects. "Nothing would make me feel better than for you to quote me saying that 1993 is going to be the year downtown," he told *The Wichita Eagle*. "But I've got some other problems right now."[85]

By the spring of 1993, there was still no private endowment for downtown development and museum support. The city's commitment to museum development and expansion, which had been included in its $75 million commitment two years earlier, had always been contingent upon the infusion of substantial private investment. "Everybody is waiting on everybody else to go first," said Council Member Stan Reeser. Alford, striking a different tone from his aggressive stance the prior year, said meekly that WI/SE would, "I hope, be supportive" of fundraising efforts, but "that is not in place right now."[86]

Back to Square One

It did not happen. The riverfront restaurant, the locks along the Arkansas, the 299-foot-tall emblem of Wichita, the amusement park, the Riverport Plaza casino—none of it happened.

In the years that followed, some minor individual elements of the DeBoer proposal did materialize, but not in the form of any comprehensive revival of Downtown Wichita. On September 20, 1996, WI/SE was quietly disbanded. As public- and private-sector leaders reflected on the legacy of the organization, they struggled to identify any tangible results that WI/SE had produced, despite over $15 million in taxpayer investment in the organization over the course of its decade of existence. "WI/SE was all about creating coalitions. That's all it was from the very beginning," said former Chairman Tom Kitch. But even as they were abandoning WI/SE, the business leaders who drove its creation were looking forward to creating a new organization to continue its work. "If you don't have WI/SE, you have got to have something," said Lionel Alford.[87]

Within a matter of months, a new group—the Wichita Downtown Development Corporation (WDDC)—would rise from the ashes of WI/SE. As I detail in chapter 4, WDDC would take up the mantle of economic development in the core that WI/SE had pursued for years with lackluster results. Driven by many of the same public- and private-sector leaders who had pushed the WI/SE agenda, WDDC would encounter economic, political, and demographic obstacles identical to those that impeded its predecessor's progress.

In the wake of this string of unfulfilled promises, leaders in Wichita came to conclude, more than ever before, that substantial progress toward a rejuvenated downtown would be largely unattainable until something was done to control or remove some of the most visible obstacles to economic prosperity in the core—the human obstacles. The struggle over how to effectively manage the problems of homelessness and poverty would figure heavily in discussions of downtown redevelopment in the twenty-first century.

REMOVING HUMAN OBSTACLES TO PROGRESS

3

The Death of Naftzger Park

On May 10, 2018, Wichita Mayor Jeff Longwell announced that the city would officially close M. C. Naftzger Memorial Park, a one-acre public park featuring a pond and a stream, winding brick walkways, and many mature trees, all enclosed by a stately fence made of brick and wrought iron. The park, constructed in the late 1970s, had been a widely recognized landmark fronting onto Douglas Avenue, the main commercial thoroughfare in Downtown Wichita, for over four decades. The park's notoriety was attributable not just to its central location or its inviting landscape, however. For nearly the entire history of the park's existence, it had been known as a prominent gathering spot for Wichita's homeless population. The stigma attached to that group, along with the periodic incidents of crime, violence, and drug activity observed within the park's walls, had drawn the consternation of municipal officials, police, developers, and city planners for years. Longwell's announcement marked the culmination of a years-long effort to finally replace Naftzger Park with a new space that would appeal to the city's professional class. "The renovated park will connect downtown destinations. It will be a gathering space for residents, businesses and visitors," Longwell proclaimed. He predicted that the renovation would "add to the great quality of life in our downtown corridor, serving everyone who lives, works and plays in the downtown area."[1]

Just hours after Longwell made his announcement, a reporter from local television news station KAKE ventured to Naftzger Park to gauge reactions to the mayor's statement from the park's users. One man who identified himself only as "D" angrily decried the announcement and the mayor's sanguine prediction. "It really doesn't make any sense," he said, "because what he's saying is probably what they said when they put this park in here."[2]

"D" was right.

Originally envisioned as an antidote to the area's reputation as Wichita's "skid row," Naftzger Park was built on a freshly cleared parcel that had previously been the site of a shelter, social assistance center, and warehouse operated by the Salvation Army; a once-grand cinema that had declined into an X-rated movie house; a seedy bar; a long-running sundries shop owned by an aging couple; and a shoeshine parlor believed by many to be a front for prostitution and other nefarious activities. The construction of Naftzger Park, first conceived as part of an expansive Urban Renewal project aimed at rejuvenating the "skid row" area, displaced some, though not all, of the services catering to the needs of the low-income men who frequented this part of Downtown Wichita. But upon its opening, the beautiful public park served as a new recreational amenity for that population. Thus began nearly half a century of tension, as the city and downtown businesses struggled to figure out how to maintain Naftzger Park as a free, open, public amenity for all, while simultaneously working to limit or eliminate the presence of homeless people within that free, open, and public space.

* * *

In chapter 2, I examined the DeBoer proposal and its promise to reinvigorate the riverfront, which sits adjacent to the western edge of Downtown Wichita. As those plans unraveled, as WI/SE (Wichita/Sedgwick County Partnership for Growth) disbanded, and city leaders regrouped, attention returned to Downtown Wichita's eastern edge, which had seen some growth in the burgeoning "Old Town" entertainment district but which remained a frequent gathering space for the city's poor and homeless, as it had for over half a century. Though concerns about homelessness pervaded the city core, no site became as clear a target for redevelopment to oust the homeless from the city center as Naftzger Park, a strategically located and highly visible space along Douglas. Increasingly, the presence of the homeless would come to be blamed for city leaders' failure to secure substantial private investment in Downtown Wichita; figuring out how to restrict the activities of the homeless, or evict them altogether, thus became the key strategy for reimaging downtown in the late twentieth and early twenty-first centuries.

Ironically, creating a space that would cater to the tastes of the middle class and drive out marginalized groups was the initial impetus for developing Naftzger Park in the first place, as it resulted during the era of Urban Renewal from the clearance of large swaths of urban territory that had made up Wichita's "skid row" in the mid-twentieth century. In this chapter I draw upon archival materials, government documents, media accounts, and my own fieldwork over the past decade to chronicle a half century of history at this location. As I demonstrate, since the 1960s this section of Downtown Wichita has been viewed by public- and private-sector leaders as critical to their efforts at sparking rejuvenation in the city's core and promoting its competitiveness with peer metro areas. At each stage in its development since the 1960s, however, the low-income and homeless people who have frequented the area have invariably been seen as obstacles to Wichita's economic development goals, and displacing them from downtown has consistently been among the top priorities of city leaders.

Wichita is certainly not the only city that has struggled to contend with the intersecting issues of poverty, housing insecurity, homelessness, and the management of public open space. Indeed, public parks have been highly visible sites of conflict over efforts to maintain public safety, ensure access to public space for various users, and promote economic development—objectives which are often at odds with one another—in cities large and small nationwide. Geographer Neil Smith opened *The New Urban Frontier,* his classic 1996 treatise on gentrification as a revanchist takeover of urban space, with an examination of the 1988 riots at Tompkins Square Park on New York's Lower East Side, demonstrating how aggressive police action to oust homeless park users and antigentrification activists served as a violent opening salvo in the push to remake the park in a form appealing to the area's growing professional class. More recently, sociologist Kevin Loughran has explored contemporary park development efforts as components of gentrification-oriented growth strategies, highlighting prominent examples in New York, Chicago, and Houston. As Loughran shows, at every step, attempts to use parks to further gentrification exacerbate urban inequalities and contribute to urban exclusion, eviction, and racial stratification.[3]

Over the past decade, as homelessness has risen to become one of the most visible—and most polarizing—issues affecting US cities, conflicts involving the police, business leaders, civil liberties activists, and unhoused people themselves have drawn scrutiny to tent encampments (and their removal) in urban centers of all sizes, geographic locations, and political orientations. Actions to take down encampments have stirred controversy at Reindahl Park in Madison, Wisconsin, at "Little Eden" Park in Dayton, Ohio, at Harbor View Memorial Park in Portland, Maine, and at Washington Square Park in Kansas City, Missouri, to name just a few examples.[4]

Though Wichita is not unique among American cities in its struggles to navigate the complex relationship between homelessness and downtown development, the history of Naftzger Park provides an especially illuminating example. The long duration of the conflicts over this space—in particular, city leaders' decision to replicate the same park-based redevelopment plan at the same location decades after it had failed to achieve its goals the first time—illustrates the limits of deliberate top-down efforts to impose gentrification upon economically fragile metropolitan areas. In this way, it contributes to my goal, discussed in the introduction, of critically evaluating the operation of the urban growth machine within a slow-growth urban environment.

Decline, Blight, and Urban Renewal in Downtown Wichita

As in major cities across the country, Wichita's growth in the mid-twentieth century manifested itself in suburbanization and sprawl; with the construction of new roads and highways, the expansion of automobile ownership, the sprouting of new suburban subdivisions, and the relocation of downtown retailers and businesses to new malls and plazas on the urban fringe, the core of the city was hollowed out. This was especially evident along East Douglas Avenue, where stores, saloons, and hotels—most impressively, the opulent Eaton Hotel—had stood for decades in close proximity to Wichita's central rail depot, Union Station. As railroad travel gave way to automobile travel, the bustling area around Union Station deteriorated. By the middle of the twentieth century, East Douglas had developed a reputation as

Figure 3.1. The Eaton Hotel and "skid row," Douglas Avenue, 1971. Source: Courtesy of the Wichita-Sedgwick County Historical Museum. Used by permission.

Wichita's "skid row," occupied by homeless and transient men, serviced by low-rent hotels, adult movie houses, and bars, and avoided and derided by respectable Wichitans (Figure 3.1).[5]

Recognizing and responding to the extent of blight in the city's core, Wichita, like many cities nationwide, pursued the path of "urban renewal," a strategy for urban reform characterized by large-scale public acquisition of parcels of land for clearance, blight removal, and new construction that first gained nationwide prominence through the federal Housing Act of 1949. In Kansas, cities were empowered to embark on urban renewal projects by the Kansas Urban Renewal Act of 1955. In 1957, the City of Wichita passed a resolution allowing for the creation of an agency dedicated to urban renewal, and the Urban Renewal Agency (URA) was established in 1958. It was composed of a five-member board appointed by the city commission. Ken Kitchen, a former Boeing aircraft employee and president of the Kansas Federation of Labor, was appointed to the URA board, and in 1967 he became the agency's executive director, a position that he would hold for over a decade, overseeing some of the most ambitious (and most controversial) urban redevelopment projects in the city's history.[6]

In line with the mission of urban renewal agencies in cities across the nation, Wichita's URA prioritized acquiring and redeveloping blighted and undervalued property in the inner city as part of a broader process of modernization designed to stave off the flight of capital and population. In May 1966, the Wichita City Commission instructed URA to survey the integrity of all structures in the East Douglas corridor "to determine if the area were eligible for federal funds under urban renewal regulations." The survey found that, of the 103 buildings standing in the area, only seven were in "good" or "fair" condition. The remaining buildings were rated "questionable," "poor," or "bad," including the once-opulent Eaton Hotel, which received a "poor" rating, "meaning it exhibited physical dilapidation or deficiencies in basic construction to a degree not warranting economic rehabilitation." In December of that year, the agency recommended that the city commission seek out collaborative relationships with private business owners to facilitate the acquisition and clearance of significant proportions of the East Douglas area to promote industrial and commercial development and expansion.[7]

City commissioners were wary to take on this task, though. The commission noted that private capital did not appear to be forthcoming, and the city was reluctant to lead the charge to seize and clear large portions of Downtown Wichita without a strong commitment from local business. Only one private developer put forward a proposal for East Douglas Avenue in 1966. This proposal called for closing the entire avenue to traffic for ten blocks and constructing "a giant downtown shopping center" straddling the entire corridor. This proposal was backed by no money whatsoever and was quickly rejected.[8]

Moreover, with several URA projects still outstanding, the city commission was hesitant to commit to a bold new endeavor. The URA board saw the situation differently, with board members expressing optimism that a city-led redevelopment effort would give entrepreneurs the confidence they needed to invest their own capital. "I think private capital will come running after the land has been acquired," said URA board member Warner Moore. The city commission conceded that the area was blighted and in need of an overhaul, but it preferred to wait for private developers to present a feasible plan for the district before asking for support from the public sector. That sentiment was clearly expressed by Mayor John Stevens, as well, who said, "I'm not so sure the city should get involved. I wouldn't want to compete with private enterprise." This public-private tension regarding who should act first presaged the prolonged standoff that would doom the DeBoer proposal decades later.[9]

With several large URA projects already underway and far from completion, commissioners seemed to be feeling a sort of renewal fatigue. "We have so many things in the frying pan right now, let's get some of them cooked," said Commissioner Clarence E. Vollmer. Professional urban planner C. Bickley Foster served at the time as the director of Wichita's Metropolitan Area Planning Commission (MAPC), the board overseeing planning and land use decisions in the Wichita region. Facing the prospect of expanded renewal efforts, Foster echoed Vollmer's sentiment, admitting that "quite frankly, with the staff we have, we're just trying to keep current with projects going on."[10]

The major benefit that the city could expect to see from redevelopment, URA argued, was vastly increased property tax revenue. In 1966, all of the property on East Douglas had yielded a combined total of just $116,000 in city property taxes; at the city's ongoing urban renewal sites, property tax revenue was expected to increase nearly sixfold after redevelopment, and URA argued that a similar increase was possible on East Douglas. For their part, local landlords were reluctant to refurbish their own properties because of the looming threat of seizure and demolition by the city and URA. "There's no sense fixing up anything if urban renewal is going to take over," said one real estate manager. Moreover, many local property owners and business owners maintained strong philosophical opposition to the idea of government intervention in the development of private land. "Number one, I'm for private enterprise. Keep the government out. I can stand an old building. I'm in one," said one local business owner. "I don't believe in urban renewal. I believe in business," added another.[11]

Private-led development, however, was not forthcoming. Only one new structure, a brick Colonial-style office building, had been built on East Douglas in recent years. (Not surprisingly, this was the only building in the area to be given a "good" rating in the 1966 URA survey of structures.) This structure housed the new headquarters of Southwest National Bank, owned by one of Wichita's most prominent families in banking, the Naftzgers. City leaders had hoped that this bank development would spark further private-led renewal on the street, but a private spending spree never materialized. Landlords attributed their reluctance to take up private redevelopment efforts to their fears that the area remained dangerous because of the continued presence of the neighborhood's homeless men.[12]

Despite its dilapidation, East Douglas had the potential to serve as the great eastern gateway to the city's central business district. The potential for profitability in the district was quite obvious; realizing that potential, however, presented a seemingly insurmountable challenge. This conundrum was expressed in stark terms in a 1967 *Wichita Beacon* editorial: "East Douglas at present offers nothing but gloom and decay. It hems in the development of downtown and must discourage some people from entering the area. Imagine the benefits, not only to east Douglas but to all of downtown Wichita if someone came up with a plan innovative and interesting enough to make a real attraction of the area!"[13] Yet no private developer stepped forward to take the lead on redevelopment. John E. Naftzger, the president of the Southwest National Bank, led a meeting of local property owners in March 1967 to trade ideas on how to upgrade the street, but this meeting yielded few concrete results, and most owners resisted the idea of large-scale urban renewal efforts.[14]

In November 1967, an audacious plan for East Douglas was unveiled. This proposal would have involved developing a new multimodal transportation hub serving the entire Wichita region at the site of Union Station. The plan would clear all but six structures in the whole East Douglas redevelopment area, primarily to make room for parking lots to serve the proposed transportation center and for a new expressway that would cut through the area. This project, like the 1967 shopping center plan, was not backed up by any money, and it never materialized.[15]

In February 1968, the president of the Wichita Area Chamber of Commerce promoted a plan that drew ideas from the earlier shopping center and transportation center visions. In conjunction with Wichita's one hundredth birthday in 1970, this project would construct a multistory mall, a transportation hub, and an agricultural hall in the East Douglas area, preserving a few older structures in order to create, as he described it, "a Disneyland-type replica of old Wichita as it stood in 1875–1880." This suggestion, too, went nowhere.[16]

With city-, MAPC-, and URA-driven redevelopment stagnating, one local bank, the Fourth National Bank, moved on its own in May 1968 to study the potential for redevelopment, hiring a New York planning firm to provide a hasty study of the area and to propose strategies for rejuvenation.

This action prompted criticism from MAPC staffers, who worried that an outside firm with little time at its disposal would return with unworkable or inappropriate ideas. And this proved to be the case, as the firm came back in July with the suggestion that URA relocate to East Douglas its already underway "Government Center" project, designed to build several large new structures to consolidate city, county, and federal offices in one location north of Downtown Wichita. As the construction of this project had already begun, this plan was utterly unfeasible and was dismissed immediately by Assistant City Manager Ralph Wulz and by Ken Kitchen, the executive director of URA. Although Kitchen rejected this idea, he did state that URA would take action on East Douglas "in the near future."[17]

By the end of 1968, then, several proposals for overhauling the East Douglas area had emerged and quickly faded. Noting the continued inaction and stagnation, *The Wichita Beacon* lamented, "Everybody talks about East Douglas . . . but nobody does anything about it." Meanwhile, the area continued to suffer from its stigmatized reputation as the city's "skid row." The prospect of Urban Renewal–led clearance activity presented a severe challenge to local business owners, who expressed a wide range of reactions, from hearty endorsement to stern condemnation. Otto Woermke, the owner of the Old Mill Tasty Shop, a soda fountain and sandwich shop, worried that such a move would cripple his business: "If they moved us out of the neighborhood it would ruin us. We've been here 36 years and we've built up our business. . . . This is our business, our home, and our work. We live upstairs." Other business owners, however, were enthusiastic about the possibility of eliminating "skid row" once and for all. Lewis Weidenbaum, who owned a pawnshop just a few doors down from the Old Mill, caustically declared that an urban renewal clearance project "can start tomorrow for all I care. The sooner the better." The manager of the Salvation Army and the owner of the Victory Theatre, both located on East Douglas, encouraged clearance. "It would be a good deal," said the owner of the theatre. "I think I'd get paid what my business is worth . . . which is nothing."[18]

One major unknown in figuring out the fate of the eastern downtown area was the future of its most prominent occupant, the Coleman Company, which had maintained its corporate headquarters and main assembly plant downtown, just one block north of Douglas, for decades. While Coleman executives expressed an interest in maintaining their headquarters downtown, they were set on relocating their manufacturing plant away from the neighborhood to an industrial park emerging out of a URA project in northern Wichita. Decisions on whether and how to redevelop East Douglas were bound up with Coleman's decision to stay or to go, and neither decision could move forward effectively without the other. This uncertainty contributed to the sluggishness and stagnation that characterized redevelopment efforts on East Douglas for the next several years.[19]

As uncertainty persisted regarding how to deal with East Douglas, URA drafted an ambitious proposal for a Neighborhood Development Program (NDP) to submit to the newly created federal Model Cities initiative. The NDP would give URA greater authority over a significant proportion of central Wichita, including the East Douglas area, which would facilitate the acquisition and consolidation of large parcels of land by pressuring owners to sell. The decision to approve the proposal for $34 million in funds from the federal Department of Housing and Urban Development (HUD) was supported unanimously by the Wichita City Commission at the end of 1968 in a rowdy meeting at which many citizens rose in heated opposition to the NDP. "This is the most vicious act of laws and regulations ever perpetrated on the American public. Its sole purpose is to destroy our rights under the Constitution. Whether it's called urban renewal or neighborhood development, it smells just as bad under my nostrils," asserted one resident, warning commissioners to "keep your dirty, grasping paws off my property and my rights." Another expressed skepticism regarding the ability of URA to use federal funds effectively, noting that "these fellows come trotting along, promising the moon and not even able to deliver the green cheese." He went on to describe the government endeavor as a manifestation of "paternalism, collectivism, socialism, Marxism and Nazism."[20]

Renewal action on East Douglas stalled for over a year until the spring of 1970, when URA filed a rather modest proposal to HUD, asking for $145,000 to survey a three-block section of East Douglas to prepare for acquisition activity. Over a year later, that application was still pending. After a year of relative inaction and upon a request from Greater Downtown Wichita, Inc.—an arm of the chamber of commerce charged with promoting downtown growth and a precursor to WI/SE and WDDC (Wichita Downtown Development Corporation)—URA agreed in 1971 to conduct another study of potential redevelopment in the entire eastern portion of the city's downtown area. Significant amounts of HUD money did not arrive, though, and plans for massive acquisition, clearance, and redevelopment by URA did not come to fruition.[21]

Continuing Frustrations, New Plans, and the Inspiration for Wichita's "Old Town"

Another year passed with little action from URA before East Douglas once again became the focus of a redevelopment push. This time, the proposal came from planners working for the Center City Steering Committee (CCSC), another group of local businessmen charged with advising the city on urban planning and development. CCSC's recommendation centered around converting a large swath of Downtown Wichita into an "Old Town" district that would preserve the "period architecture" of the buildings that remained in serviceable condition. The "Old Town" district would incorporate new museums, office buildings, parking areas, and shops, many linked together by above-ground pedestrian platforms. CCSC formally adopted the proposal in April 1972. The plan encompassed several blocks to the west of the elevated railroad tracks, with the intersection of Douglas and St. Francis serving as the hub of redevelopment efforts. "The rest of the redevelopment will not or can not take place without redevelopment of that block," said James Boyd, the chairman of CCSC. After approving these recommendations, CCSC forwarded this plan to URA and other local agencies to seek implementation. CCSC planners hoped and expected that the Old Town redevelopment would complement a touted privately funded renewal project of the charming but decrepit Eaton Hotel, situated at that critical intersection of Douglas and St. Francis. As Old Town proponents would learn for decades to come, this expectation would prove to be a consistent source of frustration.[22]

The CCSC plan was given to the planning firm Oblinger-Smith to develop a workable design for the rejuvenated district. The first phase of the redevelopment would involve the acquisition and clearing of the northwest corner of Douglas and St. Francis; after being cleared, the space would serve as a parking lot until the construction of a new structure, ideally a facility for the Wichita Art Museum. A park and underground parking garage would be constructed at the southeastern corner of Douglas and St. Francis. A remodeled Eaton Hotel would remain on the southwest corner, while the Old Town district itself would consist of just one block of intact nineteenth-century brick buildings on the northeast corner. This block of St. Francis would be closed off to automotive traffic. The plan was referred to as "Center City Development Plan—Year 2000," in reference to the long term over which redevelopment was projected to occur, and CCSC and MAPC repeatedly emphasized that this was just a guide to future development, not "an iron-clad, block-by-block specification" for the district.[23]

The planners' idea to incorporate a museum element into the Old Town design was fortuitous, as the Wichita Art Museum was simultaneously in the process of trying to find land for a new, enlarged venue to display its collection, most of which was kept in storage due to space constraints. Museum leaders and city boosters were eager to bring the museum downtown in the hopes that it would catalyze redevelopment efforts, and although at least one other downtown site was under consideration, most civic leaders in the city commission, CCSC, and MAPC favored the location on East Douglas that the Oblinger-Smith design had identified for the art museum. *The Wichita Eagle-Beacon* came out in favor of the East Douglas proposal, predicting that the art museum "certainly would do wonders for an area that presently is run-down and in need of restoration or rebuilding." Commissioners supported the plan but lamented that the city budget did not have any room for the estimated \$1–2 million cost for acquiring and clearing the land to make room for the museum. The city commission clarified that they would likely endorse the plan if the land were acquired with private funds and donated to the city. Yet after prolonged discussions and delays, the museum ultimately never moved; it simply constructed a new structure three years later at its existing location along the Little Arkansas River. East Douglas did not get its cultural catalyst, and its status as Wichita's "skid row" continued.[24]

Targeting "Skid Row"

At this point, nearly eight years had passed since discussions had begun regarding urban renewal efforts on East Douglas. Time and again, projects ranging from modest to fanciful had come and gone, culminating in the failed art museum endeavor. Frustrated public officials began speaking more aggressively about the district's "skid row" reputation and the low-income "derelict" population that many felt were responsible for it. These men, and the institutions serving them, had caused consistent consternation for both public- and private-sector leaders, who saw their continued presence as a key impediment to the acquisition of capital sufficient to fund significant land clearance and redevelopment. Al Hennessy, a former Wichita police officer and previous chairman of MAPC, was particularly vocal about the need to evict this group from East Douglas, if necessary through the use of the criminal justice system:

> East Douglas should be a showplace. It was not always a slum. At one time it was very attractive. What's the difference between these people and the people we used to call hoboes? In the old days, they slept under bridges. Now they sleep in cheap hotels on East Douglas. We just don't need a place like that. There's not an area anywhere that can't be fixed up. Wichita is a clean city and has the reputation for being one of the finest cities there is.

The "skid row" reputation of East Douglas, Hennessy alleged, was attributable primarily to the criminal activity of the area's inhabitants, and remedying that problem would require more aggressive action on the part of the Wichita Police Department. Rather than fix the problems, the police too often turned a blind eye, he claimed:

> We need to tell the Crime Commission to get off their duffs. When we start turning our heads away then we really have a problem. In my opinion, we shouldn't have such problem areas because we have the finest police department for any city our size but the officers have to worry about litigation and reprisals. You can't blame law enforcement officers. There are too many do-gooders and not enough do-righters. . . . People who say any blighted area should be left alone as a haven for derelicts are being ridiculous.

Some of those "do-gooders," including Major Joseph Irvine, the director of the Salvation Army Men's Social Service on East Douglas, disagreed with these contentions, arguing that the neighborhood served an important social need for its population and that "skid row" neighborhoods would persist. If "skid row" were cleared on East Douglas, Irvine asserted, "another one would crop up somewhere else in town."[25]

Along with the "skid row" men themselves, the shops, bars, and other establishments that catered to them also came in for criticism. The street housed several "girl shoeshine" parlors where the employees, dressed in gowns and jewelry, forcibly provided bogus palm readings to customers, ordered them to empty their pockets, rummaged through their wallets and clothing, and kept a portion of whatever money they found, oftentimes without even shining customers' shoes at all. These stores reliably generated complaints from customers to police but rarely led to any police action, since the stores attested that they were simply collecting fees for services provided. The police generally had little sympathy for the victims. One officer noted that "dissatisfied customers often are intoxicated when they go to the women and expect to get more than a palm reading," and he mused that "they are getting what they deserve."[26]

Albert Watkins and his wife had owned and operated the Watkins Sundries store since the mid-1940s in a building constructed in 1887. When the prospect of urban renewal in the area had seemed imminent in the prior decade, Mrs. Watkins seemed nonplussed: "I don't care if they tear us down. We're ready to retire anyway. I imagine we'd feel we were paid enough. We're not worried about that." Adjacent to Watkins Sundries was the Club Bar, which occupied a 1916 building that had previously housed a clothing store. The Victory Theatre, with its striking marquee, stood next door, prominently facing Douglas Avenue. The theatre had been built in 1938, and it operated continuously through the 1970s. Over that period, however, it transformed from a first-run cinema into a venue primarily for X-rated movies.[27]

Among the most prominent and controversial of the structures on East Douglas was the Johnston-Larimer Building, a former dry goods store that contained boarding rooms and social services provided by the Salvation Army. Given its mission, this building and many other nearby low-cost single-room-occupancy (SRO) hotels along the avenue were frequented by a large number of low-income men with precarious housing situations. These men—despite their stigmatized reputation—were not (mostly) itinerant drunks but impoverished, older inhabitants with few other social connections. There was a sense of camaraderie among many of them, and they, too, saw the deterioration of "skid row" and lamented the conditions affecting the area. "It isn't like it used to be. Downtown Wichita has just about gone to pot," one man said. Yet they resisted the idea of being displaced in favor of upscale new development. The Salvation Army and the other nearby SROs provided housing for these men, especially those who had substance abuse problems and found a support structure at the Salvation Army to help them remain sober. Still, the Salvation Army, along with the nearby Union Rescue Mission and the low-cost hotels, were often portrayed as impediments to the city's Old Town renewal efforts.[28]

URA stepped up again in the summer of 1974 to attempt redevelopment at Douglas and St. Francis, this time scaling back its ambition and trying simply to acquire one block of land. The agency received a $2.7 million federal grant for the NDP and hoped to use part of this money for land acquisition. However, URA emphasized that it would not take on clearance and redevelopment as an exclusively public venture; they warned that "there will be no development" without a private developer. *The Wichita Beacon* once again expressed enthusiasm that some progress might be made there, but it warned that the development must be substantial. Specifically, the *Beacon*'s editorial warned against converting the block into a park, which "might make it a loafing place for denizens of nearby Skid Row."[29]

By 1975, no progress had been made. As East Douglas continued to stagnate, frustration over the area's inhabitants reached a crisis point. Local store owners filed a formal complaint with the police department about the "drunks." In response, law enforcement leaders agreed to convene a meeting "to see what measures city police can take to get drunks off the streets." One major concern was a state law passed in 1972 decriminalizing public drunkenness, which stood in the way of police arresting intoxicated men on "skid row." In an emergency, police could take an intoxicated person into custody and bring him to a detoxification facility, but he could not be held for extended periods of time. This limitation frustrated Floyd Hannon, the chief of police:

> These guys need to be taken off the streets because they are a nuisance and also for their own protection. . . . Under the present law, we can only pick them up and take them to a detoxification center. They don't have to stay there, so before you know it, they're back out on the streets. We need to be able to put them in jail so they can be cleaned up and given a meal.

City officials and police leaders began reviewing options for creating or expanding facilities to house and treat intoxicated people picked up on the street, and they arrested some drunk men on loitering charges before promptly releasing them. *The Wichita Beacon* praised Chief Hannon for this new aggressive posture, asserting that "it is important to get drunks off the streets—for their own good and the public's welfare."[30]

At the end of 1975, URA listed Old Town beautification and redevelopment, including the construction of a new city park in the area, as one of its highest priorities. Yet once again, little tangible action was taken to bring CCSC's Old Town vision to life in place of "skid row." In August 1976, URA revealed plans to spend $1 million to support "beautification and pedestrian improvements along East Douglas." Around the same time, though, the city commission floated a plan to eliminate all on-street parking on Douglas in order to widen the street to a seven-lane thruway for several miles through Wichita. This plan provoked major consternation among small business owners, who worried that the removal of on-street parking would hurt their businesses, and *The Wichita Beacon* noted that the parking problem—and the traffic problem that the removal of parking was designed to ease—were of crucial concern "if plans to fully revitalize a central shopping district are to be realized." Once again, these ideas did not get far beyond the planning stage, and the face of East Douglas remained unchanged.[31]

The streetscaping and beautification plan announced but not executed in 1976 was again proposed in early 1977. To complement the Old Town motif suggested in the Oblinger-Smith redevelopment plan, URA would commit $800,000 for "ornamental street lamps, small trees and other greenery, benches and trash receptacles." Most local business owners supported the plan, though they voiced concerns about the upward pressure that such improvements might place on their property assessments and tax bills.[32]

Unlike many previous visions for East Douglas, this streetscaping proposal gained traction, and the city commission approved the $800,000 to upgrade the street's fixtures. While some were optimistic that this action would spur the private investment that had remained elusive for years, others were more skeptical. City Commissioner Jim Donnell, in particular, complained that all of the public investment to date had yielded little in the form of private commitment to the area. "It seems the more Urban Renewal does," he said, "the more businesses move out. Will we ever see this redevelopment really occur?" URA Director Ken Kitchen attempted to reassure Donnell and others that profound redevelopment on East Douglas was just around the corner. Designer Frank Smith of Oblinger-Smith saw this project "as the final major capital investment of public funds to bring about private redevelopment in the downtown area." The infusion of capital by private interests was seen as crucial to the success of the public investment. "Unless that happens," *The Wichita Beacon* opined, "the beautification will be largely a waste of money." Even as enthusiasm mounted in 1977, the beautification scheme that had been approved was still more than a year away from installation. Thus, yet another year passed with little visual change on East Douglas.[33]

URA's optimism about the future of Old Town increased as several developments coalesced. These included the sidewalk beautification project, the acquisition of property from the Salvation Army, which URA intended to tear down to make room for a new downtown park, and the renovation of the old Union Station and Rock Island Depot structures on the other side of the elevated railroad tracks. Additionally, a new effort arose to designate the area as a historic district in an attempt to secure special streams of funding and to impose building and renovation guidelines that would promote "activities . . . which relate to the early 1900s."[34]

Having witnessed both the promise and stagnation of redevelopment on East Douglas for years, Wichitans were understandably eager, yet skeptical, about the future. Columnist Bob Getz proclaimed that civic leaders, if they could successfully effect a turnaround of the area, "should be given a parade down Douglas." But, he insinuated, he was not holding his breath:

> I walked through that area—the 600 block of Skid Row—this week. Turned my imagination on full-throttle. Nothing happened. Got no picture. Could not begin to imagine a park, sidewalk cafes, beauty. All I could visualize was what I could see. . . . Gentlemen with stubbly beards and glazed eyes congregate in the area to break glass together. Broken bottles, broken men. . . . Bring on the face-lift, the urban surgery.

This skepticism was not limited to individual critics like Getz but was widespread in a community that had witnessed years of unfulfilled promises.[35]

By mid-1978, work was finally underway toward the creation of the Old Town aura through streetscape updates on East Douglas. With the real prospect of eviction, demolition, and reconstruction on the horizon, anxiety spread among the low-income "skid row" men of East Douglas. One resident complained about the disrespectful treatment he felt he and his peers were receiving: "I know you have to adapt to progress, but the tearing down of apartments is bad for people like us. Poor people, we are. . . . Now, what's going to happen to us? Hell, the way they're going now, there won't be a low-cost hotel anywhere and, dammit, that's what founded this town—the cheap hotel! There's no place for the poor man." Even as redevelopment loomed, however, residents and proprietors held doubts that massive renewal would succeed in ridding East Douglas of the people who contributed to its "skid row" image. Bonnie Edmark, the owner of a low-cost hotel, felt that the changes to the area would be merely cosmetic. "We're giving it a face-lift, but can you really change its old environment and the people that have spent maybe most of their lifetime in that general area? I don't think so. You only push Skid Row someplace else." One man who had recently arrived in Wichita by freight train tried to put the city's redevelopment efforts in the context of similar endeavors he had witnessed in other cities: "I've been at Tampa, Florida for the past nine winters and they tore out the Skid Row there and made a mall out of the area. And then they (the skid row inhabitants) moved over on the next street. They gotta go somewhere. Hell, they'll never get rid of the guys down here. I haven't seen a town do it yet."[36]

While there was little sympathy for the idea that these people should be allowed to stay, URA and city leaders were troubled about where they would end up after the redevelopment of the area. In October 1978, URA commissioned a study of the area and its inhabitants. The results of the study, conducted by sociologists from Wichita State University, were presented to URA the following summer. The researchers revealed that "skid row" encompassed a diverse ecological arrangement whose persistence was facilitated by the range of amenities and support structures available in the area. Massive redevelopment of the area, they concluded, would likely contribute to the departure of "transients" but would probably not cause local "skid row" residents to go away permanently. "Why should they?" said one merchant interviewed for the study. "Urban renewal came in and built them nice benches to lie on. They built a beautiful park for them to sleep in."[37]

Lester Arvin, an attorney representing the Union Rescue Mission, presented anecdotal evidence suggesting that Wichita's hospitality toward transient men had become renowned across the United States and was leading to an increase of the population due to in-migration. And police officers assigned to the area continued to complain about the lack of a public drunkenness ordinance that would allow them to arrest and jail "skid row" drunks. Reminiscing about the advantage that police had formerly had when such an ordinance was on the books, WPD Major Darrell Behrend noted to the URA board, "At least once you put him in jail, he was sober when he was let out." Behrend acknowledged that alcoholics should receive treatment and not simply imprisonment, but he lamented that under the policies in place, "we're not curing the alcoholism now, either."[38]

As part of an effort to address perceived quality-of-life concerns on East Douglas, the city began more aggressively going after nuisances—not just the behaviors of the "skid row" men but also the loitering, harassment, and delinquency of local teenagers. The police began to take serious action against the decades-old tradition of "dragging Douglas," a favorite weekend pastime of young Wichitans who gathered in groups and created significant revelry, noise, and congestion on the street, to the frustration of residents and business owners. The effort to contain the "dragging" phenomenon involved diverting cars from Douglas at certain hours as well as extending a parking ban on Douglas westward through downtown to the Arkansas River. Simultaneously, to cut down on graffiti marring the railroad underpass on East Douglas, URA installed a "graffiti board" that allowed potential artists to express themselves while keeping a new mural on the underpass graffiti free.[39]

"A Green and Tranquil Place in the Heart of the City": The Clearance of "Skid Row" and the Initial Plans for Naftzger Park

URA's boldest acquisition effort took place on the south side of East Douglas, beginning in 1976. To complement the Old Town motif proposed for the redeveloped area, URA embarked on a plan to create a new park evoking a Victorian theme on the southeast corner of Douglas and St. Francis. The agency proposed to acquire and demolish all of the buildings on that block to make way for this new park. Most of the buildings in question were key contributors to the neighborhood's "skid row" reputation. Along with the sizeable URA investment, the creation of this park was made possible by a $100,000 gift from the president of the Southwest National Bank, John Naftzger, and his family. In recognition of the family's generosity, it was agreed that the new space would be named M. C. Naftzger Memorial Park after John Naftzger's recently deceased father.[40]

It was evident from the beginning that this new park was designed as a critical component of a larger effort to remake Downtown Wichita in order to attract a more affluent set of users. The editorial page of *The Wichita Beacon* was clear about this aim: "Not only will the gift provide a green and tranquil place in the heart of the city, but it should help immensely in the efforts to revitalize downtown, for anything that makes the area more attractive and livable cannot help but increase its desirability." In June 1976, the URA board approved $642,445 for the acquisition of nine parcels of land between St. Francis and the railroad tracks. Much of this land was owned by the Salvation Army. Other acquired properties included the Girls Shoe Shine Parlor, the Victory Theater, and the Club Bar, all of which had figured heavily in reinforcing East Douglas's image as Wichita's "skid row." URA intended to acquire and clear the entire block, primarily to make room for the new urban park that officials hoped would "be a catalyst for upgrading the East Douglas area and encourage other private redevelopment in the downtown area."[41]

As plans moved forward with the park, several developers intervened, asking URA to save the five-story Johnston-Larimer building, in which the Salvation Army housed a shelter, thrift store, and social service center, and to convert it to a new use. One plan called for the construction of sixty apartments in the structure, while another proposed turning the building and an adjacent warehouse structure into a commercial center and dinner theatre. In November 1977, though, the URA board rejected both of these proposals and opted instead to raze the ninety-year-old building.[42]

A month later, however, the URA board reversed its decision on the Johnston-Larimer building and chose to seek out private developers to revamp the site. The building remained, dilapidated and empty, for over a year. As the Park Board approved final plans for Naftzger Park in 1978, URA officials suggested that if a developer could not be found for the building, they might consider expanding the park across the entire width of the block. When URA could not find a developer willing to take on the renovation project, the board—seventeen months after first voting to tear down the Salvation Army building (only to hit the pause button shortly thereafter)—again voted to tear it down in April 1979, sealing its fate for good.[43]

Early Optimism Regarding the Park's Transformational Potential

Naftzger Park was dedicated on May 13, 1979, in a ceremony featuring music from the turn of the century designed to complement the park's

"Victorian flavor." The new park was deliberately intended to evoke an "old" feel to complement the burgeoning Old Town district within which it was situated. It featured iron and brick fencing, a gazebo "painted in appropriate Victorian colors," and brick pathways winding throughout, lined with wood benches trimmed with cast iron. There were thousands of flowers and dozens of bushes and trees scattered throughout the space. A stream flowed downward through a rock formation and into a pond, at the center of which stood a tall metal sculpture of cattails (Figure 3.2). The city held the dedication in May to coincide with the annual Wichita River Festival, but the park was not actually ready to open at that time. Specially designed and crafted garbage cans had not yet arrived, and finishing touches were needed on benches, bricks, light fixtures, and a fountain. As a result, the park stood locked and unoccupied for over a month after the formal dedication.[44]

Even before it officially opened, as Naftzger Park emerged out of the rubble of the seedy bar, stores, movie house, and social service agencies that had previously occupied the block, local merchants and residents raised concerns that the "skid row" profile of East Douglas would simply return and find a new home in the beautiful new outdoor space. City officials tried to assuage such fears. URA operations officer Chung Chang stressed that the park would be closed at night and that the "transients" would not pose a safety problem for other users of the new park: "There has been a rapid change physically so far," Chang said. "Now, it's up to the merchants to make business happen and promote activities that would attract the general profile of Wichita to the area." Even before the park had opened, though, Chang acknowledged that he had "stopped two different people who were trying to steal the park benches."[45]

Local observers were pleased, expressing initial optimism that the addition of Naftzger Park really had altered and improved the character of the neighborhood. Columnist Bob Getz spent a day in the park, deliberately seeking out the spillover of "skid row" into the new area, and he was astonished when he could not find it:

> Heavy sociology was what I was after, with the accent on depravity, degeneracy and decay. . . . I waited. Started reading. Started wondering. What kind of a Big City park is this, I wondered, with not even one bum sleeping under a newspaper? . . . Time passed. A few more people came

Figure 3.2. Naftzger Park and the Eaton Hotel, early 1980s. Source: Wichita Public Library Photograph Collection. Courtesy of Local History Section, Wichita Public Library. Used by permission.

> and left. None of them collapsed in a stupor or tried to start a revolution. Getting desperate, I crossed Douglas and walked back by the railroad tracks. Maybe I could coax some seedy types to go into the park so I could write a column berating the city for allowing bums to take over the park so decent people won't go there. I couldn't find anybody.[46]

In the first few years of its operation, the Naftzger Park project seemed to have succeeded in its mission to transform East Douglas and to eradicate its "skid row" reputation. This positive attitude toward the park was short-lived, though.

Old Town's Promise and Naftzger Park's Problems

After years of conflict with the city commission, and amid growing public frustration over its slow pace and lackluster record of acquiring and redeveloping inner-city property, URA was finally dismantled in 1980. Its responsibilities were divided among other existing city agencies, and the staff of the defunct agency was placed under the direction of City Manager Gene Denton. The city commission emphasized that renewal efforts in Downtown Wichita would go on despite the elimination of URA as an independent agency, but projects would presumably be subject to greater oversight and public transparency by putting Denton in charge. The demise of URA was attributed partly to the dwindling amount of urban development aid coming to the city from the federal government, which forced URA to compete with other city agencies for a shrinking pool of money. When URA was disbanded, its director, Ken Kitchen, was given the new title of "director of downtown development" in the city government.[47]

The city finally demolished the Johnston-Larimer building, and work continued to refurbish the warehouse that stood behind it (just to the east of Naftzger Park). Redevelopment of that site, and of the Old Town district as a whole, was dealt a series of devastating blows on New Year's Eve, 1980. First, Harter, Inc., the company charged with revitalizing Union Station, filed for Chapter 11 bankruptcy protection, setting back redevelopment of that entire complex for several years. On the same day, HUD rejected a request by the city for over $4 million in federal subsidy to build parking garages for Old Town. Once again, the private investments that the public subsidy was designed to incentivize were viewed as too flimsy. Finally, the warehouse south of the Johnston-Larimer Building, which had been spared for redevelopment even as the adjacent building was torn down, burned to the ground in a massive fire. Given the magnitude of the fire, the controversy surrounding redevelopment in the area, and the confluence of the other redevelopment setbacks occurring on the same day, the fire was considered suspicious.[48]

Creating further delays in Wichita's plan for the Old Town block to the north of the new park was the city commission's requirement that local business owners' concerns over renewal activities be addressed. By 1981 the city had succeeded only in buying two empty lots in the middle of the block. Several of the cornerstones of URA's development plans—Union Station and the Old Town block—thus failed to deliver, and as a result, they failed to bring in the promised massive private investment. As larger companies and public agencies neglected the comprehensive remaking of East Douglas, individual "pioneers" invested their own money, leading to a slow but noticeable stream of development in Old Town. Arguably the most prominent of those pioneer developers was David Norris, who bought several buildings along East Douglas as well as a massive brick warehouse just south of Naftzger Park. "What this area really needs is someone with the really big checkbook to come in," Norris said. As those big checkbooks continued to be elusive, however, Norris and other smaller players pressed on. "I just figure you put your money in when you can, and if it works, it works," Norris mused.[49]

By the early 1980s, even as large-scale formal renewal efforts continued to stagnate, Wichita's Old Town area had begun to attract some investment from smaller developers like Norris adopting an "urban pioneer" spirit. They renovated some of the former cheap hotels on East Douglas, creating more fashionable living quarters for a small population of young urban professionals. Early tenants praised the vibrant feeling of downtown living. "There is so much happening downtown. . . . We walk to work, walk to eat. It's alive," one tenant said effusively. Still, pioneer landlords expressed concerns that their efforts to create a middle-class atmosphere in Old Town were threatened by the constant presence of homeless and low-income men, as explained in a *Wichita Eagle-Beacon* profile of downtown developers: "Some of the vitality isn't always welcome, the developers acknowledged. The block, its alleys and the railroad overpass just to the east are traditional haunts for transients, and the developers are rousting them out." Those landlords hoped redevelopment efforts would ultimately displace those men once and for all. One developer, who had inherited a former "skid row" hotel from her father and had converted it into upscale apartments using money obtained through a low-interest federal loan, predicted optimistically that "in another year or two, they'll all be gone."[50]

The Old Town concept had originally been proposed in the 1970s as part of a top-down effort spearheaded by URA, but even after the public redevelopment effort fizzled and URA ceased to exist altogether, the label for this area became entrenched, and the Old Town name persists to the present day. In 1983, pioneer developers, in conjunction with local business owners and young professional residents, formed the Old Town Association (OTA), a booster organization designed to promote growth on East Douglas and the surrounding warehouse district near the elevated railroad tracks. OTA expanded the boundaries of Old Town to include an area of about a dozen blocks spanning across the railroad tracks to the east. Prospects were once again bright for Old Town as new "pioneers" came to the area.[51]

By July 1983, OTA had 150 members, and the group had reinvigorated a moribund tradition in Downtown Wichita, the Downtown Farm & Art Market, which had been initiated by downtown business boosters and URA in 1976 but had fallen in popularity within a few years. An Old Town restaurant owner moved to purchase a liquor store and tavern that had tended to serve the "skid row" population to remake it into a more upscale restaurant. David Norris, who in the preceding few years had become a leading developer in Old Town (and who served as the first president of OTA), renovated the warehouse building south of Naftzger Park and leased it to a technology company from California that pledged to bring up to two hundred employees to the site.[52]

Even as Old Town continued to show the potential for middle-class reinvestment, the initial fears of local merchants regarding Naftzger Park became reality. By the early 1980s, the park did indeed serve as a central gathering spot for Wichita's homeless population. It also acquired a reputation across the region (and, some argued, across the entire country) as a welcoming place for "drifters" and "transients" to spend time without being accosted by police. Crime entered the area, and soon Naftzger Park gained notoriety as a dangerous place where visitors could be robbed or mugged. "Drifters" who arrived in Wichita and settled in or near the park frequently found themselves to be victims. "Everybody knows you can go down there and roll these guys and nothing's going to happen," said a Wichita police officer. In one case in 1982, when a forty-six-year-old man was robbed and assaulted while sleeping in Naftzger Park, the police arrested the three assailants but put the victim in jail, too, because he wanted to leave town and keep traveling to new locations, while the courts needed him to remain in order to testify. Even at the nearby Eaton Hotel, which also enjoyed a stigmatized reputation as a result of its low-income clientele, residents and employees had reservations about the park. "I've seen a lot of incidents where a guy is beat up and he comes in and cleans up in the restroom," said an employee at the hotel. "Of course, I stay out of the park. I'm not going to look for trouble." Many robberies and assaults in Naftzger Park went unreported, as the victims themselves often lived on the fringe of society, and in many cases they were friends, or at least acquaintances, of their assailants.[53]

Ultimately, even the park's original visionaries and benefactors decried what their creation had turned into. Gwen Naftzger, the widow of M. C. Naftzger, reminisced sadly as she compared the soaring original vision for the park with the disappointing reality of the park's condition just a few years after it was unveiled: "We were looking at that ugly land. It was pestering my eyes, and I wanted to do something to help it. We felt it would make that block and that district prettier, but it didn't work. Of course, it's much better than it was. But I figured a lot of people would gamble with us, and they didn't." John Naftzger, the son of M. C. and Gwen Naftzger, recounted the peril that he and his mother had felt when they visited the park dedicated to his father: "Remember when the winos came over and talked to us. We had a wonderful time. Scared to death."[54]

The larger issue of urban redevelopment on East Douglas loomed. By this point, URA had been disbanded, and despite the small projects undertaken by OTA President David Norris and other individual Old Town developers, progress in the area was slow or stalled. Still, Norris remained upbeat, asserting that Naftzger Park was "going to make it, because the area's going to make it."[55]

Growing Disillusionment and Heightened Vigilance in Naftzger Park

Naftzger Park had turned into the redevelopment proponents' worst nightmare, a "Disneyland for winos and transients who at nightfall become clients for the neighborhood's network of welfare offices and flophouses," according to a *Wichita Eagle-Beacon* description. Rather than displacing the transient population, it seemed (contrary to city officials' predictions) to be attracting more. Word purportedly spread among "drifters" across the US that the park was a hassle-free space with nearby amenities. "You've got the [Union Rescue] Mission so close, the railroad and a cheap hotel [the Eaton]," said a twenty-four-year-old Californian staying temporarily in the park. A man from Louisiana had heard about Naftzger Park from a friend in Oklahoma City while traveling: "He said the police will watch you. They won't bother you. You won't be hungry. You won't be on the streets. So far, everything he said was true."[56]

As the pace of public complaints about the park increased, city officials took action. In August 1983, the Park Department changed the opening hours of Naftzger Park. Since its unveiling, the park had been open daily from 5:00 a.m. until midnight; under the new rule, the park would open at 11:00 a.m. and close at 11:00 p.m. On paper, this new policy was designed to facilitate maintenance in the park, but users of the park sensed an ulterior motive. William "Kojak" Jackson, a frequent visitor to the park, gave a mocking interpretation of the city's motivation: "The people that come in here might be bad for our image. They probably want to get in here and drink their beer and champagne, and smoke their weed." He and other park regulars were highly critical of this move.[57]

Naftzger Park was not the only amenity on East Douglas that raised concerns that the area's "skid row" status was persisting. Along with the new, beautiful park, the area continued to contain the railroad underpass, alleys, and doorways that served as convenient sleeping quarters; a liquor store across the street from Naftzger Park; shelter and food services at the Union Rescue Mission, also facing the park; a welfare office a block away; thrift stores and other low-cost outlets to buy clothes and other necessities; and the Eaton and other cheap hotels. The police had taken steps to be more aggressive regarding loitering and other nuisance crimes, yet they still generally tolerated public drinking and intoxication. And while the Park Department experimented with opening the park later and closing it earlier, this effort had little deterrent effect on the "winos" and "transients" who frequented it.[58]

It was therefore the range of food, shelter, retail, and service amenities in the area that became the target of efforts to "clean up" Old Town. OTA officials repeatedly approached the Union Rescue Mission to urge them to relocate, but the mission resisted, claiming that the presence of the low-income and troubled population of East Douglas presented a set of important needs that the mission had set out to address. OTA President David Norris countered that the presence of the mission itself perpetuated those needs, or at least their continued presence on East Douglas: "The Mission people say they won't move as long as there's a need in the area. But their being there fosters that need—and it won't go away as long as the flophouse stays." OTA members contributed their own private money to hire a Wichita police officer to patrol the district during the holiday shopping season of 1983. Moreover, OTA officials and other Old Town proponents began to put increased pressure on Philip Kassebaum, the owner of the Eaton Hotel, to act on his longstanding, yet unfulfilled, pledge to overhaul the stigmatized hotel. OTA members doubted that his efforts were sincere. "He's hoping this area will develop, the value of his property will go up, and then he'll sell it for a profit," alleged a local business owner and OTA member.[59]

It seemed that a game of chicken had developed between Kassebaum, whose hotel anchored and towered over the rest of the area, and the public and private forces clamoring for redevelopment along East Douglas. Kassebaum maintained that his pledge to remake the Eaton into a luxury hotel was sincere but that the decrepit state of the surrounding district, as well as a lagging economy, made it impractical to pursue such a plan immediately: "We articulated our plans several months ago—restoration of the façades along Douglas, and conversion of the Eaton into a luxury hotel. But we'll do that when the economic climate is appropriate. That means when the cost of money goes down, when there are appropriate tenants who express interest, and when I see significant work being done in the area." OTA and Kassebaum thus offered competing narratives to explain the stagnation in the area: Kassebaum expressing unwillingness to significantly upgrade his structure without concomitant progress in Old Town and OTA leaders asserting that the dilapidated Eaton Hotel was the key stumbling block preventing neighborhood rejuvenation. It would be nearly two decades before this standoff would be resolved.[60]

While homeless men continued to meet and spend time in Naftzger Park, calls for evicting them came up periodically. Meanwhile, most other Wichitans avoided the park, which only served to solidify its status as a place exclusively used by the down-and-out population. Recurring incidents of crime in the park also hampered redevelopment efforts. In 1990, a group of fifteen young people attacked two men walking down Douglas near Union Station. And in 1992, Esther Moses, the elderly owner of a clothing store located across Douglas from Naftzger Park, was beaten and robbed in her own store, following a string of other robberies on the block. Still, the Wichita police were cautious not to exert too much force to expel or arrest people, and Naftzger Park retained a reputation as an open and welcoming space for low-income and homeless individuals. A 1993 *Wichita Eagle* profile of Danny Farlow, a downtown beat officer, highlighted an interaction between Farlow and a shirtless young man sitting on a bench in Naftzger Park:

> The weather had warmed up considerably by that point, but it was still cool enough to make a shirtless person seem suspicious, so Farlow stopped by for a quick chat. Asking for the young man's driver's license or other identification, Farlow assured him that "If everything's OK, I won't be bothering you anymore." . . . After learning the man wasn't

> wanted for anything... Farlow gave the ID back and offered the standard lecture on which activities should be strictly avoided in the area. Farlow also gave a brief rundown of the medical, housing and food services available in the area, along with a few other practical tips for getting by in the area, and wished the young man a nice day. The tattooed man, clearly stunned by the treatment, seemed quite sincere in wishing the officer a nice day of his own.

This open and welcoming atmosphere frustrated local business owners, but it allowed Naftzger Park to serve Wichita's homeless population for several decades as a key downtown site for gathering, relaxing, and finding resources and social services. By the 1990s, if not earlier, Wichitans often used the sobriquet "Wino Park" to refer to this small patch of green space in the city center.[61]

As local business owners grew frustrated, they pressured the city and police to take more aggressive action to remove the "winos" that gave the park its reputation. Alcohol and drug use, vandalism, crime, and violence arose repeatedly at Naftzger Park. The cattail sculpture that had originally stood in the central pond in the park was removed after being severely damaged by vandalism. While Wichita already had a city ordinance on the books banning the public consumption of hard liquor, low-alcohol beer (3.2 percent or less) could still legally be consumed in parks. In 1996, police officer James Krok, who patrolled a downtown beat including Naftzger Park, began gathering signatures on a petition to enact an ordinance that would allow him and his colleagues to make arrests for consuming alcoholic beverages of any strength within downtown parks. He said that he was motivated by persistent complaints from local business owners.[62]

In 1998, the new antidrinking ordinance sought by the police was passed by the Wichita City Council and put into effect.[63] Its proponents celebrated it as a success but were quick to assert that it was not designed to evict homeless park users. "We don't mind if they use our parks. But we want them to do it in a proper way. We want to keep a family-type orientation," said Janice McKinney, a city park employee. This sentiment was reiterated by police officer Ted Naldoza, who emphasized that the ordinance was designed "to make the park a place for everyone to visit." In an additional attempt to preempt illicit behavior, the city also increased visibility into Naftzger Park by trimming trees and bushes and by removing significant portions of the wrought iron fencing. Meanwhile, the police stepped up arrests for nuisance crimes like loitering and vagrancy.[64]

Proponents of these reforms defended them by stressing that they would facilitate greater park usage by a broader range of the population. "If diminished use of the park is because of this element being there, that's a problem," said Mitch Mitchell, president of the Board of Park Commissioners. Many local business owners also supported the new aggressive posture, including the general manager of a local restaurant, who said bluntly, "The city owns the park and we own the parking lot. If they're breaking the law, they should be reprimanded for that, and it doesn't matter to me whether they're homeless or not." The homeless and their advocates, though, saw the situation differently, believing that they were deliberately targeted for harassment and expulsion by the newly vigilant police.[65]

While stepping up enforcement actions against homeless individuals themselves, the city and police simultaneously moved to restrict the activities of organizations and establishments catering to the needs of the homeless who frequented Naftzger Park. Pressure campaigns to persuade remaining "skid row" establishments to close or relocate had been long running. Over the course of many years, Christian volunteers had come to the park on weekends to distribute food, clothing, and other services. In 1999, the police and local business owners voiced complaints about these church activities. In particular, two police officers, Chris Doyle and John Duff, whose patrol included Naftzger Park, took it as their personal mission to reclaim the park from the homeless. "We finally put the hammer down," Duff boasted. "We need to do something about the park, period." Doyle added, "I want to see more families with their kids come into the park, and it would be nice to have a jazz band play on weekends." The aggressive posture of the police received favorable coverage from *The Wichita Old Town Gazette*, a neighborhood newspaper created by and for the OTA and the young professional class it was designed to serve.[66]

Following a recommendation from the WPD, the Park Board restricted access to the park for these church groups. Along with further physical alterations designed to improve sightline visibility in the park, the board placed greater restrictions on permits for church activities. Previously available at no cost, permits to distribute meals would henceforth require a fee of twenty-five dollars per hour. Many local business leaders, including the owner of Spaghetti Works, an Italian chain restaurant adjacent to

Naftzger Park, welcomed the change. Homeless residents and their advocates, however, decried the move as a blatant attempt to evict unwanted people from the park. "They're saying there's a designated group of people the parks are for, and the homeless are not part of that. They're trying to beautify the downtown area, and homeless people are not beautiful," said Sandi Swank, who directed homeless assistance programs for Inter-Faith Ministries, a local religious and social service agency. Initially, the church groups complied with the ordinance, paying fifty dollars for a two-hour permit that allowed them to serve a turkey dinner on the weekend before Thanksgiving in 1999.[67]

Matters escalated the following month, when Inter-Faith Ministries served a turkey and roast beef dinner and, in overt defiance of the new restriction, refused to buy a permit for the privilege. "We will not pay a punitive fee that discriminates against the very people we seek to serve," the group asserted in a prepared statement. They deliberately designed their action to draw a response from the WPD. The police did not show up, but religious leaders still used the occasion to call attention to the problems of homelessness and poverty and to highlight the stark contrast between the suffering of the homeless and the increasingly upscale atmosphere the city and business leaders were trying to establish in Old Town. "People who come to Old Town to eat a sumptuous meal don't have to look at the people in the same area who can't eat or find shelter," said the Reverend Jeanette James, a Wichita pastor. "We need to think about how to treat our homeless and our poor."[68]

Negative publicity surrounding this new fee spread, and in response the city council and Mayor Bob Knight agreed to lift the fee, at least temporarily. "I don't think that having the park available for families and feeding the homeless are mutually exclusive," said the mayor. Efforts to fight homelessness in Wichita faced another obstacle a few weeks later, however, as the State of Kansas, facing a budget shortfall, slashed funds for services to the homeless and those dealing with mental health problems. Such cuts, critics worried, had the potential to drive more people onto the streets, overwhelming a system that was already incapable of effectively serving the existing need.[69]

After decades of stalling, the Eaton Hotel was finally redeveloped into an upscale apartment complex. As this redevelopment project neared completion at the end of 2000, a thorough renovation of Naftzger Park, which sat directly across the street, was planned in order to make the park more attractive for the wealthier residents who were expected to move into the new apartments. For that reason, the park was closed entirely for several months, thereby ending the weekend feedings of the homeless. More significantly, though, city leaders resumed discussions on whether to reinstate the usage fee or to eliminate that use of the park altogether. The City of Wichita had, over the years, contributed millions of dollars in public funding toward the restoration of the Eaton, and the success of that publicly subsidized project depended on the new upscale apartments attracting tenants. City leaders worried that the park's stigmatized reputation could hinder the ability to fill the new apartments. Old Town boosters' hopes were lifted when it seemed that more families and professionals were making use of Naftzger Park following the 2001 renovation.[70]

Over the next several years, the problem of homelessness, particularly in relation to Naftzger Park, received less attention in the press, but it did not disappear. In 2005, a forty-nine-year-old homeless man was beaten to death in an alley adjacent to the park. Police combed the park and other locations popular with the homeless in search of information. Meanwhile, city attorneys and police officers began to consider mechanisms for outlawing the tents and lean-tos that homeless people used as shelters in alleys, plazas, and parks. "We don't want little havens for these people," said police Captain John Speer. This was particularly true in Naftzger Park and another downtown park frequented by the homeless. "Not only do we want to clean up those two areas, in regards to trash and camping, we want to educate the homeless people that frequent those places . . . on other options than being out there," said Speer.

A year later, on a 108-degree summer day, James Geary, a sixty-four-year-old homeless man, was found dead next to the park; his death was presumed to be caused by heat exhaustion. A memorial service held for Geary in the park was attended mostly by homeless advocates, and it was used as much to vocalize discontent over the treatment of the homeless as to honor Geary's life. "James had relatives and friends. He had feelings and ideas. What he did not have was a place to live," declared the Reverend Nicolette Papanek. Commenting on the frequent deaths of homeless people on the streets of Wichita—it was estimated that Geary's was the seventh that year—Reverend Papanek called for action "to affirm their lives by making it possible for everyone to have a dwelling place."[71]

In subsequent years, Naftzger Park would be used periodically as a location for OTA-sponsored block parties, as a gathering site at the end of the annual Wichita Gay Pride Parade, and as an attractive backdrop for couples to take engagement and wedding photos. But the "Wino Park" stigma never left, even as redevelopment in Downtown Wichita progressed slowly but steadily. When a new downtown sports arena was constructed just south of Naftzger Park in 2007, some hoped that the arena construction could spur redevelopment efforts in the park, but no major changes materialized.[72]

Renewed Efforts to Reimagine Naftzger Park and New Initiatives to Curtail the Homeless

In 2010, two decades after the collapse of the DeBoer redevelopment plan, the Wichita Downtown Development Corporation unveiled a new comprehensive downtown redevelopment plan called *Project Downtown*. This $600 million plan, developed by the Boston consulting firm Goody Clancy, identified Naftzger Park as a key catalyst site that would be a cornerstone of a renewed downtown redevelopment effort in Wichita. It envisioned a redesigned and rebuilt park surrounded by new residential, commercial, and retail establishments.[73]

To complement the master plan, one proposal for the area commissioned by WDDC and designed by landscape architecture students from Kansas State University called for turning the park into "Naftzger Green: A New Vibrant Downtown Civic Space." The keys to revitalizing "Naftzger Green" were generating increased pedestrian flow to activate the site and mitigating the problems caused by what the plan called "the area's undesirable population." Eliminating those people, the plan proposed, would encourage greater pedestrian activity: "This traffic flow will pull everyday users, as well as event goers into our site and ultimately along Saint Francis with the proposed pedestrian corridor. Recognizing the site's high profile location the proposal capitalizes on that value. Currently, Naftzger Park is a popular hang out for the local homeless. Developing a more open site plan for Naftzger Park could reduce the area's undesirable population." Despite these proposals to transform this block and (proponents continued to hope) finally oust the homeless altogether, no action was taken during the five years following the approval of the *Project Downtown* plan.[74]

Still, the park's issues with violence, crime, and homelessness continued.

A fifty-five-year-old man was found dead in the park in April 2013. Two months later, a fifty-two-year-old man was beaten, knocked unconscious, and robbed in the park. Later that year, a nineteen-year-old man was stabbed following what *The Wichita Eagle* described as a "drunken fight" in Naftzger Park. Another fight led to an additional stabbing just outside the park in April 2014.[75]

In 2015, five years after the implementation of *Project Downtown* had begun, efforts to overhaul Naftzger Park and its environment once again gained momentum. Though a vision of a renewed park surrounded by mixed-use development had been incorporated into the *Project Downtown* master plan in 2010, no progress had been made in the area in the ensuing five years. In 2014, Wichita had been selected by the NCAA as a host city for early rounds of the 2018 men's college basketball tournament. The tournament games would be held in INTRUST Bank Arena, two blocks south of the park, and as part of its bid to host the games, Wichita promised to host a three-day "Fan Fest" in Naftzger Park and the surrounding parking lots.[76]

Meanwhile, plans to redevelop the large brick warehouse directly southeast of the park moved forward. Built in 1894 as the Wichita Wholesale Grocery Company warehouse, it was purchased in the 1980s by pioneer Old Town developer David Norris. In 1984, Norris renovated the building and the adjacent parking lot, which had previously been the site of the Johnston-Larimer Building and the Salvation Army warehouse that had suspiciously burned several years earlier. In the 1990s it was redeveloped into a huge restaurant called Spaghetti Works, part of a small regional chain of Italian eateries. The restaurant lasted for a decade, but after several years of sagging sales it closed in 2004. While operating the restaurant, the owners painted the name "SPAGHETTI WORKS" in ten-foot-tall capital letters on three sides of the building. Despite its official listing on the National Register of Historic Places and the Register of Historic Kansas Places under the name "Wichita Wholesale Grocery Company," it has been popularly referred to as the "Spaghetti Works" building ever since, even though the restaurant has been shuttered for more than two decades.[77]

Following the closing of Spaghetti Works, the warehouse changed hands several times, but ambitious plans to repurpose it continuously fell through, despite the 2007 construction of INTRUST Bank Arena directly adjacent to the warehouse, which proponents had argued would spark massive redevelopment throughout the area. Lighthouse Properties acquired the warehouse in 2004 with plans to develop a fashionable boutique hotel but turned around and resold the building in 2008. The owner insisted that "we don't want people to see this as a vote against the momentum building in downtown Wichita." Despite those assurances, there was, in fact, little momentum in development in that area, as I explain in chapter 4.[78]

In 2015, a new development group expressed interest in the Spaghetti Works property, and in 2016 they finalized a deal to purchase the Spaghetti Works warehouse, adjacent buildings, and the parking lot to the north that had abutted Naftzger Park for three decades. Even as they first announced their plans to transform the warehouse into an apartment building and to construct a new mixed-use development on the parking lot site, the leaders of the development team, Brad Saville and Nick Esterline, were explicit in a *Wichita Eagle* profile about their concerns regarding the homeless people who frequented the area:

> Another challenge in the area is a steady stream of homeless people in and around Naftzger Memorial Park, which is next to the parking lot adjacent to the Spaghetti Works building.
>
> "The first time we started thinking about this situation, we walked through the park," Saville says.
>
> "Quickly," Esterline adds.
>
> "We were walking a little quicker than we thought we would be," Saville says. "They're here right now because the building's vacant, and it's quiet and peaceful and nobody bothers them."
>
> He says he and Esterline have learned from other markets that homeless populations will move elsewhere once activity starts in an area.

From the start, dealing with Naftzger Park and its homeless occupants were key components of the Spaghetti Works redevelopment project, and the public park's future became inextricably bound up in many ways with the proposed private development.[79]

With the NCAA tournament (and the promised outdoor "Fan Fest") looming, city officials moved to capitalize on the Spaghetti Works redevelopment to facilitate the refashioning of Naftzger Park into a modernized space that would, according to *The Wichita Eagle*, "put Wichita's best face forward when tens of thousands of visitors and hundreds of sports reporters arrive for the March Madness basketball tournament." Tight city budgets in the past had prevented Wichita from investing large amounts of capital to substantially improve Naftzger Park. However, by this point the park sat within a TIF (tax increment financing) district approved in the previous decade to facilitate the construction of the arena (though park improvements had not previously been included as approved uses for TIF expenditures). With the anticipation that the new Spaghetti Works development would greatly increase aggregate assessed property values in the area, city leaders seized on an opportunity to tap a new potential source of revenue; they altered the restrictions of the TIF district to include park improvements among the scope of allowable expenditures.[80]

City officials anticipated that initial work to remake Naftzger Park would cost $1.5 million. Under the new TIF arrangement, the city would issue $1.5 million in new bonds, and these bonds would be paid off through revenue generated by the additional property taxes collected from projected rising property assessments that the Spaghetti Works redevelopment would presumably spur. Thus, an intricate interdependence emerged: The developers had stated that their willingness to redevelop the Spaghetti Works property was contingent upon something being done with the park and its homeless users; simultaneously, the city's ability to finance a new park that they hoped would attract a more upscale user base was wholly dependent upon the success and profitability of the new Spaghetti Works project. The park project could not proceed without the new development, and the new development would not happen without a new park. So entwined were the two projects that when the city issued a "request for qualifications" seeking a landscape architecture firm to design a new public park, applicants were instructed to send their proposals not to the city itself but rather to the offices of the Spaghetti Works developer, and the contract for the firm that was ultimately selected to design the new city-owned park was executed between the architects and the Spaghetti Works developer, not the city.[81]

Although Naftzger Park had been consistently underutilized by the public for decades, when the city's plan to level the park and rebuild it in conjunction with a new private development became public, it sparked a vibrant and at times contentious debate in Wichita. WDDC hosted a public forum in July 2017, featuring the architect hired to design the new park, Thomas Balsley of the New York firm SWA/Balsley. This forum was designed to allow Wichitans to offer their input regarding what they liked and disliked about the current park and to make suggestions for the redesign, but the architect's presentation was periodically interrupted by arguments among the audience, especially related to the fate of the city's homeless population. Taking that public input into consideration, Balsley left Wichita and returned two weeks later to present four potential designs for a new Naftzger Park at another public forum. Again, a large crowd raised pointed questions, most directly about accommodations for homeless patrons at the park.[82]

A week later, the city council approved the TIF financing plan for the park during a meeting in which two residents spoke in opposition to the project, largely on the grounds that it would displace and disadvantage the homeless. City Council Member Janet Miller, whose district included a large number of new loft apartments in gentrifying sections of Old Town and Downtown Wichita, pushed back vocally against these objections, admonishing residents in particular for their calls to include a public restroom in the new park. "People finger-paint with feces in public rest rooms. They flush clothing and other items down the toilet. They blow up toilets. They pull sinks off the walls. They do very disgusting things in rest rooms," Miller said.[83]

Alongside pushback from concerned members of the public, Balsley and the city officials promoting the redesign faced skepticism from the Wichita Design Council, a public advisory board charged with evaluating designs for city projects. Amid a prevailing public belief that the project was moving too quickly in an effort to achieve completion before the basketball tournament the following spring, the city backed off. City Manager Robert Layton acknowledged the public's concerns, and he asserted that the city, the architect, and the developer would take more time to ensure that the project was executed carefully. He also rebuffed claims that the city was undertaking the redevelopment of Naftzger Park to impress the NCAA and the tourists who would attend the basketball tournament, claiming instead that it was the Spaghetti Works development (and the TIF dollars that it would presumably generate) that spurred the city to act on remaking the park.[84]

With the enthusiasm over the rapid redevelopment deflated, several months passed with little apparent activity. The Spaghetti Works developers then surprised the city by announcing that they had halted their plans to redevelop the warehouse altogether. While they did not explain their decision, the strong links between the Naftzger Park remodeling and the private development suggested that the city's move to delay the park project likely influenced their choice. The decision to halt that project eliminated the potential for new TIF revenue, essentially dooming the park plans altogether. Within days, a large canvas sign was hung on the iron gate facing Douglas Avenue announcing that the Spaghetti Works building and adjacent parking lot were once again for sale.[85]

Then, just as abruptly as the project was called off, it was back on. In December 2017, a sweeping new plan emerged, involving the transformation of the Spaghetti Works warehouse into an upscale apartment building and the construction of a new office, retail, and restaurant complex on the parking lot directly to the east of Naftzger Park. Drawings of the plans showed that this new development would spill out directly onto the redesigned new park. In revealing the reinvigorated plan, both the developer and the city touted the inseparable links between the new construction and the park project. "We didn't want to invest a large amount of money in the Spaghetti Works building unless the park was going to be improved," said Brad Saville, one of the principals of the development team. Assistant City Manager Scot Rigby boasted that the new development's "front door is going to have this tremendous spruce-up of this renovated park."[86]

What changed between November and December to rejuvenate the seemingly dead redevelopment plan? Two important developments in the Wichita City Council were likely influential in getting the project back on track. First, the city received a petition to create a Community Improvement District (CID), a special taxing district that would apply a 2 percent sales tax surcharge on all retail sales in the area including the Spaghetti Works property. The vast majority of this revenue would go toward renovating the Spaghetti Works building and constructing a new retail and office structure on the existing parking lot—in other words, subsidizing the developer's construction costs—while 10 percent of the CID revenue would fund ongoing maintenance of the rebuilt park.[87]

The second substantial factor that had shifted between November and December related, as it had so frequently throughout the history of Naftzger Park, to the city's homeless population. Specifically, the Wichita City Council passed two ordinances directly targeting the homeless. The first, ostensibly designed to prevent dangerous collisions between pedestrians and vehicles (despite a lack of evidence that this had been a serious or growing problem in Wichita), outlawed curbside panhandling. Notably, this ordinance applied not to the entire city but only to major arterial streets with a high speed limit and to a "congested area" within the city, which the ordinance specifically defined as including all streets (regardless of speed limit, usage, or actual congestion) within the downtown core of Wichita. Although most of Downtown Wichita had for decades been generally underutilized and far from "congested," pedestrian-vehicle interactions (including curbside panhandling) were thus banned throughout downtown. This area contained many of the city's key gathering spots for homeless residents, including organizations providing food, shelter, and services as well as popular gathering sites like the central bus depot, the city's riverfront, and of course Naftzger Park.[88]

The second new ordinance, passed during the same city council meeting, was designed to "prohibit harassing or aggressive conduct for the purpose of exchanging any item between one or more individuals"—in other words, a ban on "aggressive panhandling." The vague language in the ordinance (which, for instance, made it illegal to "block, obstruct or interfere with the safe and free passage of any person by any means, including, unreasonably causing a person to take evasive action to avoid physical contact") did not specifically lay out what was meant by "aggressive" action. It thereby potentially criminalized a wide range of panhandling and other activities by the homeless that might be *interpreted* by passersby as threatening or unpleasant. Violation of the new ordinance carried with it penalties of up to $500 in fines and six months of incarceration.

Though the ordinance did not explicitly use the term "homeless" to refer to the individuals targeted, the debate in the city council chambers left little doubt as to the purpose of the new law. City Council Member Janet Miller endorsed the measure not just as a way to prevent "aggressive" conduct but also as a means of discouraging people from giving cash to homeless panhandlers altogether, criticizing that action as counterproductive: "There are lots of ways to help people who are in need, this not being an ideal one. Many times folks in these positions are not actually homeless, and so it has created some very dangerous situations, and also some difficult situations for people who are shopping and parking and walking and things that all of us want to be able to do." Both the "pedestrian safety" ordinance and the "aggressive conduct" ordinance were approved unanimously, with little debate or objection by the city council.[89]

It is not entirely clear whether the passage of these two ordinances was directly responsible for the developers' decision to restart the Spaghetti

Works project, but within days of the adoption of the new laws, the project was back on track. Even so, the delays that had occurred in late 2017 made it impossible for Naftzger Park to be rebuilt in time for the NCAA basketball tournament in March 2018. As the tournament approached, the city's initial plans to host the "Fan Fest" within Naftzger Park were moved to an adjacent closed-off street. During the tournament, the park remained open to the public, but no tournament activities occurred inside, and tall canvas banners were hung around the entire perimeter of the park, preventing out-of-town basketball fans from seeing into the public space that would soon be torn up. Though visitors were allowed to drink alcohol in the public "Fan Fest" on the street, no alcohol consumption was allowed in Naftzger Park.[90]

Soon after the tournament ended, city officials reconvened and agreed on a final design for the rebuilt Naftzger Park. The chosen design hewed closely to one of Balsley's four initial drawings, but it incorporated some elements that had been discussed at public forums the previous summer. Balsley returned to Wichita in late March to publicly unveil the design and answer questions. Very quickly the proposal obtained approval from the city's Historic Preservation Board, Design Council, and Board of Park Commissioners. The new park also received an endorsement from *The Wichita Eagle*, which wrote in an editorial that "Naftzger Park should be a jewel for years to come."[91]

Despite the approvals, the fate of the park remained in limbo. The city took no action to close the park or begin demolition for several weeks. Finally, as described at the beginning of this chapter, the mayor announced that the park would close for good on May 21. When asked by a reporter where the homeless patrons of the park would go upon its closure, the mayor indicated that no plan had been put into place, instead making a vague reference to the police unit tasked with dealing with the homeless. "We have our outreach team that has been working with a number of different entities and they've been engaged in this process," he said.[92]

Conclusion: The End of Naftzger Park and the Promise of Downtown Revival

And with little fanfare, Naftzger Park's last day came and went on May 21, 2018. News crews arrived at the park that afternoon to interview homeless

Figure 3.3. The demolition of Naftzger Park, 2018. Photo by Chase Billingham.

people, but the reporters soon went away, and the following morning demolition crews arrived and began erecting wire fencing around the perimeter. That fencing would soon extend down Douglas Avenue to the railroad bridge and around the park all the way to the Spaghetti Works building, thus finally consolidating the public park and the private development into one cohesive project. Throughout June and July, bulldozers, excavators, and men leveled the park (Figure 3.3). They began by removing a stone monument to temperance activist Carry A. Nation, all of the cast iron fixtures, and all of the brick walkways before proceeding to knock down the brick walls surrounding the park and rip out all but three mature trees. By mid-July, all that remained of the original Naftzger Park was the gazebo, which was soon relocated to another city park.[93]

In place of the eclectic tree-shaded Victorian oasis, the new Naftzger Park emphasized openness, with a flat artificial turf lawn, a stage, and a large LED screen emblazoned with the name of the local electric utility company, which had donated private funds to support the redevelopment effort (Figure 3.4). All of these elements spoke to the reimagined purpose of the park, which was designed to promote large gatherings, to sync up with programming at the adjacent arena, and to serve as a pleasant waiting area for those seeking a table at the breakfast restaurant opened in the new commercial building on the park's eastern edge. This extreme openness also facilitated surveillance, as the new park had none of the walls, bushes, trees, or rock formations that had hidden people sleeping, using drugs or alcohol, or engaging in other illicit behavior in the original park.[94]

Completed at the beginning of 2020, the new Naftzger Park was set to be

Figure 3.4. The rebuilt Naftzger Park, 2025. Photo by Chase Billingham.

unveiled to a city brimming with civic pride and excited about the future of downtown. This was no accident, as invigorating civic pride—and remedying what the city called "the perception challenge"—was a key strategy in Wichita's economic development efforts in the late 2010s; redeveloping Naftzger Park was a key component of those efforts. That "perception challenge," the string of development failures and persistent downtown stagnation that led to it, and the marketing-focused approach that city leaders developed to address it are the focus of chapter 4.

PROMOTING THE POTEMKIN CITY

4

A Region Struggling to Compete

Wichita's aviation-fueled economy was flying high following the Second World War, but, as I explained in chapter 3, by the 1960s the city core suffered from deterioration, blight, and the economic impacts of suburbanization. The Urban Renewal era helped to bring some new energy downtown, but city leaders struggled with how to deal with poverty and homelessness, particularly along East Douglas Avenue, the city's "skid row." Redeveloping that area with the creation of Naftzger Park and the incipient Old Town district did not succeed in displacing the low-income men who frequented the area. The core continued to hollow out, especially as the groundwater pollution crisis further eroded downtown property values. As discussed in chapter 2, the grand vision of Jack DeBoer was supposed to jolt Wichita back into growth and competitiveness vis-à-vis its peer regions in the early 1990s; that plan mostly collapsed under its own weight. All the while, the Wichita metropolitan area continued slipping in the interurban competition for growth, and with the failure of the DeBoer initiative, local leaders were largely at a loss regarding how to proceed in order to restore the robust growth the city had enjoyed in the middle of the century.

Wichita's leaders were right to be nervous. On a range of key economic and demographic indicators, the region was falling behind in its growth ambitions, trailing not just the major

Table 4.1. Total population in eight Midwestern metropolitan areas, 1990–2020.

	1990	2000	2010	2020	% Change, 1990–2020
Des Moines	392,928	481,394	569,633	709,517	80.6%
Kansas City	1,582,875	1,836,038	2,035,334	2,192,018	38.5%
Lincoln	213,641	266,787	302,157	340,210	59.2%
Oklahoma City	958,839	1,095,421	1,252,987	1,425,732	48.7%
Omaha	639,580	767,041	865,350	967,595	51.3%
Topeka	160,976	224,551	233,870	233,133	44.8%
Tulsa	708,954	859,532	937,478	1,015,356	43.2%
Wichita	485,270	571,166	623,061	647,599	33.5%

Source: US Census Bureau, *Census 2000 PHC-T-3, Ranking Tables for Metropolitan Areas: 1990 and 2000, Table 2: Metropolitan Areas in Alphabetic Sort, 1990 and 2000 Population, and Numeric and Percent Population Change: 1990 to 2000*, April 2, 2001, retrieved from https://www2.census.gov/programs-surveys/decennial/2000/phc/phc-t-03/tab02.xls; US Census Bureau, *CPH-T-2, Population Change for Metropolitan and Micropolitan Statistical Areas in the United States and Puerto Rico: 2000 to 2010*, retrieved from https://www2.census.gov/programs-surveys/decennial/tables/cph/cph-t/cph-t-2/cph-t-2.xls; US Census Bureau, *CBSA-EST2022: Annual Estimates of the Resident Population for Metropolitan Statistical Areas in the United States and Puerto Rico: April 1, 2020 to July 1, 2024*, retrieved from https://www.census.gov/data/datasets/time-series/demo/popest/2020s-total-metro-and-micro-statistical-areas.html.

Sunbelt destinations that witnessed monumental growth in the late twentieth century but also the smaller neighboring metropolitan regions in the Midwest and Great Plains, peers against which Wichitans often compared themselves. By the 1990s, as Wichita's growth stagnated, those peers began to pull further away, and the gaps between the rates of regional growth would expand for the next several decades.

This was evident in a measure as straightforward as metropolitan population growth, as Table 4.1 indicates. In this table, and in the tables and figures to follow, I compare trends in the Wichita Metropolitan Area against those taking place in a selection of metropolitan competitors within Kansas and neighboring states: Topeka, Oklahoma City, Tulsa, Kansas City, Des Moines, Omaha, and Lincoln. As late as 1990, Table 4.1 indicates, the Wichita region housed a population half as large as Oklahoma City, two thirds as large as Tulsa, three quarters as large as Omaha, more than twice as large as Lincoln, and significantly greater than Des Moines. In each of the following three decades, though, the region's population growth lagged behind the majority of these peers. Between 1990 and 2020, the metropolitan population in Wichita rose by 34 percent, trailing the 39 percent growth in Kansas City, the 44 percent rise in Tulsa, the 49 percent increase in Oklahoma City, and the astounding 81 percent growth in Des Moines. In the 2010s, Iowa's

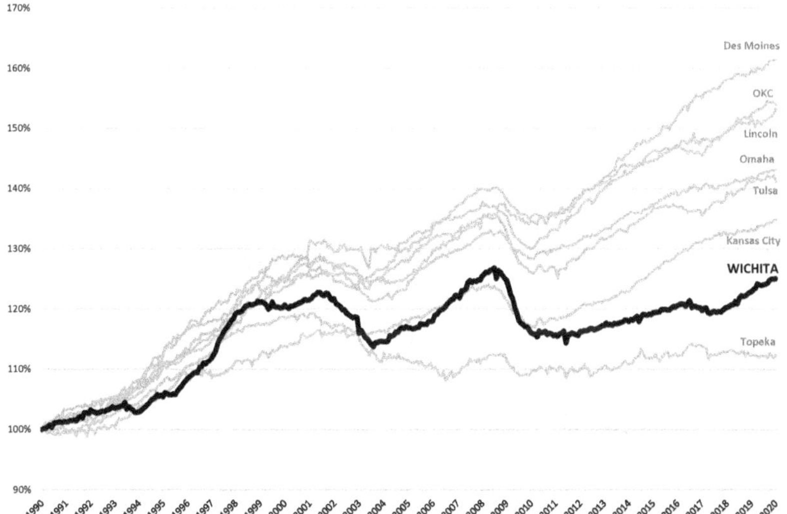

Figure 4.1. Change in total employment in eight Midwestern metropolitan areas, 1990–2020 (January 1990 = 100%).

Source: Author's calculations based upon data from the US Bureau of Labor Statistics, total nonfarm employees in metropolitan areas, seasonally adjusted data, retrieved from https://data.bls.gov/PDQWeb/sm.

capital surged past Wichita in population, housing 10 percent more people in 2020 than the Air Capital region. Even the smaller regions of Lincoln and Topeka witnessed faster population growth than Wichita in the late twentieth and early twenty-first centuries.

Similarly, in employment, Wichita's lackluster performance has been evident for decades, as Figure 4.1 makes clear. In each decade since 1990, the Wichita region has trailed the majority of this group of eight metropolitan areas in job growth. During the 1990s—a period of robust growth nationwide—Wichita's employment expansion, though strong, was lower than all but two of these regional peers. In the Great Recession at the tail end of the 2000s, Wichita's economy was hit harder than nearly all others in the region, contributing to a 3.9 percent decline in employment over the course of the decade. Then, in the 2010s, as employment again rose across the board, Wichita's economy lagged behind, outpaced in job growth by all regional peers except Topeka. All told, between 1990 and 2020, the total number of jobs in the Wichita metropolitan area rose by about 25 percent,

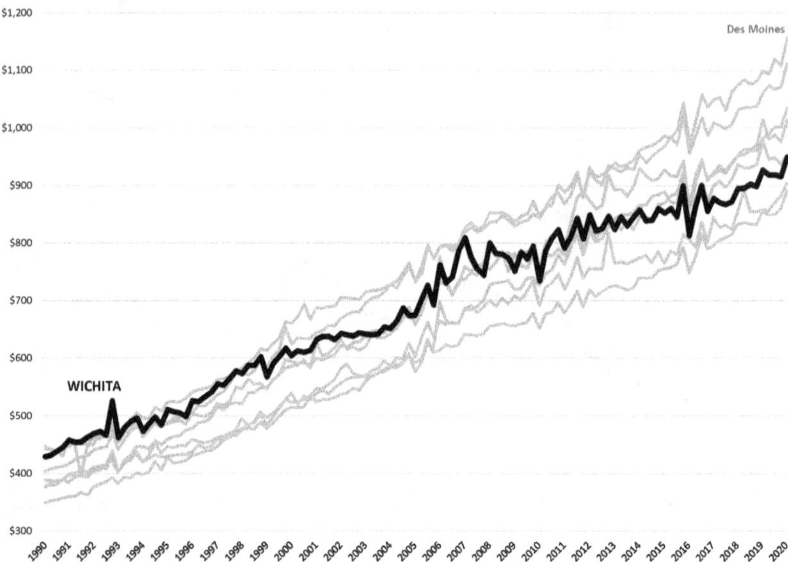

Figure 4.2. Average weekly wages for employees in eight Midwestern metropolitan areas, 1990–2020.

Source: US Bureau of Labor Statistics and Federal Reserve Bank of St. Louis, Average Weekly Wages for Employees in Private Establishments, retrieved from FRED, Federal Reserve Bank of St. Louis, https://fred.stlouisfed.org/.

outpacing only Topeka and falling far behind the 41 percent increase seen in Tulsa, Oklahoma City's 54 percent rise, and the impressive 61 percent growth experienced in metropolitan Des Moines.

Aligning with those trends in population and employment growth was Wichita's flagging performance in wages, as shown in Figure 4.2. Even in the relatively low-wage states of the Great Plains, Wichita stood out among peer regions in terms of the trajectory of wage growth in the late twentieth and early twenty-first centuries. This was somewhat surprising, given the heavy concentration of unionized manufacturing workers in Wichita's aerospace-centric economy, but it is likely that the troubles Wichita's aircraft industry faced over that period (discussed in detail in chapter 5) contributed to that wage stagnation. Among the eight metropolitan areas examined here, Wichita actually was a leader in employee compensation through the final decade of the twentieth century. In early 1990, the average weekly pay for workers in the Wichita region stood at $429, well above all regional peers except Tulsa and Kansas City. The Air Capital soon lost ground, however, as its average wages failed to keep up with the steady growth occurring in nearby rivals, especially Des Moines and Kansas City. The first few years of the new millennium were particularly hard on Wichita workers, as average wages stayed essentially flat for nearly three full years from early 2001 through late 2003, while compensation rose rapidly in other cities, especially Des Moines. By the end of the 2010s and on the eve of the COVID-19 pandemic and the economic crisis that it provoked, Wichita, a leader in worker pay three decades earlier, sat near the bottom of the pack. In terms of hourly pay, workers in the Wichita region were taking home an average of $23.01 in January 2020; this was over three dollars less per hour on average than workers in Tulsa and Oklahoma City, over six dollars less per hour than workers in Kansas City and Omaha, and nearly seven dollars less per hour than workers in Des Moines.

The Wichita region's struggles in attracting new residents, growing its workforce, and competing with its peer regions in compensating its workers were manifested more broadly in the economy, as evidenced most clearly in the housing market. Compared to the high-cost metropolitan areas in the Northeast and the West Coast, the center of the US has always been an affordable area of the country, but even among this group of relatively low-cost cities, Wichita stood out in terms of its slow growth in home value appreciation, as illustrated in Figure 4.3. This chart presents the All-Transactions House Price Index, calculated by the US Federal Housing Finance Agency to track trends in home values by comparing repeat sales of the same properties over time. The index is standardized to baseline values established in January 1995. The chart demonstrates that overall trends affecting the US housing market prevailed in each of these eight metro areas over the course of the past three decades, with generally steady growth through the 1990s and early 2000s, declines following the housing market collapse and ensuing Great Recession of the late 2000s and early 2010s, and a return to robust (in some cases, quite rapid) home price appreciation in the late 2010s and into the 2020s. Equally clear, though, is that in each era, Wichita's homes grew in value at a rate far slower than those in competing metro areas in the Midwest and Great Plains. On the eve of the COVID-19 economic disruptions, Wichita was just one of two regions in this group (along with Topeka) whose index value stood below 200.

This slow rate of home price appreciation from the 1990s to the present

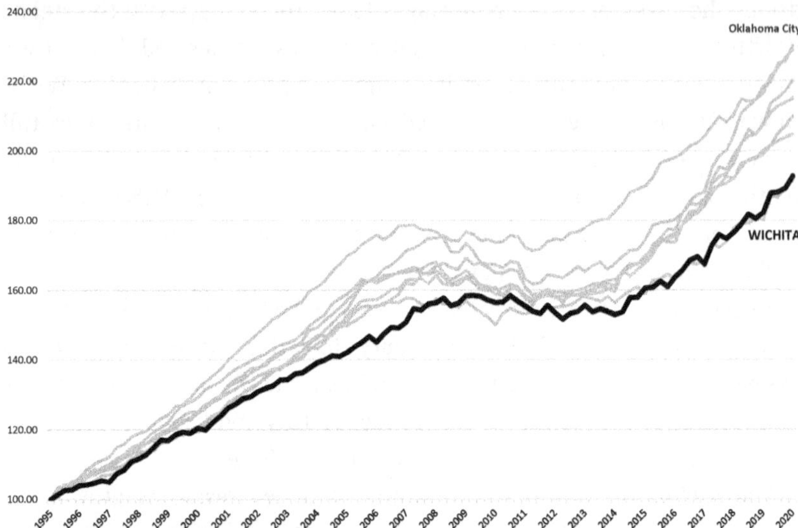

Figure 4.3. All-Transactions House Price Index in eight Midwestern metropolitan areas, 1995–2020 (January 1995 = 100).

Source: US Federal Housing Finance Agency, All-Transactions House Price Index, retrieved from FRED, Federal Reserve Bank of St. Louis, https://fred.stlouisfed.org/.

day was particularly noteworthy, given the low home prices that prevailed in the 1990s. In 1990, all of these regions had low home values, on average, and none of the other seven cities under consideration here had a median home value more than 20 percent higher than Wichita's median value of $57,000. Over the next two decades, though, interregional gaps in home values increased substantially, as illustrated in Table 4.2. By 2010, Wichita's median value rose to just $115,000, on par with Topeka for the lowest among these eight metro areas and less than three quarters the median value in the Kansas City region. As home values continued to rise at a more rapid clip across the country in the 2010s and 2020s, they tended to rise slower in Wichita than elsewhere; only Topeka experienced a slower rate of growth. As a result, by the 2020s, places that many Americans on the coasts might consider unfathomably cheap, such as Omaha, Des Moines, and Kansas City, had far higher housing costs on average than Wichita. In 2023, following a quick runup in home prices nationwide, the median home value was 32 percent higher in Omaha, 34 percent higher in Des Moines, and 41 percent higher in Kansas City than in Wichita.

Table 4.2. Median home value in eight Midwestern metropolitan areas, 1990–2023.

	Des Moines	Kansas City	Lincoln	Oklahoma City	Omaha	Topeka	Tulsa	Wichita
1990	$59,000	$66,100	$61,900	$53,900	$59,300	$55,200	$58,800	$57,000
2000	$103,300	$104,700	$105,900	$79,000	$101,000	$81,600	$85,500	$83,100
2010	$151,100	$158,000	$145,000	$121,300	$143,400	$114,900	$121,900	$115,000
2020	$193,100	$196,000	$188,700	$162,600	$181,200	$137,900	$155,000	$144,200
2023	$252,400	$265,400	$257,500	$214,700	$248,100	$172,200	$204,400	$188,200
Percent Change, 1990–2023	328%	302%	316%	298%	318%	212%	248%	230%

Source: US Census Bureau, *1990 Census of Housing, General Housing Characteristics, Metropolitan Areas*, retrieved from https://www2.census.gov/library/publications/decennial/1990/ch-1/ch-1-1b-1.pdf; US Census Bureau, "Profile of Selected Housing Characteristics: 2000," Decennial Census, DEC Summary File 3 Demographic Profile, Table DP4, accessed on July 10, 2025, https://data.census.gov/table/DECENNIALDPSF32000.DP4?q=median+home+value&t=Housing+Value+and+Purchase+Price&g=3800000US2120,3760,4360,5880,5920,8440,8560,9040&y=2000; US Census Bureau, "Selected Housing Characteristics," American Community Survey, ACS 2010 5-Year Estimates Selected Population Data Profiles, Table DP04, accessed on July 10, 2025, https://data.census.gov/table/ACSDP5YSPT2010.DP04?q=median+home+value+2010&g=310XX00US19780,28140,30700,36420,36540,45820,46140,48620; US Census Bureau, "Selected Housing Characteristics," American Community Survey, ACS 2020 5-Year Estimates Data Profiles, Table DP04, accessed on July 10, 2025, https://data.census.gov/table/ACSDP5Y2020.DP04?q=median+home+value+2020&g=310XX00US19780,28140,30700,36420,36540,45820,46140,48620; US Census Bureau, "Selected Housing Characteristics," American Community Survey, ACS 2023 5-Year Estimates Data Profiles, Table DP04, accessed on July 10, 2025, https://data.census.gov/table/ACSDP5Y2023.DP04?q=median+home+value&g=310XX00US19780,28140,30700,36420,36540,45820,46140,48620.

Decades of low housing costs were not confined to the homeownership market. Though average rents have risen roughly in parallel across most of these metropolitan areas, Wichita has consistently been a less expensive place for renters than every other region except Topeka. By 2023 it was more than $200 cheaper each month to rent the median apartment in Wichita than to rent a comparable space in Des Moines, Omaha, or Kansas City.

Economic development boosters have frequently touted Wichita's affordability and low cost of housing as a potential draw to young professionals seeking to escape from pricier parts of the country. The Greater Wichita Partnership's Choose Wichita website, designed as a central clearinghouse for the region's efforts to entice young professionals to relocate, features an entire page boasting about "how Wichita's low cost of living can let you live life to the fullest."[1] That low cost of living was deemed particularly important during the COVID-19 pandemic, when low-cost cities attempted to capitalize on the growth in remote work opportunities to persuade relocation by mobile professional workers. This effort in Wichita met with little success. By and large, the slow price appreciation is, in fact, evidence of the region's failure in that competitive effort to lure more migrants.

These diverging trends in growth also manifested themselves tangibly in the built environment, specifically in the construction of new tall buildings, particularly in the central business districts of each city. This pattern is demonstrated clearly in Table 4.3, which presents data on the number of new structures over two hundred feet tall added to the skyline of each city within each decade. The 1980s were an especially busy period for high-rise construction in Des Moines, Kansas City, Oklahoma City, and Tulsa. Though the pace of skyscraper construction slowed in the following decades in most of those cities, a significant number of new high-rise towers appeared on city skylines in the 1990s and 2000s, particularly in Kansas City. Even Lincoln added a downtown residential skyscraper over 250 feet tall in 2022.

By comparison, only two structures over two hundred feet tall have been constructed in Wichita since 1980. The most recent structure approaching that height was the Hyatt Hotel, which emerged in the wake of the collapse of the DeBoer downtown plan and soon ran into financial struggles, eventually needing to be purchased by the city in order to remain solvent. Before that, the tallest building completed was the 385-foot Epic Center,

Table 4.3. New structures over two hundred feet tall constructed in the central cities of eight Midwestern metropolitan areas, by decade.

	Des Moines	Kansas City	Lincoln	Oklahoma City	Omaha	Topeka	Tulsa	Wichita
1980–1989	3	8	0	7	3	0	10	1
1990–1999	2	2	0	0	2	0	0	1
2000–2009	0	4	0	1	2	0	0	0
2010–2019	0	2	0	2	1	0	1	0
2020–2023	0	3	1	1	0	0	0	0
Total, 1980–2023	5	19	1	11	8	0	11	2

Source: Author's calculations based upon data from Emporis, http://skyscraperpage.com, and Wikipedia.

which opened in 1987 and remains to this day the tallest building in the state of Kansas.

However, even the construction of the Epic Center, which transformed the Wichita skyline, provided an indication of the softness of the region's economy. The tower, with its unique trapezoidal peak, was originally conceived as part of a two-tower complex. Hailed upon the completion of the first tower as being "epic in proportion and epic in its confidence of Wichita's potential," the Epic Center vastly underperformed expectations, failing to fill to more than half of its capacity, selling to new owners several times in its first few years of existence, and glutting the downtown office market such that vacancies radiated outward, depressing the entire downtown core. Lofty plans for the second tower were quietly scuttled; nearly forty years later, the parcel north of the Epic Center's sole tower remains a surface parking lot adjacent to a patch of undeveloped grass.[2]

Growth Machine Politics and Civic Boosterism in the Potemkin City

By the late twentieth century, the demographic and economic trends discussed above were widely apparent, and public- and private-sector leaders worried about the region's economic stagnation. The sense that Wichita was falling behind in its competition with peer cities was palpable; that worry lay behind urgent efforts like the DeBoer plan discussed in chapter 2. Grandiose projects designed to catapult Wichita into competition with larger and more dynamic peers generally faltered, often in ways that left indelible reminders on the built environment, such as the empty tract of land where the second Epic Center tower should have stood.

For decades, urban sociologists have debated about the nature of urban growth, as I examined in chapter 1. In the late twentieth century, political economy approaches to the study of urban development posed major challenges to the human ecology perspective, which had long been dominant. Among political economy theories, none has been as influential as the "Growth Machine" model, introduced by Harvey Molotch and developed more fully in collaboration with John Logan in their classic book *Urban Fortunes*. As Logan and Molotch explained: "For those who count, the city is a growth machine, one that can increase aggregate rents and trap related wealth for those in the right position to benefit. The desire for growth creates consensus among a wide range of elite groups, no matter how split they might be on other issues."[3] The major players making up the growth coalition tend to include, on the public side, elected and appointed officials within local government and, on the private side, local banks and real estate firms, property developers, and major employers, along with chambers of commerce and other organizations designed to promote business prosperity. All of these players—despite myriad personal and professional tensions and antagonisms—come together in the service of their shared priority: encouraging robust local economic growth. In addition to these core players, a wide range of ancillary entities including institutions like local colleges and universities, locally owned retail, dining, and entertainment businesses, and local sports franchises tend to embrace the growth agenda set by the major players in this coalition.[4]

Among the most important institutions for generating the community "we feeling" that underlies booster campaigns are local media outlets. Molotch described "the metropolitan newspaper" as "the most important example of a business which has its interest anchored in the aggregate growth of the locality." Regardless of the particular businesses that succeed or fail or the specific political party that takes control at city hall, the newspaper's fortunes are tied to growth per se, insofar as that growth creates opportunities for the paper to sell more column inches' worth of advertisements to businesses and residents posting notices in the classified section. In earlier chapters, I have demonstrated how newspapers and other local media sources served as key promoters of Wichita's growth, consistently cheerleading the development that is occurring and speculating about development to come, while downplaying big plans that end up unfulfilled. That examination of the media's involvement in promoting growth will continue in this chapter and the one that follows.[5]

My heavy reliance on media accounts throughout this book is in part a methodological necessity. Journalists are the observers on the ground when major events happen, providing, it is often said, the "first draft of history." While it would be unwise to rely solely on their accounts, media sources are indispensable, particularly where the primary source record is thin. As key players in the urban "growth machine," however, it is imperative to view media messages not just as impartial sources of information but instead as data in and of themselves and to assess those messages from a critical perspective. The media have historically propped up even dubious plans for economic growth in cities throughout the US; this chapter demonstrates several examples of how that process has unfolded in the Air Capital.

The story of Wichita in the late twentieth and early twenty-first centuries helps to elucidate the options available to growth coalitions in lagging cities and the strategies undertaken to spur, cultivate, and nourish growth when possible—or, as in Wichita's case, to obfuscate, distract, and mislead the public about the scale of growth in lieu of actual, robust progress. I refer to the latter process as the "Potemkin City" strategy. It is rooted primarily in marketing, public relations, media messaging, and hollow boosterism designed to project an image of urban vibrancy, largely in the hope that creating a public perception of regional dynamism will work to persuade investors, companies, and professional migrants to invest, thereby realizing the economic development goals imagined by the local growth coalition and regularly broadcast to the public via the Potemkin façade.

In the remainder of this chapter, I explore five moments in the city's recent history to illustrate how growth interests in this one lagging urban center deployed Potemkin City strategies to mask deficiencies, encourage growth and new investment, and maintain the profitability of the business, real estate, and property development interests that form the core of the local growth coalition. I begin with a discussion of (1) the formation of the Wichita Downtown Development Corporation (WDDC), a public-private partnership tasked with rejuvenating development in the city center. The *Project Downtown* master plan spearheaded by this group set the stage for many of the strategic initiatives in Downtown Wichita that would follow. Next, I examine (2) the activities of an out-of-state group of developers who came to be known as the "Minnesota Guys." This group dominated downtown development activity in the 2000s and early 2010s as they acquired vast expanses of downtown property and promised sweeping revitalization of the entire area. I highlight the ways in which boosters and local media lionized the Minnesota Guys, and I explore how their ultimate failure, bankruptcy, and departure from Wichita set development in the city back for years. In the fallout of the Minnesota Guys scandal, WDDC and affiliated organizations within Wichita's growth coalition regrouped, promoting growth in the core with an interrelated set of initiatives, of which I examine three in this chapter: (3) The transformation of an abandoned tract of land containing an ugly sunken pit along the city's main commercial thoroughfare into a "pop-up park" space; (4) the recruitment of an economic development consultant whose evaluations and prognostications came to drive civic discourse around Wichita for many years; and (5) the harnessing of the city flag as a shared emblem to promote civic spirit and augment local pride. In each of these five moments, projecting a vision of Wichita as a thriving and dynamic metropolis took precedence over remedying the structural demographic and economic challenges impeding real robust growth. These initiatives successfully heightened a sense of community pride, but they failed to adequately halt or reverse Wichita's slipping competitiveness vis-à-vis its regional peers, as revealed in the tables and figures discussed at the beginning of this chapter.

A New Coalition Emerges to Boost Downtown

In chapter 2, I examined the formation of the Wichita/Sedgwick County Partnership for Growth (WI/SE), the public-private partnership that had championed Jack DeBoer's riverfront overhaul through the early 1990s. Following the demise of the DeBoer plan, WI/SE quietly disbanded in the fall of 1996 with relatively little to show for its work, especially in comparison to the amount of publicity it had generated. The face of Downtown Wichita had still not changed dramatically in several decades. Within months of the dissolution of WI/SE, however, a new organization was born to take its place. In the spring of 1997, many of the same leaders who had driven WI/SE launched the new nonprofit Wichita Downtown Development Corporation (WDDC), appointing as its first executive director Jerry Jones, who had moved to Wichita from Arizona just a few years earlier to take the position of vice president in charge of downtown development at WI/SE. Drawing on the findings of a consultant's report, Jones and WDDC got to work on a new strategy for improving Downtown Wichita, focusing less on a comprehensive DeBoer-style overhaul of the entire district and instead on targeted residential, commercial, retail, and entertainment development aimed at making the area more hip and attractive to young professionals.[6]

The newly formed WDDC had early success, as its launch coincided with the groundbreaking for the highly anticipated Exploration Place, a combined science museum and children's museum located on the west bank of the Arkansas River, directly across from the heart of Downtown Wichita.

The museum had been under discussion for many years and had been incorporated into the DeBoer plan, but its siting had provoked controversy, as it required the rerouting of McLean Boulevard and the obstruction of previously unimpeded river views from the west bank of the river. Designed by renowned architect Moshe Safdie, Exploration Place cut a striking image as it straddled the riverbank with its sloping concrete curves and peaks.[7]

Still, though facing Downtown Wichita across the river, Exploration Place was not itself situated within the core; a new effort was needed to rejuvenate the heart of downtown. Quickly WDDC floated a plan to impose a fee on all property owners in Downtown Wichita to support the organization's operations and its mission of promotion and marketing in order to "elevate the image of downtown Wichita." Unveiling the proposal, WDDC consultant Brad Segal argued that "downtown is only as good as it is managed and marketed." The idea of a new levy immediately met resistance from conservative business and political leaders, including Mayor Bob Knight, who viewed the proposal as a tax hike on local businesses. Protesting before the city council, prominent local businessman Willard Garvey, referring to the previous decade's escapades, accused city leaders of having "thrown millions of dollars of taxpayer money" toward futile efforts before asking them, "Why repeat the mistake?"[8]

However, more than half of downtown property owners, whose property accounted for over 70 percent of all real estate value in the area, signed a petition in favor of implementing the tax increase across the entire area, thereby establishing a business improvement district named the Self-Supporting Municipal Improvement District (SSMID). The list of SSMID supporters included the developer Dave Burk, who, more than any other person, had driven the growth of Wichita's Old Town entertainment district over the previous decade. Knight, still reeling from the DeBoer fiasco, was vehemently opposed, likening the proposal to "a rerun of a bad movie." Opponents to the proposal warned that the extra tax would prompt companies to relocate to other areas of the city where they would be free from the surcharge. As the debate unfolded, more members of the city council, who had seemed to be on the fence, began to lean against the idea of the SSMID. They ultimately rejected the proposal, cutting off the guaranteed funding stream that WDDC had been seeking. It looked as if WDDC would quickly cease to exist, or at best would continue solely on the support of volunteers.[9]

Two years passed before downtown boosters tried again. Their hopes for success were buoyed by a new advocate. Mayor Bob Knight, who had led the charge against the SSMID in 1998, ended up regretting his opposition. In an unequivocal mea culpa rarely witnessed among politicians, Knight admitted that "it was my fault the first (proposal) was stopped." This time, he pledged "to advance the momentum we have downtown." Though some business owners again opposed the reformulated SSMID proposal, Knight's support proved instrumental in ensuring its approval and implementation. Approval was speedy and less contentious for the renewed proposal, despite a petition protesting it signed by more than a third of local business owners. In 2001 the SSMID was established, generating hundreds of thousands of dollars in revenue each year, all of which flowed directly into the coffers of WDDC.[10]

Jerry Jones's tenure at WDDC was short-lived, as he resigned less than a year after the organization's formation to go to work as a private developer. Shifting his seat to the other side of the negotiating table, Jones would over the next two decades become one of the city's most prominent real estate developers in his own right, no longer the man working to facilitate development in Wichita.[11]

As a result, following the creation of the SSMID, the first task for the newly energized WDDC was to hire a full-time president, and they selected Ed Wolverton, an economic development specialist with experience in several midsized US cities. As usual, *The Wichita Eagle* was bullish on the trajectory of Downtown Wichita, touting promising recent developments and asserting in an editorial that the only thing impeding the area's success was the lack of a leader who could pull together all of those loose strands of development into a cohesive vision for the city's core. "For Wichita's sake," the editorial implored, "we hope Mr. Wolverton is that leader."[12]

Wolverton stayed in that role for nearly six years, focusing the organization's attention on marketing and promoting Downtown Wichita, attempting to recruit businesses to locate in the core and boost the area's cultural vitality with new entertainment options and events. To that end, much of Wolverton's tenure was occupied by a drive to build a multiuse sports and entertainment arena in the heart of downtown. The first decade of the twenty-first century witnessed a series of political campaigns, momentum shifts, and public votes to approve a countywide sales tax to support the arena. The original proposal, known as the "DynaPlex," fizzled as local leaders failed to develop a comprehensive financial plan to construct it. In short order, though, a new arena plan emerged from the scuttled DynaPlex proposal, and following a successful sales tax referendum, the arena began to rise from the ground just south of Naftzger Park. Eventually named INTRUST Bank Arena after the region's largest local bank, the facility generated major progress in Downtown Wichita, allowing the area to attract top-name entertainers to the city center for the first time in decades.[13]

Wolverton would not stay to witness the arena's opening, however, as he left Wichita even before the formal groundbreaking to take a new job as the leader of a similar downtown development agency in Greensboro, North Carolina. He had clashed with some local leaders over his overt endorsement of casino gambling as an element of downtown revitalization, which hastened his departure. (After his time in Greensboro, Wolverton would go on to lead parallel organizations, all pursuing the same urban economic competitiveness initiatives, in the similarly sized metropolitan regions of Wilmington, North Carolina, and Columbus, Georgia.)[14]

Replacing Wolverton was Jeff Fluhr, who like his predecessor had extensive experience guiding downtown development efforts for a midsized metropolitan region (in Fluhr's case, Baton Rouge, Louisiana, where he had worked for the previous sixteen years). Fluhr immediately set to work developing a new comprehensive plan to guide downtown development into the future. That master plan, developed by Boston consulting firm Goody Clancy, was dubbed *Project Downtown*, and it was unveiled in 2010, just two years after Fluhr's arrival. The ambitious vision, which I first described in chapter 3, laid out strategies for revitalizing various sections of the core and presented projections for plausible growth in residential, commercial, retail, and hospitality development. For the next decade, *Project Downtown* would be the sacred text guiding official downtown development policy in Wichita.[15]

Moving forward, Fluhr would be the chief navigator charting the course for Downtown Wichita's future, and *Project Downtown* would be his roadmap. Even so, a new era for the city center could not be realized until Fluhr and other city leaders pulled Downtown Wichita out from under the shadow of the boisterous, seemingly larger-than-life actors who had figured into every conversation about urban revitalization for half a decade: the Minnesota Guys.

The Dealmaker and the Visionary: The Minnesota Guys Descend on Wichita

As the first few years of the twenty-first century unfolded, Downtown Wichita continued its steady economic decline as businesses relocated to newer office developments on the east and west sides of the city or left the region altogether. In just one of a string of high-profile departures, IMA Financial Group, a commercial insurance company, announced that they would take their two hundred employees and move them to a new office building on the rapidly growing (by Wichita standards) northeastern edge of the city. Downtown Wichita had not witnessed the construction of a high-rise office tower in nearly two decades, the commercial vacancy rate in the city core had risen above 25 percent by the middle of the decade, and no one, it appeared, wanted to take a chance on the aging and inadequate buildings the central business district had to offer.[16]

Into that void stepped the "Minnesota Guys," a group of six businessmen previously unknown in Wichita who were nearly always referred to by that geographic sobriquet, a reference to their origins in the Twin Cities. In the first two months of 2005, the Minnesota Guys purchased a quarter of all of the office space in Downtown Wichita. They scooped up entire office towers at bargain basement prices, including the nineteen-story tower at 125 North Market which, when it was first constructed as the Vickers Tower in 1963, was the city's tallest building. That building—in 2005 still one of the most noteworthy landmarks on the Wichita skyline, which had barely changed at all since the 1960s—was sold to the Minnesota Guys for $150,000. The two most prominent of the partners from Minnesota, Michael Elzufon and Daniel Lundberg, boasted that they were capitalizing on undervalued downtown space in a city poised for a rebound, implying that local investors were foolish to pass on these deals and allow out-of-state investors like them to move in. "We're shedding light on what you guys aren't seeing," said Elzufon. He, in collaboration with the other Minnesota Guys, foresaw an opportunity to convert the underutilized office towers into new apartments and condos, sparking a residential revival of Downtown Wichita in an era when urban living was surging in many trendy cities across the country.[17]

Operating under the corporate name Real Development, LLC, the

Minnesota Guys continued to buy office buildings and warehouses throughout downtown, and they soon began work on their first condo conversion in a brick warehouse just south of Naftzger Park. Elzufon was excited when Sedgwick County decided to locate the large new INTRUST Bank Arena in a parcel directly adjacent to this condo conversion project. Soon, with additional acquisitions, the Minnesota Guys owned nearly 40 percent of all of the square footage in the city center, with plans to develop hundreds of condos and apartments, a new hotel, and at least half a million square feet of office and retail space. Once again, a spirit of enthusiasm was capturing Wichita's boosters, including WDDC President Ed Wolverton, who said of the Minnesota Guys, "Clearly they are accelerating that growth here." Displaying faux humility in response to a query about how much property they planned to purchase, Elzufon said coyly, "We don't intend on owning everything."[18]

The media gushed over the Minnesota Guys. *The Wichita Eagle* praised them in a multipage tribute that likened them to superheroes whom they dubbed "The Dealmaker" (Lundberg) and "The Visionary" (Elzufon). They earned the confidence of local civic and business leaders, too, with Wolverton affirming in 2005 that "everything they said they were going to do, they have done." But, as had occurred many times over the past quarter century, that enthusiasm did not appear to be reflected in the market. On their first condo conversion project, the Minnesota Guys had sold just half of the units in the first year they were available. Still, they moved forward, acquiring prominent shuttered towers fronting on Douglas Avenue and promising to convert them into luxury condominiums. Primarily in response to the activities of the Minnesota Guys, *The Wichita Eagle* boasted (echoing the pro-DeBoer spirit it had regularly applied in the previous decade) that "a new downtown is emerging, bringing new energy and excitement. Let's keep that momentum and can-do spirit going."[19]

The Minnesota Guys themselves became prominent public boosters for the city center. Elzufon went on a tour inviting businesses to relocate downtown. "Believe it. Things are happening in downtown Wichita," he told a crowd during a luncheon held by the Wichita Independent Business Association. Meanwhile, they continued their buying spree, and by the middle of 2006 they had amassed over 700,000 square feet of downtown space. Local media provided credulous coverage of their bold plans to thoroughly renovate all of that downtown office space, though eighteen months after their acquisition campaign began they had renovated only one floor of one of the downtown office towers that they owned. Another tower in their possession was so run-down that it had a tree growing out of the top floor through the roof. After a year and a half of buying and mostly sitting on their acquisitions, the Minnesota Guys unveiled a new slogan for their company: "The Downtown of Tomorrow Has Begun." While their announced plans for bold renovations failed to materialize, they continued to buy entire buildings, adding two more to their portfolio in September 2006, bringing their total space to nearly 900,000 square feet.[20]

The local embrace of the Minnesota Guys by credulous business leaders and media continued. The promotion of their work tapped into the desire for Wichita to compete against other cities by emulating those cities' successes. An advertising circular produced by Real Development appealed directly to that spirit of emulation: "When [Lundberg] came to town, he looked around and liked what he saw—a smaller version of Minneapolis, some years behind the larger city's redevelopment. What had happened in Minneapolis—conversion of industrial spaces into residential lofts, with a small business and retail component—he could make happen in Wichita."[21] *The Wichita Eagle* printed an op-ed by Michael Elzufon in late 2006 that echoed the same themes, resembling an advertisement for his company. "When Real Development first visited Wichita in 2004," Elzufon wrote, "we found a city on the verge of change—one that had experienced a downturn in the economic vitality of its downtown. Yet it was a city determined to regain footing and downtown prosperity." Not having lived through the previous two decades in Wichita, during which downtown revitalization plans—the DeBoer saga, the stalled riverfront hotel, the Riverport Plaza casino standoff—were among the most hotly contested issues in the region, Elzufon wrote as if he and his partners had just discovered Downtown Wichita and were revealing its potential to an ignorant public.[22]

Real Development did secure a tenant for one of its buildings when the Kansas Department of Corrections agreed to move its parole office into three floors of a downtown office tower owned by the Minnesota Guys. In anticipation of the move, Elzufon boasted that he and his partners would commit nearly $2 million to renovate the building. They also announced $7 million in interior and exterior renovations to their largest building, the nineteen-story skyscraper at 125 North Market. The same week that the massive renovation project was unveiled, however, one of the building's major tenants, which had occupied offices in the tower for four decades, announced that they would relocate. "Unfortunately they won't be around for the big party, but I wish them the best," Elzufon responded dismissively.[23]

When Sedgwick County voters approved the construction of the new downtown arena in 2009, it was hailed by its promoters not just as a sign of confidence in downtown growth but as evidence that downtown revitalization was already a success. *The Wichita Eagle* explicitly cited the Minnesota Guys as both recipients of and contributors to the area's momentum in an enthusiastic editorial: "We haven't even broken ground on the arena yet, and already it's delivered a huge economic payoff in downtown revitalization. Doubt that? Look at the millions of dollars in investment that just one group—the 'Minnesota Guys' of Real Development—has poured into downtown, transforming the core area with new condos and offices." But at that point, the Minnesota Guys had completed very few transformational downtown investments, though they had been in Wichita for nearly three years; for the most part, they had simply bought a lot of cheap downtown office space and held onto it.[24]

Over time, cracks began to appear in the façade of the Minnesota Guys' downtown campaign. They sought public subsidies from the city in the form of a new TIF (tax increment financing) district to help with infrastructure improvements on a proposed condo conversion project called "Exchange Place" within two historic buildings at the intersection of Douglas and Main, in the very heart of Downtown Wichita. When they were unable to secure private financing for the project from lenders, they asked the city to purchase the buildings outright and then turn around and hand the deeds to the buildings back to them. As Elzufon explained in justification for this proposal, "Getting a bank to finance a project in downtown Wichita was, 'Don't even bother.'" Soon thereafter, the real estate agent who had brokered the sale of the nineteen-story building at 125 North Market sued Real Development, claiming that his commission had been left off of the sale contract. The city council, led by a new mayor, Carl Brewer, approved both the TIF plan and the agreement to buy the two buildings and give them to the Minnesota Guys.[25]

Yet five months later, Real Development had still not begun any work on the project. "We should have started by now," observed the city's economic development director. Continuing with its pattern of credulous reporting on the Minnesota Guys, however, *The Wichita Eagle* optimistically explained that "the big news with the long-discussed renovation project at Exchange Place is that developer Michael Elzufon has redesigned the project to be bigger." In early 2008, it was revealed that the developers had not paid property taxes on the Exchange Place property since purchasing it four years earlier, nor had they paid the back taxes that were owed on the building, which they had assumed when making the purchase. "Ten thousand bills have come and gone . . . and none haven't been paid," said Steve Chaney, a Real Development partner. The property tax bills on Exchange Place, totaling $284,000, "must have slipped through the cracks," he claimed. (In its fawning coverage of the Minnesota Guys two years earlier, *The Wichita Eagle* had dubbed Chaney "The Money Man.") Despite the tax delinquency, the city council voted in the spring to approve nearly $8 million in low-interest loans to subsidize Real Development's work to rehabilitate the façades on other buildings they owned. More façade improvement loans were approved later that summer.[26]

Although their progress in redeveloping and filling their downtown spaces was slow, the appraised values on the Minnesota Guys' properties were rising quickly, as the county appraiser was interpreting the continued public celebration of Downtown Wichita's purported growth as evidence that the downtown real estate market was picking up. As a result, the Minnesota Guys were facing rising tax bills on properties that had been deemed virtually worthless when they bought them a few years earlier. By late 2008, stories in the press about Real Development focused less frequently on their purchase of buildings and increasingly on their decisions not to purchase additional downtown buildings because of an inability to secure financing. They faced a new lawsuit at the end of 2008 from a real estate agent who claimed that they failed to pay him his contracted commissions for selling condos in their buildings. Elzufon responded that the suit was meritless because he and his partners had shifted their plan for the building from condos to rental apartments after the planned condos did not generate sufficient market interest, thereby nullifying the sales contracts and the realtor's commission.[27]

Despite persuading the city government to purchase the Exchange Place buildings and give them the deed, finance a parking garage serving their apartments, and provide loans to renovate the façades, the Minnesota Guys still struggled to pay for their restoration project on these two buildings. After scrapping the condos and converting their plan to rental apartments, they applied to HUD for over $20 million in additional loans to finance the project. Elzufon called on the city government to build an even larger parking garage to service his underutilized commercial properties, because, he claimed, "Unless I can find a company with 500 employees that ride bicycles to work, we absolutely will not rent that space."[28]

As the nation's economy descended into the Great Recession in the wake of a massive housing market collapse in 2008 and 2009—and even after multiple years of evident inaction and lackluster results from Real Development in Wichita—the Minnesota Guys continued to receive glowing media coverage. A *Wichita Eagle* profile in early 2009 led with a claim bordering on the absurd: "After four years, the downtown developers known as the Minnesota Guys say they are beginning to gain real momentum." Government leaders reinforced this show of local exuberance, with the city's economic development director asserting his satisfaction with Elzufon and his partners because, in his words, "They are full of enthusiasm, and they have a big-picture view of downtown." Elzufon, who had been working in Wichita for half a decade, continued to project forward his vision of success: "Two years down the road," he proclaimed, "we're shooting for iconic. Progressive. Strong. Urban. A very upbeat, with-the-times environment." He and his partners sold a strip mall they owned in West Wichita so that they could continue "concentrating all of our efforts downtown," according to Elzufon.[29]

When in 2009 the Kansas state legislature lowered the limit that developers could seek in tax credits for restoring historic structures, developers and business leaders were furious, none more so than Elzufon, who said that this move would jeopardize the great progress that he and his company had made in Wichita. "Without [the historic tax credits], the work's just simply not going to get done in the Wichita market. The numbers do not work," Elzufon asserted. That same year, Real Development sued their insurance company for $7 million, two years after vandals had broken into the Exchange Place complex, damaged it, and stolen copper plumbing and wiring from inside. Despite their constant publicity, the Minnesota Guys had still not started any work on their redevelopment project there, meaning that the damage had not been repaired in the two years since it had occurred. The insurance company countered that the building had not been properly secured by its owners and that they were therefore not liable.[30]

In September 2009, Real Development lamented that cash flow problems and a lack of credit were impeding their ability to make progress on their lofty goals, complaining that they were unable to refinance their investment in the nineteen-story building at 125 North Market, despite the raft of public subsidies they had received. "As usual, people in Wichita don't believe in downtown," said Lundberg, chastising local bankers and investors. Soon, owners of commercial units within buildings that the Minnesota Guys had subdivided were facing foreclosure, as rampant commercial vacancies obstructed the cash flow necessary to pay the mortgages. Those owners, who had bought the properties in the buildings directly from the Minnesota Guys themselves, indicated that Elzufon and his partners had misled them about the potential profitability of commercial property in Downtown Wichita. Elzufon waved off the concerns, suggesting it was those owners' fault that they were unable to lease the spaces they had bought from him. Acknowledging the depressed market conditions, Elzufon pressed on with confidence. "If we have the wherewithal to deal with these storms but we maintain our commitment and dedication to what we're after downtown, we'll only be further ahead when things turn around," he declared.[31]

In 2010, Elzufon returned to the Wichita City Council, imploring them to increase their TIF-funded commitment to his team's redevelopment project at Exchange Place by more than $2 million. Failure to do so, he threatened, would doom the project, which he had first proposed more than five years earlier. This additional funding coincided with Elzufon's plan to increase the scope of Exchange Place—contingent upon Real Development successfully securing the HUD-backed loan that they had been seeking for over a year. Their ability to obtain the HUD-backed loan, in turn, hinged upon the additional TIF commitment from Wichita, Elzufon claimed. Real Development struggled to hold contractors (including some of the city's most powerful construction companies) at bay, as bills went unpaid and credit continued to prove elusive.[32]

City council members, especially conservatives Jeff Longwell and Paul Gray, were wary about extending more taxpayer money to the Minnesota Guys. "We can't continue to have failures and expect the [residents] to support us when we engage in a plan for downtown. There's a lot of people that don't trust us now," said Gray. On top of that, a voice rarely heard in public discussions about development in Wichita spoke up, and spoke up loudly. Americans for Prosperity, the conservative lobbying group financed by Wichita billionaire Charles Koch, took out a full-page advertisement in

The Wichita Eagle, addressing city council members directly in the form of an open letter and exhorting them to reject the deal. Real Development responded in kind by taking out their own advertisement in the newspaper, portraying the dilapidated Exchange Place property with the menacing tagline, "Is this what we want? A block of blight?" Below renderings of the proposed renovation, the ad proclaimed, "We believe Wichita wants and deserves more. A YES vote on Exchange Place starts it all." In an about-face, the *Wichita Eagle* editorial board seemed to have finally lost confidence in the developers, recommending that the city council reject the additional funding, even as they conceded that "the Minnesota Guys have done wonders for downtown Wichita over the past five years."[33]

Despite the warnings from Americans for Prosperity and *The Wichita Eagle*, negative independent analyses of the viability of the project conducted by a downtown consultant firm and a real estate economist at Wichita State University, and the publicly expressed concerns of several council members, the city council approved the additional financing for Real Development. Council Member Janet Miller, whose district encompassed downtown, dismissed the critiques as too conservative, testifying that the Minnesota Guys' five-year-old, constantly evolving plan for those properties was "going to be a catalytic project." Wary council members were swayed in part by Lundberg's declaration in the city council meeting that he had secured $700,000 in assistance from a donor whom he would not name. To cut down on costs, the developers reduced the number of parking spaces in their proposed garage that would be dedicated to public parking rather than for their own tenants. The promise of public parking spaces was one of the elements of the proposal that city leaders had originally found attractive, yet this reduction did not appear to dissuade them from maintaining their support for the Minnesota Guys.[34]

A month later, however, a New Jersey lender whom Real Development had been counting on for a $6.9 million loan reduced that amount to $4.8 million, forcing the Minnesota Guys once again to scramble to rearrange finances and search for stopgaps. Creditors were soon calling for their money. In June 2010, two California investors sued for nearly half a million dollars that they said they were owed by Elzufon and his partners; these investors were especially aggrieved, as they had also been among the buyers of units within subdivided Real Development buildings in Downtown

Wichita which had faced foreclosure the previous year. Continuing to struggle to find money, the Minnesota Guys attempted to refinance the buildings again later that summer. They needed cash to pay off vendors, which was a precondition of receiving the extra financing that the City of Wichita had approved—financing that, in turn, they needed to secure the bigger HUD-backed loan. The financial vise squeezed Real Development harder and harder, imperiling a ground floor grocery store that they had announced would be part of the development. Still, Elzufon projected his trademark confidence, proclaiming that his team had "a world-class project that will come downtown in a very short period of time."[35]

It would be another eight months before they finally obtained the mortgage that would serve as the first in that chain of obligations they hoped to navigate. Even so, their problems continued, as they were sued by a tax accounting firm they had employed to reduce assessments and tax obligations at their properties. Lundberg expressed surprise at the suit, claiming that he was under the impression that the tax firm knew "we would get to it eventually." A court ordered the Minnesota Guys to pay $28,000 to the firm in the case, which also yielded evidence that Real Development had failed to renew their corporate charter to operate in Kansas. The same week, Real Development's leasing agent quit, tenants complained about ongoing maintenance issues involving broken elevators and air conditioning systems, and the property management company overseeing several of their Wichita properties parted ways with the Minnesota Guys.[36]

After seven years, public- and private-sector leaders' confidence in the Minnesota Guys appeared to have finally dried up. While touting other developments taking place downtown, WDDC Board Chair Dick Honeyman admitted that "the Minnesota contingency has been and continues to be a problem," and he speculated that the situation would "come to a head at some point." For his part, Mayor Carl Brewer, who had voted in favor of extending greater TIF support to Real Development, stated that "the confidence we had in them is no longer there." The Minnesota Guys' primary lobbyist in city hall dissolved her association with the group after she began dating and ultimately married Wichita City Manager Robert Layton, provoking concerns about conflicts of interest. Layton, too, recused himself from all involvement in city affairs related to the Minnesota Guys, delegating that authority to an assistant.[37]

Even as the developers hinted that the HUD financing they had been seeking for years was finally within reach, city leaders' patience had mostly dissipated. They grew angrier when they learned that the Minnesota Guys, in spite of their apparent insolvency and inability to meet their obligations in Wichita, had flown to Kingsland, Georgia, to pitch that small city's leaders on a $200 million theme park project, which would also require millions of dollars in public subsidies. When prompted about his unfulfilled promises and debts in Wichita, Elzufon defended his Georgia proposal, saying, "I, too, have a right to survive." It quickly emerged that Elzufon had also pitched a downtown development project in Elmira, New York.[38]

In November 2012, after years of staving off ruin, the wheels began to come off the operation for the Minnesota Guys, as the Kansas Securities Commissioner issued a cease and desist order against Real Development, several affiliated entities, and Elzufon and Lundberg themselves related to concerns about potentially fraudulent transactions undertaken to prop up some of their struggling downtown properties. Authorities executed a search warrant at the 125 North Market skyscraper, where Real Development had its headquarters, and state officials considered criminal charges against Elzufon and Lundberg. "The Visionary" and "The Dealmaker," as *The Wichita Eagle* had labeled them in 2006, claimed that they were victims, not perpetrators, of fraud. The two had purchased life insurance policies to use as collateral in securing financing for a Wichita office building from insurance companies who they claimed had engaged in fraudulent practices. City leaders began indicating that their agreements with the Minnesota Guys were void, yet the developers persisted. "We have a written development agreement with the city and we expect them to honor it," said Lundberg.[39]

The following month, they sold three of their Wichita buildings at auction, including a building they had leased to a church that served and housed homeless people who feared eviction in the leadup to the sale. Soon after that, they sold their stake in the Exchange Place project, which they had first unveiled eight years earlier, to a Texas investor. After years of stagnation, as the Minnesota Guys' Wichita empire was nearing total collapse and as they faced charges for financial fraud crimes, WDDC President Jeff Fluhr reiterated his sunny view of the situation downtown, saying that the Exchange Place transaction "reinforces the fact that we're seeing a strengthening of the investment environment in downtown Wichita."[40]

In June 2013, Elzufon and Lundberg lost another tower to foreclosure, with their lender claiming they were delinquent on $1.6 million in loans. They were sued the following month by the owners of land leases beneath another prominent tower who claimed they had received no lease payments from the Minnesota Guys. Weeks later, they lost their biggest prize of all, the landmark nineteen-story tower at 125 North Market, relinquishing it to a lender whom they had failed to pay.[41]

Finally, after waiting in limbo for a year, Elzufon and Lundberg learned that they would, indeed, face charges for violating Kansas state securities laws. Specifically, they were charged with selling unofficial and unsecured promissory notes to raise capital for their Wichita projects. As prosecution loomed for the Minnesota Guys, Wichita city leaders, continuing to boast fancifully about robust economic growth in the city core, acted as if their nearly decade-long involvement with the group had never occurred. “It's time for everyone to move on,” said Mayor Carl Brewer. “Downtown will redevelop. Other people have interests in those properties downtown, and we're going to be all right.” Reflecting on his experiences in Wichita, Elzufon, as usual, did not mince words. “It's been an incredible nightmare. I've put everything I had into Wichita—millions, my energy, my vision. And now I—my family, my partners, everyone—are getting kicked around, dragged through the mud.” For his part, Lundberg proclaimed, “We're just about done with Wichita.” By the middle of 2014, the Minnesota Guys had lost their entire portfolio in the city.[42]

Lundberg and Elzufon may have been done with Wichita, but Wichita was not done with them. In early 2015, the charges which were expected only to carry potential fines were upgraded, as the Kansas Securities Commissioner filed sixty-one counts accounts against the two developers in Sedgwick County District Court. Alleging that Elzufon and Lundberg had committed fraud by selling unregistered securities, the state summoned the developers back to Kansas and booked them in the Sedgwick County Jail in Downtown Wichita, just steps away from the skyscrapers that had once belonged in their now-repossessed real estate empire. Refuting the allegations, Elzufon's attorney cited his client's dedication to the city and its economic progress, while deflecting blame onto government officials: “Mike has faithfully, tirelessly and passionately fought to make downtown Wichita a success for more than a decade. Make no mistake: Had the city, and the federal government through HUD, followed through as promised, investors would have seen their expected returns and Mike would be a Wichita success story." According to the state, the Minnesota Guys had lost approximately $3.5 million of their investors' money. In a separate lawsuit, Key Construction and SPT Architecture, two of the city's most powerful players in real estate construction, design, and development, sued for over $1.5 million in unpaid bills. Elzufon was surprised and personally offended by the lawsuit, saying ruefully, "I don't want to call it personal, but I worked . . . with these guys literally for ten years."[43]

In late 2015, all but five charges against the Minnesota Guys were dropped, as the Sedgwick County District Court judge found that the court did not have jurisdiction over the offenses alleged by investors in California. State prosecutors, while dropping the five remaining charges, appealed the district court's ruling to the Kansas Court of Appeals, which later reversed the lower court's decision and reinstated those charges against Lundberg and Elzufon. The case dragged on for two more years until finally the Kansas Supreme Court settled it once and for all, finding (in a divided decision) that the district court's earlier ruling had been correct and dismissing the remaining charges against the Minnesota Guys.[44]

Lundberg and Elzufon went on to new business ventures elsewhere, but the bitterness stemming from their failures in Wichita lingered. Nevertheless, the exultant boosterism of city government and business leaders, WDDC leadership, and the press regarding downtown's upward trajectory persisted, and the negative impact of the Minnesota Guys (along with the broader economic fallout of the Great Recession) provided convenient explanations for why growth in Downtown Wichita lagged behind the boosters' sanguine portrayals of the ongoing transformation of the city center. The disconnect between the growth coalition's vision of downtown and the slow pace of actual growth were epitomized in one key derelict parcel along Douglas Avenue.

Urban Boosterism and the Blurring of Public and Private Space in the "Pop-Up Park"

Perhaps no parcel in Wichita came to symbolize the city's economic torpor—or its boosters' ability to rebrand that economic failure as evidence of cultural vitality—more clearly than the "ICT Pop-Up Urban Park." This site, located right on Douglas Avenue between Main Street and Market

Street—the absolute heart of the city's central business district—had previously featured a collection of unremarkable two-story office and retail buildings. Through the 1990s those buildings, dating to the earliest era in the city's history, housed a women's clothing store, a shoe store, and other small merchants. But in 2006, just as the Minnesota Guys were touting their ambitious plans for Exchange Place located right across Douglas Avenue, owners began evicting those retail tenants. This was part of a plan to eventually tear down those structures to make way for a new parking garage that would serve a new hotel slated to be constructed in a refurbished adjacent building. The hotel was approved by the Wichita City Council, and the buildings were knocked down (over the objections of the city's historic preservation board) to make way for the garage. As a result, by 2007 a massive pit sat in the ground at this valuable location, awaiting new construction to service the anticipated hotel. Mirroring the inactivity at Exchange Place across the street, though, the hotel was never built, rendering the proposed garage unnecessary. With no alternative plans for the site, the deep pit carved into the most prominent location along Wichita's primary downtown avenue remained vacant and blighted for years.[45]

Bokeh Development, a real estate firm created by a Wichita physician and his former assistant, purchased the parcel in 2011, but like the previous owners, they did nothing with the pit for three years, allowing it to continue to languish. That changed in 2014 when outside forces stepped in, allowing Bokeh to do something with the property without having to commit significant resources of their own. The Knight Foundation, working through the Wichita Community Foundation, provided Bokeh a grant of nearly $150,000 to rework the site. Excavated dirt from a nearby construction project was donated to fill in the pit, and the grant money was used to cover the site with rock gravel, install some improvised tables made from discarded cable spools, and add a touch of greenery in the form of a few young trees in wooden planters. The result was the ICT Pop-Up Urban Park, which was designed to be a temporary placeholder before Bokeh could develop the site. ("ICT," derived from the Federal Aviation Administration code for Wichita's airport, is frequently used as a shorthand nickname for the city.) "We've always had the vision of a Class A building down there," said Michael Ramsey, the principal at Bokeh. Perpetually soft demand for commercial office space in Downtown Wichita, however, made that type of permanent structure an extremely risky investment. The Pop-Up Park was

Figure 4.4. The ICT Pop-Up Urban Park. Photo by Chase Billingham.

a much less expensive alternative that could remedy the eyesore of the pit while also potentially priming the space for more ambitious investment in the future (Figure 4.4).[46]

The idea of temporary "pop-up" architectural elements and retail spaces has become a major trend in urban planning over the past two decades, in line with similar trends referred to by labels such as "tactical urbanism," "DIY urbanism," and "creative placemaking." At the heart of these urban design philosophies lies an insurgent ethos that resists top-down bureaucratic planning boards and zoning codes. City revitalization strategies drawing upon a "tactical urbanist" ethos are often whimsical, temporary, and relatively inexpensive to implement, aiming to draw the public's attention to neglected urban spaces and spark their imagination in ways that might lead to more permanent redevelopment efforts down the road. From impromptu "parklets" installed in the street in Santa Monica to "guerilla wayfaring" signs erected to guide pedestrians in Raleigh, examples of "tactical urbanism" have abounded in midsize cities nationwide in the first two decades of the twenty-first century.[47]

Drawing inspiration from the tactical urbanism trend, the idea of a pop-up park demonstrated not just a creative solution to the blight on Douglas Avenue but also Wichita's familiarity and alignment with cutting-edge trends in urban design, allowing the city to emulate cool developments in competitor regions. In line with the emphasis on the ephemeral nature of place at the heart of the pop-up concept, the ICT Pop-Up Urban Park was intended to be temporary; the idea, if successful, could be transported from one vacant lot to the next as the vibrancy invigorated by the Pop-Up Park led to construction at other formerly derelict sites. The time frame for what was considered pop-up and temporary was unclear from the beginning, however. WDDC Vice President Jason Gregory predicted that the public could expect the ICT Pop-Up Urban Park to last between three and five years.[48]

The opening of the park was delayed slightly when the developers' original dirt donation fell through and they had to seek free fill dirt elsewhere. With the dirt and gravel finally laid into the hole, fashionable overhead string lights were added, along with chairs and a concrete ping-pong table. Because of the delays, it took nearly a year from the initial announcement before the space opened to the public, but in the fall of 2015 a festive ribbon-cutting ceremony featured speeches by city leaders, a bluegrass music performance, and food trucks.[49]

Gregory's suggested time frame underestimated the duration of the ICT Pop-Up Urban Park, which remained in place for over five years as the real estate market in Downtown Wichita continued to languish. Though the park in itself never generated the level of downtown vitality that its creators had promised, the Pop-Up Park did become a highly visible downtown space and a frequent topic of conversation in Wichita. WDDC, which had partnered with Bokeh on the project, frequently programmed the space with concerts, film screenings, and other events in its first few years of existence, but these became less common over time. Very quickly the condition of the ping-pong table deteriorated as the paddles and ping-pong balls that the organization had stored in a box underneath the table were worn, vandalized, or stolen and then not replaced. As the years passed, the Pop-Up Park's greatest success came at lunchtime during the work week, as it became the city's central spot for food trucks to gather. Given the severely limited dining options in the central business district—a Quizno's sandwich shop was arguably the only convenient lunch destination on

Douglas Avenue—the daily arrival of food trucks at the Pop-Up Park provided a greater variety of food for the area's office employees, who would frequently pack the park at lunch time on days with good weather.[50]

When the food trucks left, however, so did the people. Throughout its existence, I took regular trips to the space to observe and record details on its usage and activation. Fieldnotes from that period reveal a great deal of activity during the lunch hour on weekdays but emptiness at most other times of day and on most weekends, except for when special events were staged there. As repeated visits to the ICT Pop-Up Urban Park revealed, it was rare to see more than a few people using the street furniture, playing ping-pong, or otherwise utilizing the space in the morning, late afternoon, or evening.[51]

The Caldwell-Murdock Building, a ten-story tower constructed in 1907, sat directly to the west of the Pop-Up Park and was also owned by Bokeh Development. This structure had been completely abandoned for years before the opening of the park, and it remained empty, abandoned, and boarded up throughout the park's existence. The three-story office building on the park's eastern edge, too, remained underutilized, with a few tenants occasionally occupying some of the offices but never lasting long. In short, the park failed to catalyze significant economic activity even in its immediate vicinity, to say nothing of Downtown Wichita as a whole. Yet the inability of the park to spark robust economic growth in the area did not stop civic boosters from touting its contribution to the city's downtown vibrancy and local pride. WDDC, Visit Wichita, and local government frequently used images of the Pop-Up Park in promotional materials to illustrate the hip transformation purportedly underway in the city. Glossy photos from the park were prominently displayed in each annual publication of WDDC's *State of Downtown* report between 2016 and 2020.[52]

Public confusion over the park's origins, the city's constant promotion of the space, and the name itself led to misunderstandings regarding its ownership and control. Many in Wichita believed that the ICT Pop-Up Urban Park was, indeed, a city park. This was a reasonable conclusion, given that the Wichita Department of Park & Recreation, which maintained well over one hundred parks across the city, at times collaborated with the WDDC to program the site, and the city government frequently held press conferences, events, and announcements there. In reality, it was never a fully public space. Instead, the park relied on the continuing commitment of its owners, Bokeh Development, for its continued existence and accessibility to the public and on WDDC for most of its maintenance, upkeep, and programming.[53]

Following the death of George Floyd beneath the knee of a Minneapolis police officer in the summer of 2020, Wichita was just one of dozens of US cities to witness protests against police violence and for racial justice in line with the broader Black Lives Matter movement. Protesters in Wichita, organized by a group called Project Justice ICT, chose the prominent—and they believed public—ICT Pop-Up Urban Park as the gathering spot for a rally in August. At that rally, several Project Justice ICT leaders were arrested in the park. Two weeks after the arrests, Bokeh and WDDC announced that the ICT Pop-Up Urban Park, which they had until then continued to tout as a great asset for Downtown Wichita's revitalization, would close for good, though they insisted that the decision was unrelated to the Black Lives Matter protests and arrests. "It was always meant to be temporary," Bokeh principal Michael Ramsey said of the five-year-old Pop-Up Park; he acknowledged, however, that although Bokeh was closing the space permanently, the company had no immediate plans for development there on that potentially valuable parcel of downtown land.[54]

By the end of 2020, this key space in the heart of Downtown Wichita was once again surrounded by barbed wire fencing, with no realistic prospect for future development. In early 2021, though, a new initiative was announced. Though Bokeh continued to resist investing their own resources in their property, the Wichita Community Foundation and the Knight Foundation, which had funded the original ICT Pop-Up Urban Park, once again stepped up by providing additional grant funding for a new initiative called the Chain Link Gallery. Through this program, the foundations, in collaboration with Bokeh and Harvester Arts, an organization designed to promote the arts in Wichita, displayed artwork by local artists on the barbed wire chain-link fencing surrounding the former Pop-Up Park. While this artwork could presumably have been displayed on any surface in the city, these local philanthropies, nonprofits, and the arts community chose instead to continue to subsidize the developers' inaction. Through consistent social media marketing campaigns, they rebranded this exemplar of soft real estate demand as a cultural favor to the city and as evidence of Wichita's growing urban vitality. By its very nature, the Chain Link Gallery—which remained behind fencing with a padlocked gate and opened to the public only on rare special occasions—generated even less activation of Wichita's Downtown core than the ICT Pop-Up Urban Park had done in its five years of existence. By 2025, the space was mostly derelict, unmaintained, and rarely frequented by anyone.[55]

Through the late 2010s, the Pop-Up Park served as the most persistent visual manifestation of WDDC's attempts at generating downtown buzz via "placemaking" activities. Nevertheless, Wichita's economy continued to lag behind its peers, and in the wake of the Great Recession and the wreckage of the Minnesota Guys debacle, the city's core remained an underwhelming place. What was holding Wichita back in the interurban competition for growth, job creation, and economic prosperity? To identify the problems and figure out the solutions, the city's growth coalition enlisted an analyst who would come to take on the status of an oracle and whose prescriptions would guide economic development policy into the 2020s.

The Oracle Comes to Town

James Chung grew up in Wichita, attending the prestigious private Wichita Collegiate School before enrolling at Harvard University for both an undergraduate degree and a graduate business degree. He founded a business research and consulting firm called Reach Advisors, which first made a big splash in national media when their research revealed a provocative claim: In a reversal of decades of gender inequality, by the 2000s some groups of women were outearning their male counterparts. This "reverse gender gap," though limited to women in a specific set of age cohorts, industries, and metropolitan areas, pointed toward a future of growing power and affluence for women. Chung based this finding on analysis of data from the US Census Bureau's American Community Survey. Importantly, he extrapolated from his findings to make sweeping Richard Florida–esque statements about the diverging trajectories of American cities, as summarized in a *Time* magazine profile of his findings:

> Chung also claims that, as far as women's pay is concerned, not all cities are created equal. Having pulled data on 2,000 communities and cross-referenced the demographic information with the wage-gap figures, he found that the cities where women earned more than men had at least one of three characteristics. Some, like New York City or Los

> Angeles, had primary local industries that were knowledge-based. Others were manufacturing towns whose industries had shrunk, especially smaller ones like Erie, Pa., or Terre Haute, Ind. Still others, like Miami or Monroe, La., had a majority minority population.

The idea of the emerging "reverse gender gap" went viral in popular media, informing many cursory, thinly sourced news stories, and it served as a bedrock claim in the influential work of the journalist Hanna Rosin, including magazine articles, TED Talks, and her book *The End of Men*.[56]

The claim, however, was largely unsupported. As the sociologist Philip Cohen revealed in a reanalysis of the ACS data, the apparent "reverse gender" gap among young, single women was likely a function of the unique racial and ethnic composition of that age cohort within those metropolitan areas (within which women were disproportionately white, while men were disproportionately Latino), and it emerged due to insufficient attention to the statistical mediating effect of education. Within each category of educational attainment, Cohen demonstrated, women continued to earn less than their male peers. Though Chung reached out in a comment on Cohen's blog to defend his findings, he did not demonstrate how Reach Advisors had conducted its analysis or share any specific statistical results. Indeed, the Reach Advisors study that informed the *Time* article, setting off so much discussion and controversy, has never been seen. When an Australian news network's "Fact Check" team inquired into the study after it had informed similar claims in public discourse in that country, the network reported that "the company did not release the full research in 2010, and would not provide it to Fact Check."[57]

Nevertheless, the "reverse gender gap" story helped to propel the reputation of Chung and Reach Advisors, and with its focus on economic and demographic patterns affecting specific metropolitan areas, the firm drew the attention of economic development professionals in US cities. Chung, who grew up in Wichita and had worked briefly as a business reporter for *The Wichita Eagle* in 1989, found himself on the radar of the city's boosters and economic development proponents with this newfound notoriety.

Drawing on the recommendations of WDDC's *Project Downtown* master plan, these local leaders had begun focusing on "talent retention" as a key strategy for rejuvenating the city's core. As early as 2011, Chung was publicly affirming that focus, telling *The Wichita Eagle* in an interview that "growth simply isn't sustainable without careful thought about talent development and retention." In 2012, he was invited by the Kansas Leadership Center, a Wichita nonprofit designed to mentor civic leaders, to deliver a presentation on the impact of demographic trends in the state. Through these appearances, Chung's reputation for possessing unique insights into the Wichita economy grew.[58]

In 2014, the Wichita Community Foundation, WDDC, and the chamber of commerce teamed up to sponsor a speaker series called "Fuel the Fire," dedicated to the issue of talent retention in Wichita. The second speaker in the series was James Chung. Standing before an audience that included members of the city council and the county commission and wearing blue slacks, a sport coat, and an open-collared shirt, Chung presented a cool, business-casual appearance which, combined with his microphone head set and walk-and-talk delivery style, gave his presentation the air of a TED Talk.

Chung provided the audience some basic demographic and economic data on the Wichita region and peer cities and then sounded the alarm, explaining how Wichita was losing out to other regions because of its inability to attract and retain highly educated young professionals. His delivery, supported by PowerPoint slides filled with numbers, blended harsh critiques with the rhetoric of a motivational speaker. In closing his presentation, Chung exhorted the audience to emphasize city branding, marketing, and image:

> I know that there's a lot more to Wichita than, sort of, that negative stereotype that's out there. The problem is Wichita is not putting out a counternarrative to explain, "Why are we better than that?" And that's what I would push you to do. Think about that. What is that counternarrative where, when someone says the city's name, you get that kind of response that someone got about Des Moines? . . . They've figured out the counternarrative to sell Des Moines. It's time for Wichita to put out the counternarrative to sell Wichita.

Chung's warnings resonated with many in the community, provoking a flurry of public commentary on how to make Wichita cooler, more competitive, more welcoming, and more prosperous.[59]

These conversations also dovetailed with the arguments underlying a proposal to institute a new 1 percent citywide sales tax that would support a range of infrastructure and economic development initiatives, including the creation of a "jobs fund" to help with talent recruitment and incubation efforts. The sales tax was championed by a political action committee (PAC) called Yes Wichita, whose supporters included a long list of Wichita's biggest banks, companies, and developers, all of whom donated tens of thousands of dollars to support the proposal. All of that spending from the core of Wichita's growth coalition working in unison, however, paled in comparison to the spending by another PAC formed to oppose the sales tax named Coalition for a Better Wichita, which raised well over a million dollars to oppose the tax. Nearly all the funding for the opposition PAC was contributed by the city's homegrown powerhouse of conservative ideology, Koch Industries. In the November election, the sales tax proposal was soundly defeated by Wichita voters.[60]

In the wake of the sales tax defeat, the region's economic doldrums persisted, posing problems for business leaders and politicians but providing lucrative opportunities for James Chung, who signed a contract with the Wichita Community Foundation in 2015 to serve as a consultant for multiple years. Through this partnership, Chung would conduct research, provide recommendations, and deliver more public presentations like the one he had given the year before during "Fuel the Fire." Returning to Wichita in 2015, Chung's new presentation was called "Focus Forward," and it emphasized four key challenges that in Chung's view imperiled Wichita's future progress: the "business challenge," the "human capital challenge," the "entrepreneurship challenge," and the "perception challenge." To thrive, Wichita would have to solve these challenges by encouraging more entrepreneurship and business growth, attracting and retaining "talent," and (as he had emphasized in his earlier "Fuel the Fire" discussion) improving common perceptions of Wichita, both within the city and beyond it. Chung used an evocative line about Wichita's economy that would become a staple of his presentations and interviews going forward: "Our second-biggest export—behind aircraft parts—is talent." While he offered a few specific recommendations on how to resolve the problems he identified, he emphasized that Wichita must emulate the cooperative path of other, more successful, cities: "They put their differences aside. Leaders came together and decided, you know, we are stuck with each other, so let's make this a better city, with a lot of cooperation from the public, private and nonprofit sectors."[61]

Though his message alarmed leaders in local government, business, and economic development, Chung impressed them with his reputation as a "data guru" and via public perceptions of his impressive resume. This perception was bolstered by Chung's portrayal in local media outlets, which frequently referred to him not simply as "James Chung" but as "Harvard-trained James Chung," because he had received bachelor's and master's degrees at the university. He was alternately referred to in *The Wichita Eagle* as a "demographer" and an "economist," and his firm was described in impressive-sounding terms. The *Eagle* called Reach Advisors "a global firm that does deep-data research for Fortune 500 companies and other organizations internationally as they make investment decisions."[62]

This was a gross exaggeration. For most of its existence, Reach Advisors consisted solely of Chung and a pair of consultants. Its mailing addresses were Chung's home in upstate New York and a coworking space in Cambridge, Massachusetts, and the bulk of its previous work had consisted of advising ski resorts and museums on strategies for attracting tourists. In reporting his purported credentials and capabilities uncritically, the *Eagle*'s coverage of Chung and his firm was reminiscent of its portrayals of the Minnesota Guys just a few years earlier.

Despite Chung's sobering portrayal of Wichita, local leaders embraced him and his message, taking it as a call to action. "Regrets and recriminations must be set aside as the community replenishes its economic energy and rediscovers its swagger," wrote *The Wichita Eagle* in an editorial responding to Chung's "Focus Forward" presentation. In a second editorial a week later, the *Eagle* recommended remedying Chung's thinly sourced claim that Wichita was an "unfriendly" city by encouraging Wichitans to be nicer to each other:

> Anyone can help counter what Chung calls Wichita's "perception challenge." Volunteer for the amazing nonprofit organizations that help hold the Wichita area together and enrich its quality of life. Greet and help out neighbors, or anyone you encounter who could use a hand. Host or participate in block parties or informal neighborhood get-togethers. Don't be an aggressive driver. Start or continue one of those pay-it-backward chains of generosity at a Starbucks or other drive-through. Say "thanks."

Business leaders responded, too. The owners of Fidelity Bank created a website called The Chung Report, which featured articles about the Wichita economy designed to promote the goals recommended by Chung. Although he had no affiliation with The Chung Report, many people believed, based on the platform's title, that Chung was the website's author.[63]

Reacting to Chung's revelation that Wichita lagged behind peer regions in the supply of venture capital, a group organized by the chamber of commerce launched the E2E (entrepreneur to entrepreneur) business accelerator in 2015 to provide seed funding to new startups. The business community summoned to Wichita "1 Million Cups," a seminar popular in other cities, which was designed to bring together the city's disconnected entrepreneurs. Wichita State University expanded its campus by taking over a former public golf course, leveling it, and replacing it with what it called the "Innovation Campus," an industrial park where companies could build new facilities in close proximity to university researchers. The university president cited Chung's research on dismal entrepreneurial trends in Wichita as evidence of the need for the "Innovation Campus."[64]

Incubating a new generation of startups and providing massive amounts of venture capital; reversing entrenched demographic and migratory patterns; staving off globalization and the other international forces affecting the aircraft industry (the city's major employer and economic driver)—all of these were huge, expensive, and perhaps insurmountable tasks for a small region and its business class. As much as they worried about the "business challenge," "human capital challenge," and "entrepreneurial challenge" that Chung highlighted, city leaders therefore struggled to devise effective strategies to overcome those challenges.

But fixing Chung's fourth challenge—the "perception challenge"—was a more manageable ambition requiring far fewer resources. City leaders realized that they could make significant progress toward creating an image of Wichita as a dynamic, thriving, progressive region—a city on the move—if only they could harness the power of social media, reinvigorate the city's brand, and rally around a symbol that built on and enriched Wichitans' civic pride.

#ILoveWichita: Rallying Around the Flag

In the midst of perpetual intercity competition for residents, visitors, and investment, municipal branding campaigns are ubiquitous, as they are seen as critical components of marketing strategies aimed at attracting companies, tourists, conventions, and other out-of-town sources of spending.

These branding campaigns involve the use of slogans ("Boise: Part Rugged. Part Refined"; "Corpus Christi: Coast Your Own Way"; "Hartford Has It"), and they frequently make use of landmarks or easily identifiable symbols to promote a city's unique identity. The famous Fisherman's Memorial Statue figures heavily into promotional materials for visitors in Gloucester, Massachusetts, for instance, while the logo for the visitor's agency in Lafayette, Louisiana, incorporates an accordion and a triangle to promote the city's identification with Cajun music. In Wichita, promotional materials have frequently invoked the image of city landmarks like Century II or *The Keeper of the Plains*, but a new campaign emerged in the mid-2010s—largely in response to the challenges raised by James Chung—to integrate into the city's branding strategy a symbol that had been present, though much ignored, for many decades.[65]

In commemoration of Flag Day in 1937, Wichita Mayor T. Walker Weaver signed a resolution adopting an official flag for the city. The flag was designed by C. Cecil McAlister, a local commercial artist and sign painter, and submitted to a flag design competition conceived by City Manager Bert Wells and sponsored by an American Legion post. Over one hundred entries were submitted to the contest, and the highest-ranked entrants split eighty-five dollars in prize money. McAlister's winning design, drawing on his interpretation of Native American symbols, featured a white sun circle on a blue background, with triangular rays of white and red emanating outward toward the flag's edges.[66]

For decades, the flag existed in relative obscurity in Wichita. Though it flew outside city hall each day, was hung in the mayor's office, and was frequently displayed outside the Century II municipal performing arts center, most residents were unfamiliar with the emblem. This fact provoked periodic curiosity among local media, including one episode in 1970 in which a local radio station sent a group of young people to a busy downtown intersection with a big sign featuring the flag and the phrase, "I support this flag, do you?" The demonstration caused substantial commotion, as passersby accosted and insulted the flag-wavers, accusing them of being "a bunch of dirty communists."[67]

Like average Wichitans, city leaders generally paid little attention to the flag, and they did not see its obscurity as problematic. "There would be no reason that most citizens would probably be aware of it. Most citizens never come down here, and those that do generally aren't seeking out the city flag," said Mayor Bob Knight in 1997. Beginning in the late 1990s, though, a group of local artists led by sculptor Chris Gulick latched onto the flag, both for its intriguing aesthetic qualities and also for its potential to serve as a unifying symbol for the city and its arts community.[68]

In a quintessential example of the city's eagerness to champion itself and find points of pride, it was big news in Wichita when, in 2004, a nonscientific online poll conducted by the North American Vexillological Association ranked Wichita's flag the sixth best city flag in the United States behind the flags of Washington, DC, Chicago, Denver, Phoenix, and St. Louis. A *Wichita Eagle* article on Wichita's place in the online ranking encouraged readers to go to the website to vote for the Wichita flag. Following that notoriety, the city's flag gained a little more visibility, especially as a few small boutiques like The Workroom, run by Wichita artist and entrepreneur Janelle King, began selling stickers, pins, patches, and other memorabilia emblazoned with the flag.[69]

Despite that incipient energy, "Flag Fever," as it would come to be known, did not fully grip Wichita until the following decade, and the driving force behind the flag obsession that would eventually overwhelm the city came not from the artists but from the business community and the Wichita Regional Chamber of Commerce. These groups saw the emblem as a potential antidote to the perceived lack of civic pride identified by James Chung. The original "Fuel the Fire" presentation by Chung occurred in the fall of 2014; by the following spring the chamber of commerce had created the Twitter account @WichitaFlag and had begun promoting the hashtag #ILoveWichita. Wichitans were encouraged by the chamber of commerce to use the flag as a symbol of their own civic pride (Figure 4.5). "Wichita needs to work harder at voicing our pride in our city. We need to be more vocal about what makes Wichita the best place to grow companies, careers and our families," wrote a chamber executive in an op-ed in *The Wichita Eagle*. "Let's wave our flag and demonstrate our pride in the people and places that make Wichita so special."[70]

King, the shop owner who had been an early proponent of the flag, embraced the popularity that the chamber's campaign had invigorated, and her store, which had begun as a quirky all-around interior design destination, quickly morphed into a flag-centric gift shop. "It's not that the merchandise is really what's driving it. It's the pride," King said. She added, in a sentiment speaking directly to the talent retention crisis highlighted by

Figure 4.5. #ILoveWichita sign featuring Wichita flag at the Wichita Regional Chamber of Commerce headquarters. Photo by Chase Billingham.

Chung, that the Wichita flag and the civic pride it engendered meant that "we don't have to move to another city. We can be a cool city." King contracted with the chamber of commerce to produce Wichita flag buttons for chamber events.[71]

Within a matter of months, the flag, once an obscure relic, was everywhere in Wichita. Homes throughout the city, especially in older central neighborhoods, hung it on their porches. Thousands of cars sported novelty flag license plates on their front bumpers; following a campaign spearheaded by City Council Member Bryan Frye, one of the flag's most vigorous advocates, the State of Kansas approved a new state license plate bearing its image, and thousands of Wichitans paid the additional fee (a portion of which went to support the Wichita Parks Foundation) to adorn the rear bumpers of their cars with those tags. For his part, Frye regularly appeared at events wearing a custom-made full Wichita flag business suit. Elements from the flag were incorporated into the crest of the naval vessel USS *Wichita*, the logo of the city's professional soccer team, the jersey worn by the mascot of the city's professional hockey team, and the poster art for the annual Wichita River Festival. Dozens, perhaps hundreds, of people got Wichita flag tattoos.[72]

Local media published dozens of articles on the flag—accounts of the theft of a flag from a business, reports of various places around the world where Wichitans had taken photos holding the flag, and examinations of how people around town had incorporated the flag into their home Halloween decorations. Together Wichita, a business coalition organized by the chamber of commerce, purchased more than three dozen Wichita flags and donated them to the city to fly in front of police stations, fire stations, and recreation centers. As Wichita prepared to play host to an early round in the 2018 NCAA men's basketball tournament (previously discussed in chapter 3), the city's daily newspaper made sure to inform out-of-town visitors of the flag and its local importance with a full-page article on the subject. The article featured a revisionist history that elided the active role that the chamber of commerce had played in pushing the importance of the symbol, emphasizing instead a tale of organic resurgence in local vexillological ardor:

> Over the past several years, it's become a much-worn, oft-painted, frequently flown sign of local pride. And because of its resurgence in popularity, it'll be easy for you to take some of it home with you. . . . About three years ago, . . . the flag went from obscure to everywhere. A local entrepreneur began selling "flag swag" out of her custom drapery and upholstery store, and it became a thing. Soon, everyone everywhere was selling and buying items emblazoned with the Wichita flag.

"Flag fever" may have been a deliberate marketing campaign by business elites and not a spontaneous display of organic pride, but it was undeniable that thousands of ordinary residents embraced the symbol and felt more positively about the city. In other words, the Chamber's #ILoveWichita and Wichita flag campaigns did work successfully to remedy Chung's "perception challenge."[73]

Pride in Wichita surged, as attested by the many residents who said so in media reports; so did perceptions of pride, as assessed by city leaders and editorials celebrating the perceived increase in pride and tying it explicitly to the growing prominence of the city's flag. A *Wichita Eagle* editorial explained, "There is a growing sense of pride in Wichita and its institutions. The city of Wichita flag is becoming ubiquitous." Janelle King echoed that sentiment, writing in an op-ed that "Wichita is having a civic pride moment. This is seen in the emergence and love of our city's flag." The Greater Wichita Partnership convened a Perceptions Task Force, which hosted "Pride-in-Place Meetups" featuring speakers from the chamber of commerce, Visit Wichita, and other affiliated organizations. The first speaker in the series was Janelle King, highlighting her work promoting the flag as a driver of improved perceptions of Wichita.[74]

The saga of the Wichita flag culminated in 2020, when local documentarian Julian Liby produced *Welcome Home, Wichita*, a thirty-minute film that documented the rise of flag enthusiasm and its role in turning around the city's misfortunes. Featuring interviews with Chris Gulick, Janelle King, representatives from Visit Wichita and the chamber of commerce, Mayor Brandon Whipple, and a remote cameo appearance by James Chung himself, *Welcome Home, Wichita* reminded Wichitans of why they had fallen in love with their flag and explained how it had been instrumental in transforming perceptions of the city.

The film opened with a montage of young people discussing why they had been disenchanted by the city and had left Wichita for opportunities in other locations. "This wasn't a long-term place to live for basically anyone I knew," said one young woman. The perils facing the city due to the "perception challenge" formed the backdrop of the film's premise—James Chung's name was mentioned within the first three minutes. As Chung explained, he and his team then set about "processing ridiculous amounts of data. . . . We ran three years of heavy analysis." A soft mournful dirge played in the background of the film as Sheree Utash, the president of WSU Tech, a two-year vocational training school in Wichita, said solemnly, "James brought a reality to this city that jolted us, and it jolted us to action."[75] Most of the remainder of the film dealt with the city's efforts to address the "perception challenge," focusing primarily on the role of the Wichita flag in furthering those efforts. The tone of the film's music shifted as those same formerly disgruntled residents recounted how their views of the city had evolved. "Wichita isn't boring! We're way cooler than people think we are," said one young woman. "I'm not sure we need to stay humble about how great Wichita is anymore," said Whipple. "This is our opportunity to really show off our city."[76]

At the height of Wichita's flag craze, James Chung returned once again in 2018 for a much-anticipated presentation at the city's brand new central library; indeed, his appearance was the library's first public event, and the room was packed with several hundred Wichitans eager to hear his assessment of their progress. Chung was pleased with the surge in local pride, epitomized by the ubiquity of the city flag, noting that "the city is feeling less negative and more optimistic." Still, his message remained somber, as he told his audience that "the Wichita way is not working." All attendees left the meeting with a custom-made deck of commemorative trading cards designed by the Wichita Community Foundation. Called "Truth *and* Dare," each card featured both a "truth" about Wichita, featuring factoids from Chung's presentation, and a "dare" about Wichita designed to prompt its reader to get more engaged in the community—"Invite a neighbor to your house for a meal," read one card.[77]

For many in a city riding a wave of civic pride, Chung's continued scolding was disheartening. As *The Wichita Eagle* summarized the message and its reception in an editorial, "a native Wichitan came home this week and attempted to slap some sense into his city. He did it with numbers and charts and detail, the way a Harvard-educated researcher slaps." While leading figures in the business community and local government expressed dismay at some of the depressing trends that Chung discussed, they remained optimistic that the city was headed in the right direction. Addressing the "perception challenge," largely via the success of the Wichita flag campaign, was setting the stage, many believed, for robust economic growth to come. "Perception's the leading indicator. You're not going to get a business person to invest more in a town they don't believe in. It's just not going to happen," said Aaron Bastian, the president of one of Wichita's largest banks.[78]

Conclusion: A Newly Confident Air Capital Enters the 2020s

As the 2010s drew to a close, robust economic growth nationwide had finally remedied much of the painful fallout from the Great Recession. The US unemployment rate had fallen to its lowest level in half a century, and the economy in Wichita grew in line with that national trend. Yet, as all of the indicators reviewed at the beginning of this chapter illustrate, the Wichita region continued to trail competitor metro areas in expansion and prosperity.

The city skyline had barely changed since the 1980s, as the Epic Center (the half of it that had actually been built, that is) remained the tallest structure on the horizon. The Pop-Up Park—though certainly less blighted than the deep derelict pit it replaced—continued to take up space that ought to have given way to more intensive development. And the downtown residential population, though rising, was not as high as leaders had hoped for or projected in the *Project Downtown* plan.

Yet it was undeniable that the city's economy had advanced during the rapid growth of the 2010s. The aircraft industry, buoyed by global economic growth, showed strong projections of continued prosperity, boosting confidence in the economy of the Air Capital of the World. Thanks in large part to the city's love for its flag, Wichita had beaten back the "perception challenge." Furthermore, economic progress was beginning to show in the built environment of the urban core. As outlined in the introduction, Wichita had replaced the aging Lawrence–Dumont Stadium with a state-of-the-art facility and had used it to lure a Minor League Baseball team to the city for the first time in decades. Public- and private-sector leaders were setting the stage for the unveiling of the grand Riverfront Legacy Master Plan, which would pump hundreds of millions of dollars into the urban core in a sweeping transformation of the river corridor. Voters had just elected a progressive young mayor, Brandon Whipple, who promised to champion new ideas in order to promote the recruitment and retention of young talent. And, as discussed in chapter 3, the troubled Naftzger Park had been bulldozed to make way for a new mixed-use development linking the heart of Downtown Wichita to the Old Town district. Wichita, it appeared, was primed to move beyond the "Potemkin City" approach to promoting downtown vitality and ready once again to generate real economic growth in its core.

Taking office at this optimistic moment, Whipple immediately had the opportunity to showcase a thriving new era in Downtown Wichita's growth as the city prepared for a major gathering scheduled on March 12, 2020. The celebration would feature music, food, and fireworks in commemoration of the ribbon-cutting at the newly rebuilt Naftzger Park. As the date of the park's unveiling approached, however, cases of a new and poorly understood virus, which had already wreaked havoc in other countries and in major urban centers in the US, began circulating in the city. With public health experts cautioning against large gatherings of people, the new mayor took to Facebook to announce the abrupt cancellation of the Naftzger Park ribbon-cutting event.[79]

The COVID era had begun in Wichita.

BUILDING A LEGACY IN THE POST-PANDEMIC CITY

5

Filling the Hollow Core

Thirty years had passed since Jack DeBoer introduced his ostentatious riverfront redevelopment plan, which failed to materialize in a comprehensive form. In the intervening decades, Downtown Wichita continued to languish. Office vacancy rates remained high, and the bare parcel where the second Epic Center tower should have stood presented a constant reminder of the lack of growth. Despite Chris Cherches's homegrown solution to the Gilbert-Mosley crisis, groundwater pollution continued to make investors skittish and depressed property values. Low prices for office property did attract investors in the 2000s—most notably, the Minnesota Guys—but as the extent of their financial troubles became more apparent, and as their audacious promises to revitalize Wichita failed to materialize, the community felt more demoralized than ever about the state of downtown.

On a typical day, there was little to see and little to do in Downtown Wichita; one could walk for blocks down Douglas Avenue in the middle of a weekday afternoon and not pass another human being, and it had been that way for years. In fact, the city took decisive action in the 1990s to use public art to try to counteract that lifelessness—a blatant deployment of the "Potemkin City" strategic approach that I described in chapter 4. Making use of a donation from the DeVore Family Foundation, the city purchased several dozen bronze statues crafted by artist Georgia Gerber and installed them along several blocks of Douglas Avenue between 1997 and 2001. The idea was to "to help the sorry-looking sidewalks in the middle" of downtown, as *The Wichita Eagle* described the strategy. Dick DeVore, who purchased and donated the art, said at the time, "I think that that Douglas streetscape and this art project is going to be just another piece of the catalytic puzzle that's going to help drive downtown."[1]

Many of these sculptures originally included water elements so that passersby could interact with them. At the corner of Douglas and Main stood a bronze businessman with his shoes off soaking his feet in water (Figure 5.1). Nearby, two bronze children crouched low to the ground, dumping out cups of water. A little bronze girl held a balloon over a fountain of water, and a small bronze boy pushed a small bronze car with water splashing onto it, which kids could sit in while turning the steering wheel, pretending to drive.

Describing a visit to Wichita in his influential book *What's the Matter with Kansas?*, journalist and commentator Thomas Frank said of Douglas Avenue, "These days the street is lined with bronze statues of average people, apparently so it doesn't look quite so eerily empty." That observation was not quite accurate. The statues were not explicitly designed to fill in the emptiness on their own. Instead, they were initially designed to be interactive, to attract people downtown so they could interact with the bronze figures and enliven their experience of being downtown. But with so few human beings around, Frank's description ultimately became the reality. These still lifes depicting vibrancy presented an ossified portrayal of what Douglas Avenue used to be and might one day become again, but this was not reality. Their constant presence and immovability highlighted, in contrast with lived reality, the absence of people and the absence of human movement around the statues.[2]

By the 2010s, though, as Wichita's leaders felt buoyed by the resurgence in local pride, energized by the community's embrace of the city flag, and encouraged by the evangelizing of James Chung, attention shifted back to revitalizing the Arkansas River corridor. With construction underway on the new baseball stadium along the west bank of the river, residents were eagerly anticipating the arrival of the city's new baseball team, Wichita's return to minor league baseball, and the potential for commercial development to rise around the stadium. In the Delano neighborhood, adjacent to the stadium on the west bank, the city had recently completed construction

Figure 5.1. Still life statue on Douglas Avenue. Photo by Chase Billingham.

on a new central branch of the Wichita Public Library, and a large apartment complex called River Vista had gone up along McLean Boulevard, obstructing the riverfront views from that road that had been such a controversial sticking point during development debates in the 1990s.

In comparison with this collection of activity on the west bank, the east bank of the river, which housed the core of the downtown business district, remained mostly unchanged over the previous several decades. George Laham's proposed casino had never materialized; Jack DeBoer's fanciful WaterWalk complex had stalled so completely that only one structure—a seven-story condo building emblazoned at the top with the words "WaterWalk Place," despite being situated nearly a quarter mile from the water—had been completed; and the sixteen-story Hyatt Hotel had (as its skeptics long predicted) required constant public subsidy since its construction due to low demand. (It would ultimately come to be owned by the city.) Contrary to the original plans for the tower, the Hyatt, though built adjacent to the river, was aligned so that most of its guest rooms faced the elevated highway to the south and the convention center to the north, with few direct views of the Arkansas flowing nearby.

The most troubling element of the entire area, in the eyes of economic development boosters, was also the most noteworthy. Indeed, it was arguably the most recognizable structure in all of Wichita: the iconic blue-domed Century II Convention and Performing Arts Center.

If Downtown Wichita was going to regain its vibrancy and luster, something had to be done about Century II. Remaking this area could jumpstart economic growth in the city and make Wichita more competitive with the peer metropolitan regions that it hoped to emulate. But lurking beneath any attempt to turn Wichita into a bustling twenty-first century city was the reality that its economic base was firmly rooted in the aircraft manufacturing industry that had propelled the city's burst of growth in the twentieth century. Its status as the "Air Capital of the World" was what made Wichita truly distinctive, and if the aircraft industry faltered, it would jeopardize any chance to build a new economy for the technological age. Wichita was thus perpetually caught between the twin goals of mimicry and unique authenticity. Leaders frequently touted the need to "diversify" the economy beyond its reliance upon the aerospace sector, and attracting young professional "talent" to accomplish this goal would require offering the same downtown consumption amenities on display in more dynamic regions. Yet simultaneously, thoroughly remaking downtown to further that goal would require stable and robust local economic prosperity, which could only occur if the region's key economic driver—its unique strength in aerospace—remained healthy.

That dilemma would come into full relief as a new plan to reenvision the city core came head-to-head with a series of crises affecting Wichita's largest employer. This chapter details the intersection of those forces and the ways in which they reflected the perpetual push and pull between the urges of replication and distinctiveness. In the first half of the chapter, I detail the saga of the Riverfront Legacy Master Plan, whose unveiling I discussed in the introduction. This sweeping proposal to recreate the city's downtown core promised to bring Wichita into the twenty-first century, improve the city's competitiveness, and position it to draw the young professional workforce that would generate economic prosperity for the next generation. In the chapter's second half, I examine the struggles of the region's key industry and, in particular, its largest employer, the aircraft manufacturing firm Spirit AeroSystems. Despite contributing enormously to the metropolitan area's prosperity for decades, a string of crises affecting that company and the sector more broadly threatened to undermine the region's economic future while also scuttling any hopes for downtown riverfront rejuvenation. These two sagas overlapped and influenced one another, and they were both heavily affected by active resistance and adversity—in Spirit's case, from labor unions, business partners, and federal regulators, and in the case of the riverfront plan, from a dogged and influential activist and historic preservationists dead set against the demolition of Century II. Overhanging all of these struggles was the COVID-19 pandemic, which disrupted every aspect of the economy and society, upended assumptions about urban economic development, and presented a series of dire challenges that Wichita's public- and private-sector leadership continue to contend with to the present day.

The Big Vision: Unveiling the Riverfront Legacy Master Plan

Following the momentum created by the stadium, library, and apartment complex on the west bank of the Arkansas River, attention returned in earnest to the east bank in 2019. A coalition of the region's economic development organizations comprising the core of Wichita's growth machine—the Greater Wichita Partnership, the Wichita Downtown Development Corporation, the Wichita Regional Chamber of Commerce, the Wichita Community Foundation, and Visit Wichita, in consultation with city and county government—announced the Riverfront Legacy Master Plan (RLMP). This plan, when complete, would reimagine more than half a square mile of land, tying together disparate elements already existing, building new facilities, and reorienting the street grid to create a more cohesive, vibrant, and attractive urban environment that could catalyze further economic development initiatives in the urban core.[3]

The groups behind the RLMP initiative committed hundreds of thousands of dollars to studying the area, planning potential uses of the land, and conducting public outreach campaigns. They contracted with the Kansas City architecture firm Populous to lead the design effort. Local business leaders exuded confidence and optimism about the plan. "We're looking at this as a once-in-a-generation opportunity. You just don't get to redevelop riverfront development hardly ever," said Jon Rolph, the chair of the board of the Greater Wichita Partnership. The city and county governments put substantial money into the planning process, too, despite objections from

County Commissioner Lacey Cruse, who complained that the RLMP board, which consisted of thirteen men (including Rolph) and two women, was insufficiently diverse.[4]

In the summer of 2019, Populous hosted a public meeting to reveal their initial conceptions for the RLMP, drawing an overflow crowd of hundreds of interested Wichitans. Populous founder and principal Todd Voth exhorted the crowd to be bold, telling them, "You can have a wimpy vision and you get a wimpy result. You need to think about the big vision for the future. And when you do that, you will create your future in a way you never imagined. And I wholeheartedly believe that Wichita can do that." Echoing the rhetorical legacy of Jack DeBoer, Voth added, "This momentum only happens every once in a while and we need to make the most of it." It was clear from that first public meeting, though, that Century II and the striking brutalist building that had formerly housed the central public library would not likely survive RLMP's redevelopment vision.[5]

RLMP was oriented around the perennial goal of remaking Downtown Wichita in a manner designed to appeal to young "talent." It had emerged following the results of Project Wichita, an initiative launched in 2018 and headed by banking and business executives to gauge public sentiment regarding how to move the region's economy forward. Building on the "big wins and increasing pride" that the city had experienced in the preceding years, Project Wichita issued a survey to thousands of respondents, asking them to list their top priorities for regional investment going forward. When the results of the survey came in, the Project Wichita report revealed the "Top Ten Essential Investments" that residents had named in their responses. New performing arts and convention facilities were not among those "Top Ten Essential Investments"; nevertheless, a "world-class facility to highlight our exceptional performing arts" and "a state-of-the-art convention center to host local, regional and national events" were the first two priorities listed in Project Wichita's "Quality of Place Action Plan," which was designed to "invest in ourselves to create a vibrant region, help retain and attract talent, and strengthen our communities." Though "Quality of Place" was just one of five "Action Plans" put forward by the Project Wichita report, it was effectively the only one that was ever pursued. The cornerstone of the "Quality of Place" strategy was the Riverfront Legacy Master Plan, which Project Wichita leadership announced just a few months after releasing its final report. "Retaining and attracting talent to our region is a priority, and it's clear that the riverfront is important to a diverse group of people," stated Project Wichita cochair and local bank president Aaron Bastian in a press release that largely contradicted the results of Project Wichita's own resident survey.[6]

Emerging out of the Project Wichita recommendations, the RLMP coalition consisted of all of the central players in Wichita's growth machine: City and county government, the chamber of commerce, WDDC, the Greater Wichita Partnership, Visit Wichita, and the Wichita Community Foundation, and it quickly pushed forward the conflicting yet complementary themes of urban authenticity and urban mimicry that I discussed in earlier chapters. At the top of the list of "Planning Principles" guiding the development of the riverfront plan was the purported need to "enhance Wichita's reputation as a gathering place in the Midwest, while celebrating our authenticity by creating a diverse district characterized by regional innovations in arts and industry." Meanwhile, in a series of repeated posts on social media, the coalition drew attention to the deployment of similar strategies in other regional metropolitan areas, highlighting the ways in which new convention and performing arts centers had sparked economic growth and urban vitality for Wichita's competitors. "In 1993, Oklahoma City made a conscious decision to invest in themselves," the coalition wrote on social media, noting how "the community passed MAPS 4, a nearly $1 billion plan, due to the momentum and positive economic benefit of the previous plans before it." The coalition then invited social media followers to view the RLMP proposal, which represented Wichita's attempt to duplicate Oklahoma City's success.[7]

When members of the public read about RLMP on social media and jumped in with critiques—in particular, emphasizing that due to Oklahoma City's larger size the situations within the two cities were not directly comparable—they received a rejoinder from prominent local lawyer, auctioneer, and realtor Ty Patton, an active leader in the chamber of commerce. "People are fond of saying that 'Wichita isn't Oklahoma City.' Thats [*sic*] true. But Oklahoma City wasn't Oklahoma City in the early 90s," Patton wrote. "OKC looked at the issues plaguing their city and made a conscious and bold decision to invest in themselves. That investment is what helped turn OKC into the success it is today. There isn't any reason the ICT can't duplicate that success." Patton chimed in again when RLMP posted similar information about Tulsa's successful urban investments. "We can either draw inspiration from what our sister cities are doing or we can look for reasons it won't work in the ICT. We've spent a long time finding reasons to say no. Let's try something different," he encouraged RLMP's critics. In this fashion, project proponents repeatedly returned to the need to emulate other cities' successes as the most straightforward path to realize RLMP's goal to "enhance Wichita's reputation as a gathering place in the Midwest."[8]

The proposal faced criticism from many in the public, who frequently expressed concern about the contradiction inherent in the twin goals of creating something unique and iconic in Wichita while simultaneously striving to replicate the models of regional peer cities. "My question is why do you guys want Wichita to be as good as these other cities should we not strive to be better?" wrote one commenter on an RLMP social media post. "This plan could be Anywhere, USA," noted another. A third critical commenter begged city leaders to "stop trying to be OKC and start being Wichita." Heywood Sanders, a nationally renowned scholar who has published widely on the convention industry and its role in urban economic development, followed the RLMP debates in Wichita closely, and in an interview with *The Wichita Eagle*, he derided the idea of using a new convention center as the centerpiece of an economic development strategy aimed at attracting young "talent" to the city. "The relationship between young talent and the size or relative newness of a convention center is something that escapes me," he told the *Eagle*. "If you want to be unique, you build on your strengths as a community, and you don't try to do exactly the same thing that literally everybody else is doing." In a poll conducted by the newspaper, only 39 percent of respondents supported razing Century II, while more than half endorsed restoring or repurposing the round building.[9]

The Resistance: Celeste Racette and "Save Century II"

While there was widespread skepticism about the proposal, by far the most formidable challenge to RLMP came from Celeste Bogart Racette, a retired accountant and auditor whose father, Vincent Bogart, had served as a city commission member and as mayor during the 1960s, when Century II was planned and erected. Racette had shown up at Populous's initial public presentation with historical documents and photographs, seeking to protest the demolition of Century II, but RLMP leaders had kicked her out of the meeting. Fuming, she organized a meeting of her own, featuring presentations by historic preservationists and architects regarding the importance and local significance of the structure. She formed a new organization of her own—"Save Century II"—aimed at raising public awareness regarding the structure's history and significance and campaigning to keep it out of the path of the wrecking ball. Racette went before the Wichita City Council, alleging that RLMP "appears to only have one purpose—public relations for the razing of Century II and the building of a new arts center."[10]

From that moment forward, Racette would remain an incessant thorn in the side of business and political leaders in Wichita. Michael Monteferrante, the chair of the chamber of commerce and a member of the RLMP board, wrote an op-ed in *The Wichita Eagle* pushing back against Racette's charges, asserting that "no decisions have been made or even proposed—not about CII or any other part of the plan," affirming that RLMP and Populous were merely striving to follow the will of the city's residents and would be as open and transparent as possible. Susie Santo, the president of Visit Wichita and one of just two women on the RLMP board, seconded Monteferrante's claims, saying that "anything's on the table" and that, contrary to Racette's accusations, there was no definitive plan to raze Century II.[11]

Public assurances about an open-minded conversation notwithstanding, RLMP leaders consistently highlighted the shortcomings of Century II in public discussions. As a convention and exhibition space, Century II was too small to attract some large conventions, tourism and convention leaders asserted; furthermore, its odd circular configuration impeded the efficient use of space that convention planners valued. As a performing arts space, Century II was also deficient. The circular structure was divided into several sections like the slices of a pie; this left all of those spaces with inadequate backstage areas, which were crammed into the small center of the building, and sound from one slice of the building frequently bled into other areas. In addition, the loading docks for Century II were awkwardly positioned, preventing the largest trucks from pulling right up to the designated loading area and forcing them instead to park for hours or days at a time on the public plaza facing Douglas Avenue.[12]

Confirming skeptics' worst fears, following months of public hearings, surveys, and project development, RLMP and Populous returned in November 2019 with five alternative proposals for the east bank of the Arkansas;

only one of the five retained Century II as a refurbished and repurposed performing arts center. Even this one option seemed to be a mere concession designed to silence critics; Populous continued to disparage the structure, saying they could not identify a way to reuse the building efficiently even if it were retained. Another heated public hearing ensued at which the main source of argument among attendees revolved around whether to retain or demolish Century II. Bill Warren, the owner of a local chain of movie theatres, alleged that city leaders simply lacked creativity, while County Commissioner Michael O'Donnell—himself a member of the RLMP board—decried the entire process and said that the planners and economic development boosters were out of touch with the community and the more pressing needs of its residents. Most city and county officials remained cautious and noncommittal; they worried that tearing down Century II would anger their constituents, even as opposing exciting new development would cause consternation and make them appear complacent. Their ambivalence also stemmed from their knowledge that public investment on the scale being proposed for the RLMP proposals would require tax increases, possibly necessitating public votes on the project. These same concerns had sunk many ambitious proposals in the past, including the DeBoer plan.[13]

Following their receipt of public input, Populous and the RLMP leaders quickly narrowed the five options that they had presented to the public down to one final proposal. As expected, the final plan for the east bank of the Arkansas eliminated Century II and the former library building. Indeed, the only existing structures that would be preserved under the final plan were the Hyatt hotel and Jack DeBoer's WaterWalk condo building. The remainder of the space would be leveled and repurposed, with a new convention center, new performing arts center, and new retail and office spaces, all surrounded by new parks and connected via a reconstructed street grid. Most of the land incorporated into this vision was owned by the city, but a substantial portion was still owned by DeBoer after years of inaction on the WaterWalk complex, so he stood to gain tremendously from the overhaul. At the end of 2019, DeBoer, by then over eighty years old but still displaying his trademark exuberance, announced that he would construct a new office tower—the most luxurious and prestigious building the city had seen (or, in DeBoer's words, class "double-A")—on his undeveloped land in conjunction with the RLMP initiative. He displayed no nostalgia for Century II.

"Let's not build any more temporary buildings that people get emotional about. Let's just do it right," he said.[14]

Many people were indeed emotionally attached to Century II, and DeBoer, Populous, and the RLMP leadership did not anticipate the tenacity of Racette and her Save Century II movement. As the year 2020 began, her supporters fanned out across Wichita, gathering signatures on a petition to trigger a ballot referendum that would allow voters to decide whether or not to permit the city government to tear down Century II. Racette and her followers were initially told by county election officials that they would need to obtain signatures from at least 5,022 voters (10 percent of the number of voters in the previous city election—a heavily contested mayoral race with above-average turnout—in which 50,214 people had cast ballots). They soon learned, however, that the election office had given them inaccurate information and that the true number of signatures they would need was far higher—25 percent, not 10 percent, working out to 12,554 signatures—because the type of initiative they sought would create new law rather than merely overturn a city council vote. Soon, yard signs featuring the slogan "SAVE CENTURY II," set against a Wichita flag background, appeared in front yards across the city as Racette's petition drive accelerated (Figure 5.2).[15]

On January 10, 2020, as I discuss in more detail in the second half of this chapter, Spirit AeroSystems, Wichita's largest employer, announced that it would lay off 2,800 workers, more than one-fifth of its local workforce. In the wake of several deadly crashes over the previous months, Boeing all but ceased production of its 737 MAX aircraft, the bulk of which was assembled by Spirit workers in Wichita. Economists projected that the Spirit layoffs could have huge economic ramifications for the region as the effects of the income loss rippled through other sectors of the economy and adversely affected municipal revenues. Spirit's announcement rattled nerves across Wichita. Four days later, RLMP and Populous unveiled the final approved designs for the east bank of the Arkansas River, along with the price tag: $1–1.2 billion. This sum, they suggested, would be paid for with a countywide sales tax increase, a diversion of hotel tax revenue, a tax increment financing (TIF) district that would divert property tax revenue, and a community improvement district across all of the riverfront that would impose a 2 percent sales tax surcharge on top of the elevated base sales tax rate. As working-class Wichitans worried about the looming

Figure 5.2. The Save Century II movement. Source: Photo by Lynda Rathbone. Used by permission.

threat of unemployment, lost income, and a prolonged regional economic downturn, RLMP leader Jon Rolph stressed the need to push forward with the bold, publicly financed downtown revitalization plan. "Wichita is really at a crossroads moment. You feel all this energy and civic pride about where we're going and what we can be and how we might want to invest in ourselves," he said, adding that "we can't afford to do nothing."[16]

As Racette and Save Century II continued with their effort to gather signatures, they pressed forward on another front, too: working to get the structure, designed by architect John Hickman and influenced heavily by the style of Hickman's teacher Frank Lloyd Wright, added to the National Register of Historic Places. RLMP and Populous dismissed Hickman's legacy and the influence of Wright as insignificant. "I used to play football, and I actually trained with Barry Sanders's brother, but I was no Barry Sanders. So to me it's different. You have Frank Lloyd Wright—wonderful architect—but students are students," said Brandon Johnson, a member of the Wichita City Council and the city's representative on the RLMP board. To make sure he was not misunderstood, Johnson emphasized that he "would not classify it as a historic structure." Historic preservationists disagreed, with one preservationist (who was working with Racette to prepare the Historic Register nomination paperwork) asserting that the round building was "about as historic as it gets in Wichita."[17]

Not Throwing Away Their Shot: RLMP and the *Hamilton* Factor

A major focus of the controversy surrounding the Riverfront Legacy Master Plan, the fate of Century II, and the future of Downtown Wichita surprisingly involved the hit Broadway musical *Hamilton*. The hip-hop extravaganza based on the life of Alexander Hamilton, created by Lin-Manuel Miranda, had taken Broadway—and later the entire country—by storm in the 2010s, but Kansans were aggrieved that the traveling company had never performed in Wichita. While the small size of the regional market had made *Hamilton*'s producers determine that playing in Wichita was impractical (this was the primary factor underlying one of the other most common grievances in Wichita, the absence of a local franchise of the national chain restaurant The Cheesecake Factory), RLMP advocates and their allies in Music Theatre Wichita, the local theater troupe that performed musicals on the Century II stage, blamed Century II. The configuration of its stage, its loading docks, and its backstage capacity were at fault for *Hamilton*'s perennial avoidance of the city.

Wayne Bryan, the artistic director of Music Theatre Wichita, said explicitly that "because of the shape of our stage, shows like *Hamilton* and *The Phantom of the Opera* cannot come to our theater." Darryl Kelly, an RLMP board member, capped off a published satirical open letter penned by a Wichitan in the year 2070 with the following postscript: "P.S. I know in 2020 the play 'Hamilton' was extremely popular. Well, in 2070 it is still going strong. It has become one of the longest running shows in history. Unfortunately, I had to take my family to Tulsa to see it." Even the city government (the owner of Century II) perpetuated the charge that their own deficient facility impeded their residents from viewing *Hamilton*, asserting in a post on the city's Twitter page that "we have been turned down . . . due to the facility not being able to accommodate their stage needs." In this way, *Hamilton* assumed an outsize role in debates about the future of Wichita. If Wichita wanted to compete with other cities—that is, if it wanted its residents to be able to access Broadway-quality entertainment without having to send them to Tulsa or other more successful cities—Century II had to go.[18]

As the debate over Century II and its inability to host *Hamilton* reached a crescendo in early 2020, the American Theater Guild, which produced touring stage shows in the Midwest, made an announcement that was simultaneously exciting and embarrassing for Wichita: *Hamilton* was, indeed, coming to town in the 2021–22 season, and they would put on a full (not scaled-down) version of the production right on the Century II stage. Century II's backers seized on the announcement. "This is vindication—total vindication, with a capital 'V,'" said Celeste Racette, taunting her RLMP antagonists. Obviously, whatever its real structural deficiencies, the Century II building itself was not the major obstacle to Wichita's ability to attract investments that were common in other major cities. It appeared unlikely, however, that *Hamilton*'s commitment to come to Wichita would sway either proponents or opponents of Century II to change their minds about the fate of the domed structure. As City Council Member James Clendenin explained, "Most people are where they're going to be on this," and they were unlikely to budge.[19]

The Fight for Century II and the Fight Against COVID-19

The layoffs at Spirit AeroSystems and other large aircraft manufacturers may not have slowed the RLMP proponents, but the COVID-19 pandemic did. As in most places across the United States, initial reactions to the emergence of the novel coronavirus, first in China and then in other countries in Asia and Europe, sparked some concern and discussions of the need to take precautions, but the full scope of the disease's potential impact was not originally appreciated. Very quickly, as cases began surging in US cities—and, importantly, as the first cases appeared in Wichita—local leaders began to realize that containing COVID-19 and making adjustments to manage its impact would become their top priority. Responding to denunciations of his support for RLMP from a campaign challenger, Sedgwick County Commissioner David Dennis was dismissive: "I have enough to worry about. Trying to fight COVID, trying to balance budgets, trying to do everything else that we do. . . . Right now, for us to worry about Century II is not our worry."[20]

Growth proponents in Wichita could brush off critics in the public, and they were poised to expend considerable energy putting down Racette's legal challenge in order to clear the way for replacing Century II. In early 2020, though, the combined crises of the 737 MAX grounding and the rapidly spreading pandemic posed a formidable pair of challenges that they could not have foreseen. As city leaders began to better understand the scope of the COVID-19 pandemic and the economic disruptions that it provoked, discussions regarding grand riverfront redevelopment plans ground to a halt. The pandemic decimated the travel industry, prompted an abrupt end to in-person conventions, provoked a widespread shift to remote work and online shopping, and eliminated the ability to put on concerts, plays, and other events requiring large, dense, in-person crowds. These priorities—conventions, performances, office occupancy, and retail activity—lay at the heart of the RLMP proposal. It became clear that demand for all elements of this downtown overall would be nearly nonexistent for the foreseeable future, so the RLMP initiative went dormant. The coalition made its last official statement on social media on March 20, 2020, promising that "once we come out from this unprecedented time, we will take the next steps to move this plan forward."[21]

Though many initially expected the COVID disruption to last only a few weeks, the pandemic dragged on for several years, and so did its impact upon the convention industry, public gatherings, office occupancy rates, and other essential ingredients for downtown economic growth. With more urgent demands to confront, including widespread public consternation over mask requirements, business closures, and vaccines, Wichita's leaders had little time or energy to devote to riverfront redevelopment, and the hundreds of millions of dollars in private fundraising needed to realize the project were not forthcoming during a long stretch of economic uneasiness. In addition, public sentiment was widely split on the fate of Century II, with a substantial proportion of the city population dead set against its removal. As a result, even if RLMP had been financially feasible, implementing it would likely have proven highly unpopular. Thus, despite periodic exhortations from a few city leaders to get the plan moving again after the COVID pause, the Riverfront Legacy Master Plan—like the RTKL plan, the DeBoer Plan, the Riverport Plaza Plan, and the WaterWalk plan before it—fizzled. RLMP's March 2020 social media post announcing a temporary pause in the early days of the pandemic would be the last content the coalition would ever post, an enduring testament to the latest in a string of scuttled ambitions along the banks of the Arkansas.[22]

As it disrupted the normal operation of the economy, the pandemic threatened to wreak havoc on municipal finances, especially due to the impact of depressed retail activity on local sales tax revenue. Like local governments across the country, Wichita faced a looming revenue hole which, combined with the statutory requirement to operate on a balanced budget, required substantial cuts to expenditures. City Manager Robert Layton and his staff held a series of tense and difficult retreat meetings with members of the city council, presenting them with a range of expenditure items that could be reduced to close the impending budget gap. Among the biggest and most controversial items that the council considered, and ultimately adopted, was the privatization of the management of Century II. For decades the city government had operated the publicly owned facility and subsidized several million dollars in operating losses, which made it possible for Century II to play host to performers and shows that otherwise might not be made available to the people of Wichita. Privatizing the operation of Century II and removing that annual public subsidy would help Wichita balance its budget during the pandemic, but critics like Racette feared that it might be just the first step toward an ultimate strategy of selling the facility altogether, thereby hastening its demolition by private developers.[23]

The privatization plan spurred on the work of Save Century II. Racette succeeded in persuading the Wichita Historic Preservation Board to recommend both Century II and the former public library building for listing on the National Register of Historic Places, despite objections from the RLMP backers and the city government. That same week, after early worries about their ability to collect more than 12,000 signatures as required by law, Racette and her collaborators revealed they had in fact received more than 17,000 signatures toward their cause, overcoming the additional obstacle caused by residents' reluctance to open their doors to petitioners during the pandemic.

It was clear that Racette had cleared the hurdles put in front of her to get her proposed initiative placed on the next electoral ballot. Rather than accepting that Racette had accomplished the necessary tasks that they had required of her, though, the City of Wichita instead filed a lawsuit challenging the content of Racette's petition (after city staff had previously approved it and allowed her to begin collecting the necessary signatures). City attorneys argued that the initiative was invalid because it permitted citizens to make administrative law on issues that required a level of professional expertise not possessed by most average voters. Striving for a compromise, Wichita Mayor Brandon Whipple and the city council pledged to permit a nonbinding vote on the city ballot if a plan to demolish Century II were proposed in the future. Racette denounced the council's legal challenge, calling it "a slap in the face" to the 17,000 Wichitans who had signed her petition.[24]

Nevertheless, the Sedgwick County District Court judge ruled in the city's favor, finding that the petition was improperly worded and therefore void. Save Century II leaders vowed to fight on, asserting that "the battle over the future of Wichita continues." Racette appealed the decision to the Kansas Court of Appeals, but she lost there, as well. While Save Century II had not succeeded in requiring a public vote before the historic building could be demolished, the primary focus of Wichita's growth coalition had shifted away from the riverfront and toward the spiraling crisis at the region's largest employer, Spirit AeroSystems, detailed below in this chapter. As the pandemic raged on into its second year, the ambitious Riverfront Legacy Master Plan remained in a holding pattern, and no plan to demolish Century II or the former library building (which had been converted temporarily to serve as the county's main site for COVID-19 vaccine distribution) appeared imminent. Whipple, who clashed frequently with Racette during her near-weekly diatribes in front of the city council, cited the nonbinding vote that the council had pledged to hold as evidence that Century II was not in danger and that, by extension, Racette's movement was obsolete. "We have saved Century II. Century II is absolutely saved," Whipple told *The Wichita Eagle*.[25]

By the beginning of 2021, the city had issued a request for proposals for a private firm to contract with the city to manage and operate Century II. Later that year, the city council selected ASM Global, the same company that managed operations at the county-owned INTRUST Bank Arena, to run the facility. ASM pledged to reduce Century II's operating losses, in part by laying off the city employees who had staffed the facility. Despite some consternation over this arrangement, the contract with ASM—and perhaps more importantly, the allocation of several million dollars to repair and upgrade the building, including resurfacing the iconic but deteriorated blue dome roof—provided concrete evidence in support of Whipple's boast that he and his colleagues had "saved Century II." At the same time, though, by early 2021 two members of the city council who had been most heavily invested in RLMP were already calling for the project to proceed, and they went to the state capitol to testify in opposition to proposed legislation that would have constrained municipalities' power to tear down historic structures.[26]

RLMP Redux (and Reduced)

Nearly three years after the original Riverfront Legacy Master Plan had gone dormant, Populous returned to Wichita with a new plan. This time, there was no packed auditorium, no reverent applause for the city, no "Bravely Onward" t-shirts—just the architects and Wichita City Manager Robert Layton presenting a much more modest vision of east bank redevelopment before the city council. The revised plan was notable not just for the initial RLMP elements that had been removed but perhaps more importantly for what had been put back in: There, in the heart of the planners' new designs, stood the blue dome of Century II, alongside the old central library building and the existing Bob Brown Convention Center. All of these structures would be gutted and redeveloped. The convention center would be substantially expanded, the library would become an event space, and Century II would feature a massive ballroom with sweeping river views to support social functions complementing major conventions. Significantly repurposed, the structures would endure, a testament to Racette's tenacity, the enduring scars of the pandemic, and the business community's inability to push through its vision of the downtown of the future. "We have heard loud and clear that this civic icon deserves to stay, and it deserves to be a beautiful piece of architecture that can live on for the next generation," Populous principal Adam Paulitsch said reverently of Century II as he unveiled the scaled-down proposal to the city council.[27]

In many ways, this reduced vision for riverfront redevelopment reflected a concession to the rebuke that RLMP and city leaders had received from Racette and other skeptical Wichitans. The revised project was comparatively tame and far less transformational. Nevertheless, the same aspirational rhetoric and the same framing of the project in terms of interurban competition persisted. "I really want to talk about Oklahoma City," Paulitsch asserted in his presentation to the city council. "I had the pleasure of being the lead designer for that project, so I've seen that city grow. Wichita right now is where Oklahoma City was eight years ago." Bryan Frye, arguably the most enthusiastic proponent of RLMP on the Wichita City Council, maintained his enthusiasm in describing the impact that this less ambitious plan could have on the city. "We don't want to settle," he explained. "I think this vision—whether or not all of this comes to fruition—is a vision that doesn't settle.... We know that there's a business case to be made for making this investment, not only for the economic output, but also for the psyche of our community. And that we are a world-class, leading city."[28]

The revised plan appeased many of RLMP's most ardent detractors. "I'm so thrilled they finally ... realized how beautiful the library was. And also they now realize how beloved Century II is. They could have done that the first time around," Racette told *The Wichita Eagle*. In addition, the new proposal had the benefit of being far cheaper, with a proposed price tag of just $400 million (approximately one third as much as the original RLMP would have cost). Even at this reduced cost, however, neither Populous nor the city manager could say definitively where the money would come from. City officials hinted that a dedicated sales tax would likely be necessary to support the project, but approving such a tax would require a vote of the public.[29]

Following this unveiling, no further action was taken. By the end of 2025, the east bank of the Arkansas River looked nearly exactly as it had for the past quarter century. The blue dome of Century II received much-needed repairs, but no action was taken to reimagine or repurpose the structure. Directly adjacent, the brutalist former central library building remained where it was—empty, abandoned, and subject to frequent vandalism (Figure 5.3).[30]

The Air Capital in Crisis: Growing Without Boeing

As detailed in chapter 1, Wichita's identity as the "Air Capital of the World," though perhaps hyperbolic, was by no means farfetched. For decades, the region has served as one of the world's great hubs of aircraft manufacturing, and the concentration of the aircraft manufacturing sector in Wichita was rivaled in the US only by the Seattle region. As such, Wichita's

Figure 5.3. Vandalism at the former central public library building, 2025. Photo by Chase Billingham.

economic prosperity and growth were tied intimately to the fortunes of the local aircraft firms, especially Boeing. When Boeing, which had operated in Wichita for more than eight decades, finally left the city for good in 2012, the departure resulted in the direct loss of only about 2,000 jobs. This relatively modest job loss, however, masked the true impact of Boeing's withdrawal for several reasons. First, the departure of one of the country's most important and powerful corporations took a significant psychological toll on the city's economic identity and pride. Second, Boeing had already shed thousands of jobs in Wichita following the industry declines caused by the terrorist attacks of September 11, 2001, and the Great Recession in 2008 and 2009. Finally, and perhaps most importantly, Boeing had already had one foot out the door since 2005. In that year, Boeing had spun off its commercial manufacturing division in Kansas and Oklahoma, leading to the creation of an entirely new firm called Spirit AeroSystems. Though it would never employ as many workers in Wichita as Boeing had at its peak, Spirit would quickly take its place as the region's largest employer and, by consequence, as the linchpin of the Wichita economy.

Upon the creation of this new company, over 7,000 Boeing workers in Wichita became Spirit employees, and they continued doing the work that they had previously done at their Wichita plant—building the fuselages for Boeing aircraft, especially the 737, the workhorse of Boeing's fleet—but now as part of a Boeing contractor and not a branch of the company itself. As arguably the most important link in Boeing's supply chain, Spirit benefited from "life-of-program" contracts that effectively guaranteed work for the company as long as Boeing sustained operations of the 737 and other airframes constructed by the Wichita company. Spinning off Spirit was designed largely as a move to bolster Boeing's profits via maximizing "return on net assets." With this splintered arrangement, Spirit was responsible for building approximately 70 percent of the 737 structure, while Boeing retained the responsibility of assembling the final completed planes in its Seattle facility from the components shipped by Spirit and its other suppliers.[31]

With this arrangement in place, Spirit's place in the Boeing supply chain was secure. Long freight trains topped with massive, wingless airplane fuselages regularly flowed through Downtown Wichita from Spirit's plant on the south side of the city northward en route to Seattle, and though there was only a small handful of cities to which air travelers could fly directly from Wichita's airport, Alaska Airlines added a weekly nonstop connection between Seattle and Wichita in 2016, further cementing the links between the headquarters of Boeing and Spirit. In many ways, then, the fortunes of Spirit—and by extension the entire Wichita economy—were intimately bound up with the fortunes of Boeing.[32]

The High Stakes of the City Boundaries

As such, Spirit's success was in Wichita's interest, and Wichita made sure to demonstrate its appreciation. The city government routinely included Spirit among the recipients of a generous array of economic incentives designed to facilitate the company's growth, its workforce development, and the construction of new facilities, but perhaps the city's biggest act of generosity was an act of exclusion. In 1979 and 1980, Wichita's major aircraft manufacturers—Beech, Cessna, and Boeing—established "non-annexation agreements" with the city government. Wichita, continuing to grow over the decades through the annexation of previously undeveloped rural land, had begun to encroach on the sprawling plants, which had been constructed in rural territory outside the city limits. By pledging not to annex this land, the city exempted these companies from millions of dollars in property taxes that they would otherwise have to contribute toward municipal operations. These agreements emerged largely to put to rest the companies' threats to leave the region if the city attempted to tax them. The deals would last for twenty years, at which point they could be renewed. After its original creation in 1980, Boeing's non-annexation agreement was extended for another twenty-year term in 2000; at the time of this renewal, another 114 acres of land that Boeing had expanded into were added to the 835 acres previously protected by the agreement.[33]

The perpetuation of the non-annexation agreements became conspicuous as the city limits continued to sprawl outward in the late twentieth and early twenty-first centuries. Still today, the amoeba-like blob of Wichita's municipal boundary is punctured by holes of unannexed territory, and the southeast boundary of the city sprawls less than the fringe in other directions, in large part because of these agreements. Their renewal has never been seriously called into question, lest the companies use an annexation proposal as a pretext for leaving the region altogether in pursuit of more generous government subsidies elsewhere. The city has lost out on untold amounts of potential revenue through these agreements; nevertheless, proponents argue, by enticing these companies to remain in Wichita, the agreements provide enormous economic benefits to the region that far outweigh the forgone tax revenue.[34]

In 1997, though the various non-annexation agreements were not set to expire and require renewal for more than two years, the Wichita City Council nevertheless preemptively adopted a resolution pledging to continue the agreements when the time came. This commitment, the resolution asserted, was rooted in the success the aircraft manufacturers had achieved in growing the workforce of Wichita: "The three aircraft manufacturers . . . have been the primary contributors to the community's healthy economy. . . . Boeing Wichita has grown from 7,000 employees to more than 21,000 in the last 20 years. . . . It is anticipated that the three companies will continue to create jobs and invest in capital which will further increase the local tax base." That anticipated future growth did not materialize. Shortly after the renewal of the non-annexation agreements, the terrorist attacks of September 11, 2001, provoked a severe curtailment of air travel and aircraft manufacturing. The city council's adoption of the resolution pledging its support for these companies and for the non-annexation agreements had occurred in December 1997; total employment in the Wichita metropolitan area in aerospace product and parts manufacturing would peak one year later, in December 1998, at 47,600 employees. But by the middle of 2003, following the renewal of the non-annexation pacts, that employment total had fallen by more than a third, to just over 30,000 employees.[35]

The following years were marked by mergers, departures, and reorganizations. Raytheon, which had purchased the Wichita-based Beech company in the 1980s to form Raytheon Aircraft, divested of this division in 2007, leading to the creation of a new company, Hawker Beechcraft. Ailing under debt following the Great Recession, Hawker Beechcraft laid off thousands of workers in the late 2000s and filed for bankruptcy in 2012, and in 2014 the much smaller remaining company was acquired by Textron Aviation, the conglomerate that had previously purchased Wichita's Cessna aircraft company in 1992. For their part, Cessna (under Textron's control) also shed thousands of jobs in Wichita in the late 2000s and early 2010s. Arguably the biggest shock to the local economy came with Boeing's departure. All this economic turmoil—downsizing, changing hands, and leaving the region altogether—came in spite of Wichita's generous incentive packages and despite the pledge to never annex the manufacturing plants into the city and extract property tax revenue from the companies.

By the time the second twenty-year interval had passed on the non-annexation agreement for the Boeing Industrial District in late 2021, Boeing had long since disappeared from the region, and the facilities and territory that had previously been occupied by Boeing were under the control of Spirit. In the wake of the COVID-19 disruptions to global air travel and the deadly debacle involving the 737 MAX (detailed below), Spirit laid off thousands of workers. In 2016—despite being exempt from nearly all city property taxes—Spirit had again received a generous package of financial incentives from the city government in the form of industrial revenue bonds to support the construction of new facilities on the condition that it grow its Wichita-area workforce over the following five years. Yet by 2021 Spirit employed just 9,000 people in Wichita, approximately 2,000 fewer than it had in 2016 and less than half the total that Boeing had employed when the non-annexation agreement had previously been renewed and the city council proudly "anticipated that the three companies will continue to create jobs."[36]

Nevertheless, the city council pressed forward with another twenty-year renewal of the non-annexation agreement. When City Council Member Jared Cerullo had the temerity in the meeting to raise the prospect of not renewing the agreement, a Spirit executive responded by threatening that the company might leave the region altogether if its property tax exemption were not extended for two more decades, telling the council that "all these things count in terms of consideration of where we put the work." To reflect the new reality, the Boeing name was erased from the non-annexation district, which was renamed the "Aerospace Industrial District." In addition, Wichita granted Spirit an extension on its employment growth projections, forgiving the company for circumstances deemed out of its control.[37]

Boeing and Spirit: The Special Relationship

The "life-of-program" agreements between Boeing and Spirit provided a sense of stability for the Wichita supplier, and so long as Boeing thrived, Spirit, its employees, and the Wichita economy shared in its prosperity. A strong symbiosis formed between Boeing and its most reliable supplier. When, for instance, a tornado struck Spirit's Wichita facility in 2012 and caused significant damage, the company barely missed a step, ramping production back up within a matter of weeks and preventing delays on Boeing's production line. Still, strains emerged, particularly when Spirit was stretched too thin working on several Boeing programs as well as fuselages for other manufacturers, leading to a loss in Spirit's productivity and a drop in its stock price in the mid-2010s. Boeing began extracting more profit by demanding cost cutting measures from its suppliers, severely straining the relationship between Seattle and Wichita. A new agreement was negotiated in 2017, but Spirit sued Boeing in 2018, alleging that Boeing had withheld payments owed to its Kansas supplier.[38]

Despite the tensions, cooler heads prevailed. The lawsuit was settled, claims of liability were dropped, and another agreement for pricing and deliverables was forged at the end of 2018. Things were back on track. Days before Christmas, Spirit announced that it would add 1,400 more jobs in Wichita, on top of 1,000 additional hires it had promised the prior year, and would invest approximately $1 billion in new facilities at its Wichita location. Wichita Mayor Jeff Longwell lauded Spirit's leadership, saying that the manufacturer "is the kind of company that under promises and over delivers." For his part, Spirit CEO Tom Gentile pointed to major backlogs of aircraft orders as evidence that there would be plenty of work to do for years to come in what he called "the golden age of aviation." A new arrangement with WSU Tech, the local technical college, promised to rapidly train new workers who wanted to enter the field of aerospace manufacturing. These new opportunities for manufacturing jobs would generate positive ripple effects throughout the Wichita economy, Longwell predicted.[39]

Eighty-one days later, Ethiopian Airlines Flight 302 dove into the ground at nearly seven hundred miles per hour just six minutes after taking off from Addis Ababa Bole International Airport, instantly killing all 157 people aboard.[40]

America's Most Exposed Region: The MAX Disaster and Its Impact on the Air Capital

If the crash of Flight 302, a newly built Boeing 737 MAX 8 aircraft, had been an isolated incident, it may have had little effect beyond generating sympathy for the victims of the air disaster. Instead, the incident drew immense scrutiny due to its close similarity to another air catastrophe that had occurred just five months earlier, when Lion Air Flight 610 plunged into the Java Sea just minutes after leaving Tangerang, Indonesia. That flight, also aboard a brand-new MAX 8, resulted in 189 deaths. In both cases, the MAX jets experienced malfunctions soon after takeoff in the Maneuvering Characteristics Augmentation System (MCAS), a flight control and aircraft stabilization mechanism Boeing introduced in its MAX jets. Designed to prevent aircraft from stalling by rising too quickly, MCAS would automatically engage to push the nose of the plane downward. It was deemed likely that MCAS engaged on both flights, possibly triggered by faulty sensors. Flight records indicated that in both cases the pilots struggled to regain control of the aircraft from the MCAS system, with which they were not thoroughly familiar, as their aircraft nosed down toward Earth.[41]

The Lion Air crash occurred about two months before Gentile touted the new "golden age of aviation" in Wichita. When the Ethiopian Airlines jet came down in a strikingly similar manner, it was immediately clear that Boeing—and its most important supplier—were facing a major crisis. Anecdotal reports from other pilots indicated that the two crashes were not the only incidents of automatic nose-down behavior in the MAX 8. Within days, the Federal Aviation Administration (FAA), following the lead of government agencies in countries around the world, ordered the grounding of all Boeing 737 MAX 8 planes. Many nations banned the aircraft from flying in their airspace altogether. In Wichita, Spirit's plans to ramp up production from an average of fifty-two MAX fuselages per month to fifty-seven grew uncertain. Just weeks later, Boeing announced that it would slow MAX production to forty-two planes per month, but Spirit maintained that they would continue creating fuselages at their prevailing rate—fifty-two per month—in order to maintain their workforce. Surplus aircraft fuselages would be stored on site in Wichita until Boeing was ready to take them. Despite implementing some cost cutting measures, Spirit executives resisted the idea of layoffs, and they expressed confidence that they could press on with the major hiring spree that had driven so much enthusiasm at the press conference with city and state officials a few months earlier, when Longwell had touted the company's ability to "under promise and over deliver."[42]

That show of confidence became harder to maintain, however, as the MAX grounding dragged on. In June, Spirit announced that it would save money by moving its employees to a four-day work week through the summer, cutting the pay of its unionized workers by 20 percent. The company offered a voluntary retirement package to several hundred seasoned employees. As spring turned to summer, and the MAX remained grounded, the plan to escalate the rate of production was pushed back even further. As summer turned to autumn, hopes of a timely return to a normal production schedule frayed. The number of completed fuselages stored in shrink wrap on the Spirit tarmac rose into the dozens, a glaring reminder of the corporate paralysis effected by the MAX disaster. And as autumn turned to winter, the situation grew even more dire when Boeing, facing an indefinite timeline for recertification of the aircraft, opted to pause MAX assembly altogether. Within weeks, MAX fuselage assembly halted at Spirit's Wichita plant, while ninety completed fuselages sat idle on the tarmac, awaiting delivery to Seattle at some uncertain point in the future.[43]

At the beginning of 2020, Spirit began offering voluntary buyouts to employees, and local government and business leaders recognized that a looming regional economic crisis was on the horizon. A few days later, the company announced that it would lay off 2,800 employees in Wichita, along with more at its other locations. Due to the outsize impact of Spirit on the local supply chain and other elements of the local economy, analysts estimated that the Spirit job cuts could ripple through the economy, resulting in thousands of additional lost jobs throughout the region. The economic threat was compounded by Wichita's second largest aircraft producer, Textron, which had recently announced hundreds of layoffs of its own. Preparing to take office in just a matter of weeks, Wichita's newly elected mayor, former State Representative Brandon Whipple, exuded confidence. He boasted, "We build airplanes better than anyone else, and we design airplanes better than anyone else," pledging that the city would "respond with every tool we have." Other local leaders echoed these sentiments, confidently asserting that the region would bounce back stronger than ever once the MAX crisis had passed and promising that over the long term they would work to diversify the economic base so that the region would no longer be so vulnerable to downturns in the aircraft industry. This boast about Wichita's distinctive manufacturing prowess—"We build airplanes better than anyone else"—would become a common (and increasingly unbelievable) refrain in the years to come, as the industry, and the city whose economy it drove, would be battered by crisis after crisis.[44]

State and local agencies mobilized swiftly to offer assistance to affected workers. A coalition of over a dozen government agencies unveiled a strategy dubbed the "Air Capital Commitment," working to expand unemployment benefits, halt eviction proceedings, and provide free tuition and waive application fees to dismissed employees for retraining at WSU Tech, among other benefits. Because Spirit had maintained its production pace when the MAX was first grounded, creating a backlog of dozens of fuselages sitting on its tarmac, it would likely be several years—even after the jet was finally recertified by the FAA—before Spirit would again be able to resume its high rate of production and bring back those it had dismissed. Unfortunately for Wichita, its economic troubles were highly localized because they were tied to this specific crisis. A Wells Fargo financial analysis labeled Wichita the country's metropolitan area "most exposed" to economic harm stemming from the MAX disaster. Around the US in early 2020, the economy was enjoying robust growth, which meant that workers laid off in Wichita had ample opportunities to pursue careers elsewhere, thereby threatening the city's ability to retain its skilled employment base.[45]

Acknowledging this dilemma, Spirit CEO Tom Gentile implored laid off workers to remain in Wichita in the hopes that the company could rehire them when production resumed. Though the backlog of fuselages assembled during the MAX grounding would slow the pace of recovery at Spirit, the company announced at the end of February 2020 that it would begin resuming MAX production the following month, fueling hopes that the crisis would soon be behind it. Those hopes were short-lived, however, because very soon Wichita would not be unique among metropolitan areas in facing economic turmoil.[46]

The Prolonged COVID Pause

In only a matter of weeks, COVID-19 had gone from an alarming but distant news story affecting other countries to a catastrophe sweeping across the United States. In mid- to late December 2019, several cases of an unknown respiratory condition emerged in the city of Wuhan, China. The first death from the novel coronavirus was reported in China on January 11, 2020. Two days later, the first case outside of China was confirmed. Within a week, the first case on US soil had been identified, and by the end of January, new cases were developing in the US among people who had not traveled abroad, indicating growing domestic community spread of the virus. Over 1,000 people had died across the world by mid-February, even as leaders in Wichita continued to voice optimism about Spirit's ability to recover from the temporary pause in MAX production.[47]

The first case of COVID in the state of Kansas was confirmed on March 7, just days after Spirit's announcement that it would soon resume MAX production. By March 19, the virus had arrived in Wichita. As the virus quickly burst out of control across the country, including in Wichita, Spirit's plans to ramp production back up were scuttled. All Boeing production in Seattle was halted in late March, and Spirit followed suit, stopping assembly at its Wichita facility. Spirit's shutdown announcement came on the same day that Sedgwick County's public health officer issued a stay-at-home order for residents of the county. Simultaneously, Kansas Governor Laura Kelly limited gatherings to no more than ten people, echoing similar restrictions placed on large gatherings by public officials nationwide. In an abrupt about-face, Spirit, which had been hoping to recall workers laid off following the MAX grounding, furloughed all of its employees working on Boeing aircraft, leaving them without pay for weeks as work stopped altogether at the South Wichita plant. Textron, too, furloughed thousands of aircraft manufacturing workers.[48]

In April, as the country adjusted to the reality that the struggle with COVID would be a prolonged one and that the economy would have to find a way to reopen while maintaining precautions to preserve the health of employees, Boeing announced it would restart production on many of its models. Spirit responded by initiating a slow process of calling back some furloughed workers, though the timeline for restoration of 737 MAX production remained unclear. The president of the union representing Spirit machinists took a cautious tack in evaluating that program, telling *The Wichita Eagle* that "if another mistake is found, or another defect, or if we just encounter another problem, . . . we're going to be right back in this pickle."[49]

The enthusiasm engendered by the recall of some employees was short-lived, as the company did, indeed, find itself in a particularly bitter pickle. Within two weeks, Spirit was offering voluntary layoffs to engineers working on the MAX project as the program's delays dragged on. Spirit announced nearly 1,500 additional (nonvoluntary) layoffs the next day. The company found a way to keep some workers on the job despite the interruptions in aircraft manufacturing by converting some of its facilities and training several hundred workers to produce much-needed ventilators for patients suffering from acute respiratory distress—a symptom of COVID-19 infection. While important, noble, and necessary, this shift was not enough to sustain many employees, and in June the company furloughed nearly 1,000 additional workers. Nearly 500 more permanent job cuts followed in July. By this point, the MAX had been totally grounded across the US and most of the world for well over a year.[50]

The pandemic caused massive economic dislocations across the world, prompting national-level responses needed to secure the fortunes of businesses, business owners, workers, institutions, and communities. All local economies suffered because of the lost business revenue, which translated into slumping municipal revenues as dependable revenue streams like sales taxes stagnated. At the same time, though, Wichita's aircraft-centric economy remained uniquely vulnerable because of both the pandemic-induced slump in air travel and the prolonged grounding of the MAX. As a result of this dynamic, the perennial dilemma facing city leaders—the struggle to balance the pursuit of uniqueness and authenticity, on the one hand, and the urge to emulate peer cities, on the other—reemerged with a new fierceness.

It manifested itself as always in the form of debates over whether, and how, to "diversify" the local economy and make it less susceptible to the ups and downs of the aircraft industry. "A more diverse economy is better in the long run," asserted Andrew Nave, a vice president at the Greater Wichita Partnership. At the same time, the region's identity as the "Air Capital of the World" was so closely associated with the industry that leaders were loath to distance the city too much from its historic economic base. As the Spirit layoffs began to take shape in early 2020, the city's new mayor, Brandon Whipple, touted the industry and its employees, repeating the mantra, "We make the best airplanes in the world." State Representative John Carmichael echoed this sentiment, also boasting that "we make the best airplanes in the world." But Carmichael added a caveat, noting that maintaining such a specialized workforce "without diversification of the economy" would inevitably "have an impact" if that workforce were adversely affected by a downturn in the industry.[51]

Machinists on Strike

The FAA finally approved the 737 MAX to return to US airspace in November 2020, more than a year and a half after it had grounded the plane. While this marked an important milestone, it did not solve Boeing's problems, as the company still had to work to regain the confidence of travelers and the business of airlines that had previously canceled MAX orders. Boeing had a large number of MAX jets that it been unable to deliver during the grounding, so it took some time before the MAX recertification resulted in gains for Spirit in Wichita, but by the middle of 2021, economic analysts were predicting that local aircraft companies would soon see renewed job growth. Despite continued financial underperformance, Spirit did report a rise in the number of aircraft delivered by mid-2021. In the summer of 2021, the company announced that it planned to grow its workforce by more than 4,000 employees by 2024, which would largely (though not entirely) restore the company to its employment level before the pandemic and the MAX disasters. Production levels and corporate revenue continued to edge upward, and Spirit and other large manufacturers in Wichita received tens of millions of dollars in federal COVID relief funds through the Aviation Manufacturing Jobs Protection Act to retain employees and stabilize operations. It appeared as if, with the massive disruptions largely in the past, Spirit was on its way back toward profitability and Wichita's economy was headed toward stability.[52]

Ramping up production was not an easy task after such a long pause and after shedding so many experienced manufacturing employees. Spirit worked to bring on and train new employees, but profitability remained elusive, with several quarters of disappointing earnings reports. Meanwhile, the unionized machinists who remained, and who had endured several years of anxiety over their careers, grew increasingly impatient, as they had been working under the same contract for well over a decade. The situation was tense as contract negotiations opened in early 2023, and the union membership voted to authorize a strike vote in the event that the bargaining process did not yield progress on their key concerns, which focused primarily on compensation and health insurance coverage contributions.[53]

Following weeks of negotiations, the company put forward its last and best offer, which included substantial pay increases, annual cost-of-living adjustments, and a $7,500 ratification bonus for every employee if the union voted in favor of the contract. They did not. In the wake of heated meetings and tense exchanges on social media, the machinists union overwhelmingly rejected Spirit's contract offer, and though some employees worried that they were unlikely to receive better terms after a protracted standoff, the union membership swiftly voted to strike, all but halting Spirit's ability to function and creating enormous new challenges for Boeing as well.[54]

The next day, orange mesh fencing went up all around the Spirit plant as the company planned for picket lines. In the blistering heat of the Kansas summer, hundreds of strikers walked up and down the street hoisting their signs (Figure 5.4). Mayor Brandon Whipple, out of the country trying to tout Wichita's economic competitiveness at an aircraft industry conference in Paris with a delegation of the region's economic development promoters, reiterated his frequent boast about the city, asserting confidently, "Global companies know that we have the best advanced manufacturing workforce in the world." A striking worker echoed the critical importance of the work done by Spirit's employees, telling *The Wichita Eagle*, "If something goes wrong with something we build, a lot of people can get hurt and killed, but they want to pay us barely more than some fast food workers start at."[55]

Within days, both sides had returned to the negotiating table, hoping to resolve the dispute swiftly. Though the rejected contract had reflected the

Figure 5.4. Striking machinists at the Spirit AeroSystems factory. Source: Photo by Travis Heying. Courtesy of *The Wichita Eagle*. Used by permission.

company's "best and final offer," as workers picketed outside and the machines idled, Spirit negotiators offered significantly more generous terms, including higher wage increases, a higher cost-of-living adjustment, the elimination of mandatory overtime provisions that had been in the original contract offer, and the preservation of prescription drug benefits that had been removed in the earlier offer. In short, the striking union workers got nearly everything they had demanded when they rejected the initial contract agreement as inadequate. Union members approved the revised contract, and the strike that had temporarily paralyzed much of the US aircraft manufacturing industry ended within a week. Though short-lived, the strike did significantly depress earnings for a company that was already financially vulnerable following years of adversity.[56]

Defects Undermine Wichita's "Air Capital" Renown

Even as Spirit worked to return to normalcy and settle its labor disputes, further obstacles arose that impeded its profitability, tarnished its reputation around the world, and posed significant challenges for the Wichita economy. In April 2023, Spirit discovered defects in some fittings installed by the Wichita manufacturer on 737 fuselages. Though the defects were not deemed critical to the safety of the aircraft, they still needed to be repaired, which slowed production at Boeing and Spirit once again. Further investigations revealed that the installation of the defective fittings affected aircraft built over the span of several years, thus expanding the scope of the remediation effort required. On top of that, the newly negotiated labor contract stood to increase Spirit's annual wage and benefit costs by upwards of $80 million, putting further strain on the company's bottom line.[57]

Spirit's stock price plummeted. After climbing steadily throughout the 2010s and reaching a high above $105 per share at the beginning of 2018, Spirit shares had collapsed, at one point in early 2020 trading below $15 in the wake of the MAX disasters and the pandemic, a decline of nearly 90 percent in the span of two years. Over the next year, as the company appeared on track to resume normal production levels, the stock rebounded somewhat, reaching $50 per share in early 2022. But as the MAX grounding dragged on, and especially following the strike, the stock fell dramatically once again. On September 21, 2023, Spirit's stock price again dropped under $15. CEO Tom Gentile, who had taken the helm at Spirit in 2016, brought the company to new heights of profitability and then weathered crisis after crisis, had finally overstayed his welcome with weary shareholders and directors, and he abruptly resigned two weeks later.[58]

Since Spirit had been spun off from Boeing's Wichita operations in 2005, the fortunes of the two companies had been tightly bound together, so as Spirit suffered, so did Boeing, whose patience with its Kansas supplier was wearing thin. With Gentile out, Spirit and Boeing forged a new agreement through which Boeing injected millions of dollars into Spirit to aid its recovery, renegotiated pricing structures on Spirit's Boeing deliveries, and gave Boeing greater operational control over Spirit's management. Spirit was required to demonstrate sufficient success at remedying its defects on Boeing fuselages, and a timeline was established for Spirit to reimburse Boeing for the cash provided to stabilize the supplier. Once more, despite a slew of travails, Wichita's leading employer appeared to be righting itself and correcting course.[59]

But Spirit's troubles were not over. In a terrifying midair ordeal just days into the new year of 2024, passengers aboard an Alaska Airlines flight over Oregon panicked as a door plug—a piece of the fuselage that could if needed be taken out to make way for a mid-body door—flew out of the plane in an explosive burst, leaving a gaping hole in the side of the 737 MAX 9 aircraft through which passengers watched the ground approach as the pilots carefully returned to the airport. Fortunately, no one was injured in the incident, but it drew renewed attention to the MAX's troubling safety and maintenance record, and the FAA immediately stepped in and once again grounded dozens of 737 MAX jets nationwide, ordering inspections of the planes' door plugs. Other airlines flying the MAX 9 voluntarily discontinued use of the jets temporarily in order to perform their own inspections.[60]

As part of the 737 MAX fuselage, the door plug was assembled and installed in Wichita by Spirit workers. Finger-pointing between Boeing and Spirit ensued as investigations revealed that the plug on the Alaska Airlines flight had been removed once the structure reached Seattle and then reinstalled but without the necessary bolts to hold it in place securely during flight. The FAA ordered extensive audits of the production facilities of both Boeing and Spirit, identifying a large number of lapses in safety protocols at the Wichita facility. Meanwhile, current and former employees emerged as whistleblowers, one after another, alleging major quality control issues in the production of the jets—issues which appeared to result from heavy corporate pressure to speed up the pace of assembly at the cost of cutting corners.[61]

Boeing, Spirit, and the Fragile Future of the Air Capital

Spirit AeroSystems had been born nearly two decades earlier as an attempt by Boeing to save money on production costs as it prepared to eliminate its own presence in Wichita. The symbiosis between Boeing and its Wichita supplier developed into what *The Air Current*, an aircraft industry newsmagazine, called "the most important industrial relationship in U.S. aerospace." However, as a retired Boeing executive explained to *The Air Current*, the companies had maintained "a strained relationship for a long, long time."[62]

After years of turmoil and crisis, that strain grew increasingly unbearable, especially as the defects, errors, and delays at Spirit—once Boeing's most reliable partner and supplier—took a rising and destabilizing toll on Boeing's profitability. Spinning off its main supplier no longer served Boeing's purpose of cutting costs; quite the opposite, the relationship was becoming a liability, and in early 2024 discussions began in earnest to reverse

Figure 5.5. Air Capital Boulevard. Photo by Chase Billingham.

the split and bring Spirit's operations back in-house through a reacquisition of the company. Such a move would allow Boeing to exert more direct control over production, as it had before the spinoff, but executing the acquisition was heavily complicated by the fact that Boeing, though Spirit's largest customer, was not its only client; the Wichita manufacturer maintained many other military and commercial contracts, in particular with Boeing's primary competitor, Airbus. As negotiations over a possible merger continued through 2024, navigating the process of disentangling Airbus's needs became one of the major obstacles to a deal.[63]

While those negotiations proceeded among company executives, Spirit workers continued to face the fallout of the lapses in manufacturing safety, most notably the Alaska Airlines incident. With the federal government escalating its inspections of Boeing jets, the pace of delivery slowed, and Spirit again faced a backlog of inventory. In May 2024, the company announced that it would lay off over four hundred workers at its Wichita facility. Just one year after celebrating the monumental concessions that they had won in their new contract with Spirit, Wichita's aviation workers once again confronted the threat of widespread job loss.[64]

Wichita, meanwhile, responded with its standard array of laudatory comments about its own distinctiveness and the unique skills of its residents. "Wichita has many opportunities for our skilled workforce," newly elected Mayor Lily Wu proclaimed on social media. "This is a reminder of the need to come together as a community to support our friends and neighbors. WE have one of the best skilled manufacturing workforces in the world, and WE will emerge from this stronger."[65]

As the heat of late spring descended on Wichita, hundreds of Spirit employees opened letters containing pink slips, and with the outcome of the Spirit reacquisition negotiations still uncertain, the fate of the city's largest employer—and its core industry as a whole—hung in the balance. Seemingly oblivious to the turmoil to come, members of the city council gathered at the Kansas Aviation Museum in southeast Wichita to unveil the renaming of a major thoroughfare, which would henceforth be known as "Air Capital Boulevard" (Figure 5.5).[66]

CONCLUSION

Of Busts and Booms

In the eyes of its loudest boosters, Wichita, Kansas, is one major economic triumph away from becoming the next great American city—and it has been for over half a century. Perhaps it was always so. When Marshall Murdock was pontificating about the marvels of the young "Peerless Princess of the Plains," Wichita was an isolated cow town on the prairie whose recent cattle-fueled boom was on the verge of turning into a prolonged bust. Murdock published his boast that Wichita was "born booming" at the end of 1886; just months later, a poem mocking the puffery of that self-proclaimed boomtown circulated across newspapers in Indiana:

> A lady teacher in one of our schools,
> Announced a prize for an essay on fools.
> A precocious kid, with hand upraised,
> Thus spake as the teacher stood amazed:
> "The biggest fools I ever saw,
> Invested their money in Wichita."[1]

The lofty aspirations of the growing city took physical form in the organization of Fairmount College, the predecessor to the institution that would later become Wichita State University. Atop the heights of Fairmount Hill stood the impressive façade of Fairmount Hall, the centerpiece of the prospective campus. Erected in the late 1880s, it then sat unfinished, boarded up, and hollow for several years. It was "a fitting symbol of the busted boom—a grim shell with no students," wrote historian Craig Miner.[2]

Following the boom and bust of its fitful early development, though, Wichita did grow steadily in the early to mid-twentieth century, bolstered by the economic engines of agriculture and warehousing, petroleum, and manufacturing—especially the nascent aircraft manufacturing industry, which thrived in the region, particularly during and following the Second World War. Certainly, Wichita's growth far outpaced that of many competing Midwestern boomtowns whose hometown newspapers had lampooned its early speculative real estate bust. It was in this era that the "Air Capital" moniker took flight, and the city has clung tightly to that label ever since, even over the past several decades as its major aircraft companies extracted concession after concession from local government while subjecting the local economy to major periodic shocks following layoff announcements. Recently, the relationship between Wichita and the corporate sector has increasingly seemed like a one-sided love affair. This relationship has been my primary focus throughout the preceding chapters.

Excavating the Future in an All-American City

Urban theorist Mike Davis included the subtitle *Excavating the Future* on his magisterial 1990 opus *City of Quartz*, a sprawling and dizzying social and cultural archaeology of greater Los Angeles. "The best place to view Los Angeles of the new millennium," he wrote, "is from the ruins of its alternative future." Indeed, the broader Los Angeles School of urban studies that informed (and was informed by) so much of Davis's work took as its charge the dissection of sociopolitical and cultural currents in LA in the service of "excavating the outlines of a paradigmatic postfordism, an emergent twenty-first century urbanism."[3]

I have pursued a similar objective in this book. Though by no means as comprehensive as Davis's urban vision or as philosophically sophisticated as the theorists of the Los Angeles School, my work has aimed to peer into the modern history of one modest metropolitan region in the American heartland in order to pull out trends in urban economic development, design, and culture that course throughout the urban landscape of the twenty-first century. Wichita is, of course, esoteric in many ways. Its isolated location, the legacy of the impact of conservative social policies and cultural mores, and the immense reliance upon one core industrial sector have put Wichita on a distinctive trajectory throughout its modern history. These unique characteristics, especially the last one, helped to propel Wichita's growth and success in the mid-twentieth century, but they also left it uniquely vulnerable to downturns in the aerospace manufacturing sector, to such an extent that it became the nation's economically "most exposed" metropolitan area following the 737 MAX grounding crisis.

But Wichita is also akin to small and midsized metropolitan areas nationwide in important ways, and it prides itself on a sense of middle-American normalcy. The first sentence on the Wichita Regional

Chamber of Commerce's "Welcome to Wichita" web page touts the fact that the city has "been named an All-American City five times since 1962." Wichita has struggled historically with many of the same challenges that have affected urban communities large and small in the United States—blight, decline, middle-class flight, sprawl, urban renewal, environmental degradation, and fiscal strain, to name just a few—and for the most part (the city's handling of the Gilbert-Mosley groundwater pollution crisis was a notable exception) its strategies for handling these challenges have reflected urban "best practices."[4]

Following the end of the Urban Renewal era, federal support for urban infrastructure and social services declined substantially. Metropolitan areas across the nation that had previously counted on the direct infusion of federal cash and the oversight of federal bureaucracy to help them advance were left to forge their own prosperity, setting off a new era of interregional competition. This competition was fueled by influential trends in urban planning and governance rooted in an acknowledgment that in an increasingly postindustrial, knowledge-based economy, ensuring economic prosperity required cities to attract and retain smart, technologically savvy, and mobile young professionals. Discovering, cataloging, and appealing to the tastes of these talented professionals took on enormous importance within urban economic development agencies. As consumer research revealed that, on the whole, those professionals eschewed the homogeneous suburban enclaves that their parents had preferred, opting instead for "authentic" urban neighborhoods like those championed by the great chronicler of urbanism Jane Jacobs, cities went to great lengths to facilitate the gentrification of older central neighborhoods by marketing them as unique, distinctive destinations. Of course, ironically, by replicating such "best practices" across the metropolitan landscape, urban real estate developers, economic development boosters, and city governments facilitated the progressive homogenization of urban life, further flattening regional distinctions.

As explained in chapter 1, one aim of *All-American City* has been to delve into Wichita's recent history in order to advance the project of "conjunctural urbanism" established by geographer Jamie Peck. That project involves a process of midlevel theorizing, highlighting individual cases in order to establish patterns of homogenization and regularity in contemporary entrepreneurial urban governance. Demonstrating the spread of "ordinary entrepreneurialism," as Peck describes the prevailing trend in urban leadership, can best be accomplished by illustrating how individual cities engage in "repetitive emulation, 'transmission effects' and reactive adaptation," which despite appeals to uniqueness and authenticity, end up "yielding a narrowing of development agendas, imaginaries and pathways."[5]

In my view, there is no clearer manifestation of that "repetitive emulation" than this appeal to organizational "best practices." Indeed, each year the Mayors Business Council (a branch of the US Conference of Mayors, a lobbying organization representing municipal interests) publishes a "Best Practices Report," which highlights "innovative public/private partnerships submitted by the Mayors Business Council to inspire other cities and companies." The 2024 report drew attention, among other projects, to San Diego's partnership with a private video surveillance company, Grand Rapids' deal with a private digital revenue collection company, and Reno's contract with a private solar power company to put solar panels on a public parking structure. By disseminating details about these types of arrangements to city leaders nationwide, organizations like the US Conference of Mayors help to orchestrate that "narrowing of development agendas" identified by Peck.[6]

Like all organizations, city governments do not generally attempt to devise original solutions to the problems that they face. Instead, they borrow strategies observed in other places that have dealt with similar issues, or they follow guidelines disseminated by professional organizations and taught to their staffs in the management textbooks used in professional schools, or they abide by rules set for them by higher levels of government. These tendencies toward imitation, rule following, and organizational conformity work, over time, to make urban policies and practices increasingly similar across places that were previously more idiosyncratic.

Urban Authenticity and Homogeneity, Past and Present

Homogenization of urban space is not a new phenomenon. These tendencies toward replication have long been in existence as modernity and modern capitalism have spread across the world. Describing the replication he observed across European cities in his 1890 book *The Laws of Imitation*, the French sociologist Gabriel Tarde remarked, "The modern continental tourist will find, particularly in large cities and among the upper classes, a persistent sameness in hotel fare and service, in household furniture, in clothes and jewelry, in theatrical notices, and in the volumes in shop windows." But as the journalist Kyle Chayka has argued, this tendency has been vastly accelerated over the past few decades by the impact of the internet and social media, and the ultimate effect is to flatten all aspects of culture, filtering out all but the safest and least disruptive cultural artifacts and homogenizing contemporary life.[7]

In Chayka's view, our experiences are more and more being curated by the algorithms that fuel social media and other online resources. This affects our decisions as consumers, because so much of the content we view comes to us in the form of "recommended for you" options on TikTok, Instagram, Amazon, YouTube, and other sites. But it also affects what is produced for us, because businesses are subject to the same algorithmic pressures. They see what consumers are doing, recommending, and liking on social media feeds, and they feel pressure to offer consumers experiences that align with those demonstrated tastes.

The influence of algorithms increasingly makes all places feel more and more the same across the globe. When traveling from city to city, Chayka recounts,

> I often typed "hipster coffee shop" into the search bar as a shorthand because Yelp's search algorithm always knew exactly what I meant by the phrase. It was the kind of café that someone like me, a Western, twenty-something (at the time), Internet-brained millennial acutely conscious of their own taste, would want to go to. Inevitably, I could quickly identify a café among the search results that had the requisite qualities: plentiful daylight through large storefront windows; industrial-size wood tables for accessible seating; a bright interior with walls painted white or covered in subway tiles.[8]

What is perhaps most remarkable of all, though, is the decentered and unguided manner in which the diffusion of these trends has yielded this progressive homogenization. Interrogating the mechanisms that produce this sameness, Chayka writes, "These cafés had all adopted similar aesthetics and offered similar menus, but they hadn't been forced to do so by a corporate parent, the way a chain like Starbucks replicated itself.... Instead, despite their vast geographical separation and total independence from each other, the cafés had all drifted toward the same end points." They do so, he argues, to bring themselves into greater alignment with patterns that are producing the most engagement with users via social media.

This applies to places, as well. As urban analyst and strategist Sarah Barns has explained, the proliferation of digital culture and the ubiquity of technological devices and connected apps mediate the experience of contemporary urban life. City governments themselves increasingly develop and disseminate digital platforms and apps to facilitate residents' access to city services. These tendencies generate a digitally integrated contemporary urban experience that Barns terms "platform urbanism," which augments the influence, via digital user interfaces, of consumer ratings and rankings, intensifying competition not just between commercial establishments within cities but between cities themselves. Sociologist Matt Patterson has used the term "scoreboard urbanism" to characterize this competitive impulse. Patterson's research draws attention to a "feedback loop between digital scoring systems and spatial practices," as "scores provide a clear, unambiguous target that focuses and amplifies the drama, while also giving it a broader audience and allowing it to spread from city to city." This process tends to have a homogenizing influence on places as they jockey to improve their scores on a range of rather arbitrary metrics. Moreover, it dovetails with individuals' experience of the city, which is often mediated through social media networks and guided by the recommendations of social media influencers.[9]

Though standardization and homogenization are not new phenomena in the modern world, they have thus been taken to new extremes in the digital age. Throughout this book, I have examined the history of economic development initiatives, economic growth and decline, and inequality as they have played out in one modest Midwestern city in order to draw out key moments when the impulses to replicate the successes of other places have collided with the urge to stand out and forge a more distinct identity. This tendency is likely to grow even more acute into the future.

Retracing Our Path

My effort to juxtapose the competing impulses toward authenticity and replication began in the introduction, as I discussed the unveiling of the Riverfront Legacy Master Plan and the dedication of the new Minor League baseball stadium. In that introductory chapter, I highlighted the linguistic gymnastics that city leaders and professional consultants undertook to frame urban development strategies that they had pulled from well-worn playbooks as innovative interventions that would set Wichita apart from its peers.

In chapter 1, while also synthesizing key concepts and theories drawn from urban sociology and related disciplines, I went back to the nineteenth century to trace the raving boosterism—embodied most fervently in the bombast of *Wichita Eagle* founder Marshall Murdock—that drove growth and speculation in Wichita and other boomtowns throughout the westward-expanding United States. Bitter intercity rivalries (as illustrated by the "biggest fools" poem above) drove cities to magnify their own attractiveness while denigrating peers. This was not mere bluster; there were high stakes involved in these battles over growth in the form of real estate profits, economic prosperity, and the securing of desirable new amenities like railroads, waterworks, and colleges, which city builders knew would be critical both for sustaining a high quality of life for existing residents and for propelling growth. Standing out against the competition was critical, and Wichita was quite lucky when a confluence of factors—terrain, existing industrial infrastructure, and the genius of people like Clyde Cessna, Walter Beech, and Lloyd Stearman—set it apart from its peers as a leader in the burgeoning aircraft manufacturing industry. Aerospace supplied a true mark of distinction that would grow even more profound with the mobilization for US entry into World War II, which solidified the city's identity as the "Air Capital of the World."

Beginning before the city's founding in the mid-nineteenth century and extending through the end of the twentieth, chapter 2 examined Wichita's ambivalent relationship with the Arkansas River. Though the riverfront location was the major factor prompting the original development of a town at this location, throughout its history the Arkansas has not played a prominent a role in the city's growth and sustenance, industrial and commercial activity, or tourism and recreation, as major waterways have in other cities. By the 1980s, as many US cities were undertaking waterfront-fueled redevelopment schemes, Wichita's downtown-adjacent riverfront remained mostly untouched and ignored. Led by entrepreneur and developer Jack DeBoer, the business community pushed hard to remedy that perceived competitive disadvantage in the late 1980s and early 1990s with a massive redevelopment plan that would have fundamentally transformed the center of the city, emulating other cities' waterfront successes in order to put Wichita on a more competitive footing. At the same time, with the three-hundred-foot-tall *Keeper of the Plains* as its centerpiece, the DeBoer plan strove to highlight a distinctive local landmark that might make the city stand out. Ultimately, trepidation on the part of local government and hollow promises from the private sector doomed the ambitious project, and Downtown Wichita and its riverfront entered the twenty-first century looking very similar to how it had looked in the last decades of the twentieth. Just beneath the surface of the downtown redevelopment struggles loomed the Gilbert-Mosley groundwater pollution crisis, which the city responded to in a way that was truly unique and distinctive—though not completely effective in securing Wichita's financial future or easing the fears of would-be investors and developers.

Along with groundwater pollution, downtown boosters in Wichita dealt with decades of frustration over the persistent presence of poor and homeless people in the city core. In chapter 3 I concentrated on the actions undertaken by business and government leaders over more than half a century to oust and regulate low-income and homeless people, who were concentrated in the eastern portion of Downtown Wichita that had been eyed for redevelopment since the 1960s. In fits and starts, the new district known as "Old Town" came to life through the second half of the twentieth century, yet concerted efforts to evict homeless people and eliminate the institutions that served their needs failed in removing them altogether. Conflicts over the presence of homeless individuals were most acute at Naftzger Park, an outdoor space designed in the late 1970s to promote middle-class reclamation of the area. The park appeared after the demolition of a city block filled with services catering to the needs of low-income men staying in single-room-occupancy hotels. Although the elimination of needed services did make the area less hospitable to the unhoused, it did not succeed in ushering in widespread gentrification to the neighborhood, so business leaders teamed up with the city in the 2010s to implement the same strategy again, bulldozing the original Naftzger Park to make way for a new park designed to support middle-class retail, dining, and residential amenities. Urban governance strategies aimed at marginalizing, criminalizing, and displacing the homeless from gentrifiable space are widespread across the United States, and as such, Wichita's treatment of those vulnerable people was of a piece with patterns observed in cities nationwide.

Especially in the twenty-first century, Wichita's antihomeless campaign was bound up with renewed efforts to create a new and distinctive downtown environment that could position the city more effectively to compete against its peers for residents, jobs, and investment. Those efforts, and their lackluster results, were the subject of chapter 4, which focused on Wichita's struggles to reinvigorate downtown development in the twenty-first century. In the wake of the failure of the DeBoer Plan, the lingering impacts of the groundwater pollution crisis, and a sluggish economy, Downtown Wichita continued to stagnate, and property values remained very low. Into the breach stepped the Minnesota Guys, whose sweeping acquisitions and lofty promises generated newfound confidence in the region's economic future. But as the hollowness of their promises became evident, and as the Minnesota Guys left town with creditors and law enforcement in pursuit, local leaders struggled to clean up the mess and restore real, solid economic growth to downtown. In the absence of that robust investment, the local growth coalition instead promoted "Potemkin City" strategies rooted primarily in marketing efforts. These strategies—in particular, the promotion of the city flag as an emblem around which the city could rally—were targeted primarily at solving the "perception challenge" identified by the much-heralded consultant James Chung. Thanks to the success of these efforts, civic pride surged in Wichita in the late 2010s, and in conjunction with a growing economy, the city was finally poised to embark on a major reenvisioning of its downtown core—the Riverfront Legacy Master Plan. The project would both replicate the successes of competitor cities and, its proponents hoped, set Wichita apart from those competitors by offering a distinctively unique urban experience along the banks of the Arkansas.

As I revealed in chapter 5, however, immediately upon its announcement, the Riverfront Legacy Master Plan faced a cascading set of obstacles that proved too difficult to overcome. These involved some of the same barriers to execution that had plagued the earlier DeBoer riverfront plan—resistance from the public (especially Celeste Racette and her Save Century II coalition), inadequate financial commitment from the business sector, and wavering enthusiasm from public officials. More consequential, though, were the calamitous impact of the COVID-19 pandemic and the unforeseen series of crises that unfolded at Wichita's largest employer, Spirit AeroSystems. Once again, struggles related to uniqueness and competitiveness came to the fore. The city's heavy reliance on its largest and most important industry, aircraft manufacturing, made it particularly vulnerable to disruption when that industry fell on hard times as a result of the pandemic and the prolonged grounding of the 737 MAX. The thing that truly set Wichita apart from its peer regions—its hard-won identity as the Air Capital of the World—turned into a liability as the aircraft manufacturing sector suffered. As other metro areas continued to grow and expand, Wichita faced an uncertain economic future. Beyond the woes of that one specific industry, deeper challenges tied to a fragile philanthropic ecosystem and a prevailing conservative ideology have posed major structural impediments to regional prosperity in the contemporary economy.

Political and Philosophical Impediments to Prosperity in Wichita

Analyst James Chung caused a sensation across Wichita when he delivered his "Focus Forward" presentation in 2015. In order to compete in the twenty-first-century urban marketplace, Chung said, Wichita would have to address and remedy four fundamental challenges: the "business cycle challenge," the "human capital challenge," the "entrepreneurship challenge," and the "perception challenge." For each challenge, he laid out policy recommendations. Fixing the "business cycle challenge," for instance, required seriously evolving the region's economic base beyond its heavy dependence on aerospace in order to be less susceptible to the booms and busts of that particular industry, while remedying the "human capital challenge" involved investing much more in education and skill development.[10]

These were huge lifts that would require hundreds of millions of dollars of investment from the corporate sector to be successful, yet Wichita's business community had shown time and again that it was not willing to open its wallet as frequently as business leaders in other communities. The reticence of the private sector to spend had sealed the fate of Jack DeBoer's riverfront vision in the early 1990s, and it reappeared in the 2020s as backers of the Riverfront Legacy Master Plan struggled to identify just where the money would come from for that ambitious project. In a stark and revealing 2020 investigation, the *Los Angeles Times* juxtaposed the philanthropic endeavors of Wichita's oligarchs against those in one of its key Midwestern rivals, Omaha. For decades, Warren Buffett has utilized his fortune to invest hundreds of millions of dollars into the civic infrastructure of Nebraska's largest city and inspired other wealthy Omahans to do the same. By contrast, the libertarian ethos of Wichita billionaire Charles Koch has informed a minimalist and privatized approach to philanthropy. While he and his family have certainly been generous in some aspects of their giving, broad investments in Wichita's public infrastructure and civic sphere have not been the target of much of Koch's largesse. These differing philanthropic philosophies radiated outward, with tangible impacts upon the two cities. Research on regional philanthropic giving found that Omaha tended to generate several times more giving per capita than its Kansas peer. This was reflected, too, in Chung's analysis of community foundations in various Midwestern cities. The Wichita Community Foundation had amassed assets of just $80 million by 2018, he found, compared to total assets in excess of $1 billion in the Omaha Community Foundation and $545 million in the Des Moines Community Foundation.[11]

Perhaps most importantly, Wichita's conservative political climate consistently evinced a firm opposition to taxation. Wichita-area legislators voted overwhelmingly in favor of the notorious income tax "experiment" championed and signed into law by Governor Sam Brownback in 2012, which drastically reduced state income tax rates for high earners and corporations. Moreover, as sociologist Daniel Alvord has revealed, the Wichita Chamber of Commerce, far more than other regional chambers of commerce across Kansas, lobbied aggressively in favor of the legislation. Despite Brownback's assurances that the massive income and business tax cuts, aimed primarily at high earners, would provide a "shot of adrenaline" to rejuvenate the state's economy, the "march to zero" tax experiment did no such thing; instead, as many fiscal analysts had predicted, it cratered the state's revenue, leading to large cutbacks in government services, especially public education. Five years later, some Republican legislators joined Democrats in reversing the tax cuts, even mustering enough votes to override Brownback's veto of this repudiation of his signature policy achievement.[12]

As state legislators worked to reduce state income taxes, at the local level the primary focus was on property taxes. The city, county, and school district governments overseeing policy in Wichita prided themselves on holding their property tax rates steady for decades, and as city and county revenues rose in tandem with rising property values, elected officials faced pressure from conservative activists to lower property tax rates in order to minimize the burden on residents and businesses and to put a check on the growth and size of government. The result, not surprisingly, was a threadbare provision of public services. The relative paucity of city services in Wichita, compared to peer cities, was apparent across a wide range of quality-of-life measures, but it was particularly noticeable in the city's anemic public transportation system. Wichita Transit has perpetually received far lower levels of funding than public transit agencies in cities of similar size across the nation, including among competitor regions in the Great Plains and Midwest, resulting in a network of buses that runs only once per hour six days a week, shuts down on holidays, operates only into the late afternoon, charges comparatively high fares, and provides scant coverage in most neighborhoods.[13]

While concerns over property tax appreciation and government spending are widespread across municipalities, they take on heightened fervor in a city where power is widely diffused and local government is heavily dominated by conservative Republican politicians. Decision-making power, control over public agencies, and taxing authority in Wichita are divided between the city government and the government of Sedgwick County, which includes not just Wichita but also a handful of small outlying cities (it would be a stretch to call them "suburbs") and vast expanses of sparsely populated rural territory. The five-member county commission, each of whose districts encompasses both urban and rural territory, perennially consists of a Republican majority averse to taxation and wary of some of the city's more cosmopolitan impulses. (As of 2025, the commission comprises five Republicans and zero Democrats.) Although the city contains a higher proportion of liberal and Democratic voters than the outlying county, the sprawling geography of Wichita's six city council districts also tends to produce Republican majorities. Perhaps more importantly, the council, led by a very weak mayor, exercises limited power, existing primarily to oversee and ratify the executive decisions of the unelected city manager, who arguably holds the most power in city affairs.[14]

The conservative anti-tax ethos poses significant challenges to the region's ability to remain competitive, and it frequently pits factions of the business and political leadership against one another. As described in chapter 4, the 2014 referendum to impose a new 1 percent sales tax across

Sedgwick County to generate funding for water infrastructure, public transportation, and economic development initiatives generated a heated and expensive campaign, led on the pro-tax side by business leaders affiliated with the chamber of commerce and led on the anti-tax side by PACs associated with the Koch empire, which greatly outspent proponents and soundly defeated the proposal. In a place so wary of income taxes (as the Brownback experiment showed) and property taxes, however, sales tax proposals tend to be the only politically viable option for generating large amounts of public revenue for major projects. After years of debate and political wrangling, the construction of INTRUST Bank Arena was finally made possible after county voters agreed in 2004 to a temporary 1 percent sales tax surcharge to fund the construction.[15]

Since then (as that failed 2014 referendum illustrates), voters have generally been wary of new sales tax proposals as well. Enthusiasm surrounding the Riverfront Legacy Master Plan flagged when it became clear that the bulk of the funding for it would likely come from new sales taxes. And so, in the face of persistent budget constraints and both structural and attitudinal limits to the introduction of new taxes, Wichita, like many other cities, has relied increasingly on debt financing and user fees to generate the revenue for the special projects designed to make the city more competitive and attractive to young "talent." Most major downtown development projects in recent decades have made ample use of tax increment financing (TIF) as well as sales tax and revenue (STAR) bonds. Both of these mechanisms typically involve issuing debt and committing future revenue (property tax in the case of TIF, sales tax in the case of STAR bonds) to pay off the debt. As such, these mechanisms offer the veneer of free revenue without subjecting residents to noticeable tax increases. However, by diverting revenue toward paying off project-based debt, these mechanisms withhold funds that would otherwise go to support core governmental services, including schools, streets, sewers, and public safety, and as such they indirectly place additional strain (often lasting decades) upon municipal budgets.

These financing mechanisms—as well as the widespread use of "community improvement districts," which impose additional sales taxes upon retail purchases within a delimited geographical area and direct that tax surcharge toward repaying developers and supporting infrastructure maintenance—represent clever attempts by local government to find the revenue necessary to finance new development amidst the backdrop of widespread antipathy toward broad-based taxation. Each of these tools narrows the scope of responsibility for the support of new development, driving urban development further and further toward an individualized pattern of user experiences supported by user fees.

Of course, aversion to broad-based taxation on income and property is not unique to Wichita, and frustration over taxation permeates even the most progressive parts of the US, just as it does the most conservative. But conservative political atmospheres serve as incubators for anti-tax activism. The domination of city and county government in Wichita by very conservative politicians empowers these sentiments and allows them to thrive. Wichita sits at the epicenter of the Koch ideological empire, embodied in powerful organizations like Americans for Prosperity and the Kansas Policy Institute, a think tank and lobbying organization whose mission is to promote Kansans' liberty and "allow them to keep more of what they earn." As such, among American cities, it is uniquely beholden to a supercharged libertarianism that by design places major constraints on the ability of local government to make new investments.[16]

Pervasive anti-government sentiment could plausibly open the door to a libertarian ideal, facilitating new growth and development fully funded by the private sector. Yet in practice that type of development, free from government funding, has been hard to come by in Wichita. As discussed throughout this book, the private sector has been wary of footing the bill for major public investments. As a result, local taxpayer support has been essential to the creation of any momentum for any development in Downtown Wichita for over half a century, from the Urban Renewal–led creation of Century II and Naftzger Park to the government-funded cleanup of the Gilbert-Mosley groundwater plume, through to the creation of INTRUST Bank Arena and the new baseball stadium. None of these projects, which have yielded substantial private profits, would have been able to move forward without local government taking the lead and leveraging tax dollars. The retention of the city's aircraft manufacturers, the lofty ambitions of the Minnesota Guys, and the bold vision of the Riverfront Legacy Master Plan—all these efforts and more, whether ultimately successful or not, hinged upon the provision of massive amounts of financial support from the public sector.

But as noted above, and as confirmed by Chung and other analysts,

Wichita's business and banking community, while often talking a big game about dynamism and distinctiveness, has tended to be skittish and reluctant to spend the large sums necessary to realize bold new initiatives in the city core. While exuding confidence during the unveiling of big and expensive plans, time and again the growth coalition's exuberance has deflated when faced with the challenge of raising needed taxpayer dollars in a tax-averse region of small government advocates. It is reasonable to suspect that, public-facing bluster notwithstanding, business leaders and growth advocates are well aware of the fundamental economic fragility that has afflicted the region for decades, and they are hesitant to invest their own dollars in big projects that may not ultimately yield the major economic returns that their glossy prospectuses anticipate.

This reality, I suggest, is the primary underlying cause of the "Potemkin City" growth strategies that I outlined in chapter 4. Laudatory press coverage of underleveraged developers, hashtags and themed social media accounts, civic pride campaigns highlighting the city flag, the relabeling of a prime undeveloped downtown parcel as a "Pop-Up Park"—all of these examples and more represent attempts to promote an impression of robust growth without committing the actual financial assets necessary to generate that growth. In short, building is expensive; marketing is cheap.

Solving the "Perception Challenge" on the Cheap

Of the four "challenges" identified by Chung, the one that Wichita most successfully remediated—indeed, the only one that received any sustained collective attention at all—was the "perception challenge." Through the prolonged and intense dissemination of public relations campaigns, Wichita's leaders truly did spark a resurgence of local pride that has persisted to the current day. While a low level of local civic pride was a genuine problem affecting Wichita, it did not emerge from nowhere. Wichitans felt genuine dissatisfaction with a place whose volatile major industry caused periodic shocks to the local economy and whose local government offered fewer and worse quality-of-life amenities than other American cities of similar size. Such deficiencies were quite noticeable to residents as they traveled for work, vacationed, and visited friends and family in other metropolitan areas. By working to reverse the "perception challenge" without first engaging in the harder and more expensive work necessary to reverse the other problems that Chung correctly identified, Wichita's boosters made the city feel better about itself. But it was a Pyrrhic victory; these endeavors did not yield significant progress toward shoring up the city's vulnerable economic base. Rather than heeding Chung's advice and acting on his most daunting and expensive recommendations, the business and philanthropic community exalted the figure of Chung himself, turning the very act of retaining him as a consultant into a component of the coordinated marketing campaign to boost city pride.

To a significant extent, then, the social media–fueled convergence in urban design and amenity trends identified by Chayka, Barns, and others may be explained by private-sector frugality and cost aversion spilling over into public-sector austerity within tax-averse and financially vulnerable cities. Copying is cheaper than innovating; established consumer tastes are safer bets than risky avant-garde experiments; and filter-heavy social media marketing is far less costly than the boring and invisible infrastructure upgrades, staff salaries and benefits, and new capital construction and maintenance expenses needed to build, grow, and sustain the city.

The Ungentrifiable City

Place-based marketing campaigns, incentive programs designed to lure young professionals to relocate with monetary rewards, and hasty efforts to produce suites of consumption amenities like those in competitor cities are founded upon a baseline principle that cities can engineer economic prosperity through deliberate gentrification. Whether it is more accurate to view gentrification as a supply-led or demand-led phenomenon is one of the longest-running sources of contention within the social science literature on urban social change. It is certainly clear that in prosperous, dynamic, growing metropolises, the supply-side forces of urban real estate development, banking, business, and local government frequently come together in the form of growth coalitions to enact sweeping territorial change in inner-city neighborhoods. In the final analysis, however, gentrification cannot fully flourish without some demand from consumers of the real estate, retail, culinary, and cultural amenities that those growth interests are supplying.[17]

Decade after decade, Wichita has failed to attract young white-collar professionals in large numbers. Repeated calls to "diversify" the economy have faltered. When a midsize data security firm expanded into Wichita in 2021 and pledged to add a few dozen new jobs, the city greeted the announcement with a jubilant press conference featuring US Senator Jerry Moran, Mayor Brandon Whipple, and Lieutenant Governor David Toland, who boasted that "we will always be the Air Capital of the World, but we can be the capital of other sectors as well." Elected officials gathered again for another press conference in 2023, when Wichita-based semiconductor assembler Integra Technologies announced that, conditional on the provision of a raft of state and local incentives and the firm's selection as a recipient of funding under the federal CHIPS Act, they would construct a new facility and add over 2,000 new high-tech manufacturing employees to the region's economy. "Our region hasn't seen anything this transformative in years," exclaimed Kansas House Speaker Dan Hawkins about the heavily subsidized Integra plan. More than two years after the ecstatic press releases, however, Integra had yet to be approved for CHIPS funding, and they had not broken ground or added any new jobs. In these examples and others, Wichita's leaders talked a big game about "diversifying the economy" but made little tangible progress toward that goal.[18]

As the COVID-19 pandemic normalized remote work for white-collar employees across the world, many places featuring relatively low cost of living capitalized on the trend to try to promote local growth by appealing to workers in high-cost regions, coaxing them to relocate and work remotely while saving money. Wichita leaders recognized this opportunity, developing the "Choose Wichita" website (discussed in chapter 4) to lure these professionals. This effort generated modest results. Unlike other cities, including Tulsa and Topeka, Wichita did not offer direct cash payments to potential migrants. With its harsh climate and conspicuous absence of proximate beaches, mountains, hiking trails, and other natural amenities, the region was at a comparative disadvantage relative to other US destinations for remote workers. And unlike smaller and cheaper industrial cities on the fringe of major metropolitan areas (such as Newburgh, New York, the subject of Richard Ocejo's recent research on small-city gentrification), Wichita is too geographically isolated to serve as a convenient escape for those priced out of larger, high-priced cities nearby.[19]

Although many large corporations called Wichita home in the mid-twentieth century, even in their heyday they had felt little desire to locate substantial corporate offices downtown. The large aircraft manufacturers concentrated their corporate offices on their sprawling airstrip-adjacent campuses. For its part, Koch Industries occupied a five-story downtown structure for decades until that building, next to the newly built Century II, came down following a long and contentious acquisition struggle with the Urban Renewal Agency. Rather than remaining downtown, Koch built a suburban-style low-rise campus in the late 1960s on the north side of the city, and they have remained there ever since. Other major Wichita-born companies, like Pizza Hut and Coleman, made similar suburban moves. Eventually, both Pizza Hut and Coleman, as well as Rent-A-Center, were purchased by larger corporations, depriving the city of its corporate headquarters status altogether. Following the unraveling of the DeBoer riverfront plan in the early 1990s, attention turned to what to do downtown without the revitalization promised by the proposal. County Commissioner Billy McCray publicly called on the city's big companies to invest in the core and locate major office functions there, but corporate leaders brushed McCray's concerns aside. The result has been a big city with a perennially sparse downtown, as I examined in chapter 4.[20]

The conversion of a few old office and warehouse buildings into loft rental apartments has led to a modest increase in the downtown population over the past decade, but the total number of people residing downtown remains well below 3,000, less than 1 percent of the city's population. Deprived of much of its prior corporate entrepreneurial fortitude, featuring few natural or cultural amenities to lure and retain young professional "talent," steeped in a deeply conservative milieu often at odds with the "tolerant" ethic that (in Richard Florida's influential formulation) is a key component of twenty-first-century urban economic vitality, and devoid of critical public infrastructure thanks to underinvestment by stingy and tax-averse local governments, Downtown Wichita has been effectively gentrification proof.[21]

However, that is true only insofar as gentrification is conceived as a process involving the influx of affluent new residents and the introduction of a range of new consumption amenities oriented toward their tastes. In previous historical and sociological research on development in Downtown Wichita, I have demonstrated the structural impediments to substantial gentrification in the Air Capital, but I have also made the case for a broader conceptualization of the idea of gentrification, one that involves attending not merely to visible signs of socioeconomic ascent but also to (sometimes subtle) changes in the overall socioeconomic trajectory of a geographic area. Even if affluent professionals and retail outlets catering to them do not appear en masse, a steady process of gentrification can still be underway if efforts to eliminate those at the lower end of the socioeconomic spectrum from urban territory are successful.[22]

As I explained in chapter 3, that strategy has been at work in Wichita for well over half a century. It began with the Urban Renewal–era efforts to raze the "skid row" area of East Douglas Avenue and build Naftzger Park in its place; it continued with the campaigns to launch the idea of "Old Town" in the imaginations of Wichitans, the relocation of the Union Rescue Mission, and the prolonged struggle to wrest control of the Eaton Hotel from Phil Kassebaum and evict the low-income men who inhabited that deteriorated building; it persisted in the codification of new anticamping and antipanhandling ordinances designed to criminalize the activities of the homeless people who continued to occupy the area; and it culminated in the replacement of the original Naftzger Park with a new and even more sanitized space once the first park had become a haven for unhoused Wichitans. Public- and private-sector leaders have pursued a relentless campaign to oust the poor from the city core and prime the area for upscale redevelopment. Even in the absence of a critical mass of stereotypical "gentrifiers," these activities represent aggressive actions that fall under the umbrella of the broader process of urban gentrification.

Despite consistent action over the course of many decades to clear the path for gentrification, rejuvenation within Downtown Wichita has been a slow, fitful, uneven, and generally unimpressive process. Empty buildings abounded throughout the area even before the COVID-19 pandemic, when many cities experienced a vacancy crisis as commercial properties suffered from the pivot to working at home, and commercial vacancy rates remain high today. Even by the standards of the US—a country whose urban fabric was torn apart in the twentieth century by the obsession with accommodating automobiles—Wichita stands out for its autocentric identity. Roughly 60 percent of downtown parcels are dedicated to parking; a lack of demand and economic activity has generally stalled any attempt to redevelop those parking lots into higher-value structures.[23]

By 2025, more than a decade after creating the "Pop-Up Park" on a key parcel right in the heart of downtown—a stopgap before anticipated construction of a high-value new structure—the owners of the property had still taken no action to develop the property. It sat dormant and derelict behind a chain link fence. Some new development projects, including an osteopathic medical school complex, have been completed, and a new medical science construction project stemming from a collaboration between two public universities has begun, but no significant downtown development project has moved forward without massive public subsidy, and private-led commercial construction in Downtown Wichita remains anemic. Following the collapse of the Riverfront Legacy Master Plan, Century II still stands and continues to operate, though the iconic former library building sits vacant and abandoned with no realistic plans in the works for either repurposing or demolishing the facility. There are few full-service restaurants and no major retailers to be found in the core, and the nearest full-service grocery store is two miles away from the city center.

What's Wrong with Being Boring?

In the 2010s, during the wave of campaigns to reignite civic pride, a local graphic designer began marketing bumper stickers stamped with the phrase "WICHITA IS NOT BORING" in black capital letters on a white background. The message of the bumper sticker was a pointed protest against a common sentiment echoed among young people who grew up in the region and fled, seeking more exciting lifestyles elsewhere. Of course, "boring" is a subjective evaluation, but the need for a graphical rejoinder to counter the "boring" stigma provided strong evidence that Wichita was in fact, in the eyes of Wichitans, rather boring.[24]

Boring. Lame. Flyover. These are pejorative terms used to describe places that fail to adequately provide consumption amenities that middle- and upper-class people have learned to expect, based upon their own consumption experiences in other cities. With such consumer demand among affluent residents and visitors in place, the provision of these consumption experiences becomes a major goal of real estate developers and economic development agencies. Growth proponents are not wrong to prioritize this aspect of economic development. Visitors do notice when they cannot access their favorite retail or dining chain upon arriving in a new city, and residents develop a frustrating sense of local inferiority when they cannot frequent the same restaurants, stores, concerts, and sporting events that they see their bigger-city peers enjoying in mirthful social media posts.[25]

Consumption-oriented economic development, gentrification-fueled growth, and competitive boosterist energy all make sense—arguably they are vital—within the entrepreneurial paradigm that has held sway over the urban landscape in the United States for more than half a century. As the federal government, under both Republican and Democratic administrations, has pulled back many direct investments in the nation's cities (for instance, phasing out the Great Society–era Model Cities program), ended the period of centralized urban renewal, enacted severe reforms to welfare programs, and retreated from the direct provision of public housing, cities—and the poor and working-class people who inhabit them—have increasingly had to fend for themselves and chart their own path to prosperity. Though boosterism has always been a defining feature of American urbanism, the entrepreneurial turn has ratcheted up the stakes of inter-city competition, tying metropolitan regions' fortunes to their ability to successfully lure businesses and professional "talent." As Florida and others have correctly observed, this situation inevitably produces "winners" and "losers" among cities that are vastly unequal in their ability to supply the amenities needed to have a chance in that perpetual competitive struggle. Almost by definition, this paradigm erects nearly insurmountable obstacles for "boring" cities.[26]

This presents a fundamentally unjust situation for those who, by accident of birth, find themselves living within smaller, less economically dynamic regions. The traditional solution favored by economists for individuals facing this dilemma is simply to relocate in search of preferable opportunities elsewhere, and the slow population growth and net domestic out-migration experienced in Wichita (not to mention struggling small cities and rural communities all across Kansas and other agricultural states) indicate that relocation remains a common course of action. But, of course, such an individual-level reaction to economic conditions is not feasible for entire established neighborhoods and communities, and the prosperity and vitality of communities should not hinge upon the presence or absence of Starbucks, a new convention center, or *Hamilton*. We need new, robust, twenty-first-century paths to prosperity for cities that are sleepy, mundane, and just plain boring.

Policy Agenda for a Boring Urbanism

How can we respond, make Wichita and cities like it thrive in the decades to come, and promote prosperity for urban dwellers across the United States?

Rather than haughtily protesting that "WICHITA IS NOT BORING," it would be preferable to promote new policies that allow boring places to flourish. The remainder of this conclusion addresses that policy agenda along with challenges to its implementation.

Regarding Wichita specifically, the structural impediments to advancing the region's economic competitiveness are widely acknowledged and have been documented for years by analysts, consultants, and economists. In his study of regional economic clusters across the United States in 2001, economist Michael Porter offered the following diagnosis of the problems facing the Air Capital:

> The region is facing a shrinking workforce and relatively few new firms are being formed. Wichita's good wages and steady economic growth are mainly the result of past innovation, and Wichita is lagging today as an innovation center. In order to grow, or even maintain economic prosperity, the region needs to improve its innovative capacity through greater R&D spending, greater investments in local research and development institutions, enhanced workforce training, and more institutions for collaboration. A bold, highly coordinated economic development strategy will be needed if Wichita is to sustain its success over the coming decade.

Porter went on to identify key challenges placing the region at a competitive disadvantage, including a lack of access to skilled labor and weak labor force training; a low rate of research, development, and innovation; a relatively small pool of investment capital and angel investors; and poor transportation infrastructure, especially (ironically) in terms of air travel service.[27]

Most of those issues remain in place today, and they have been identified by other analysts, including Chung. Addressing those challenges—investing in the workforce, infrastructure, and research, and truly diversifying the economy beyond its reliance upon aircraft manufacturing—will all be critical if the city's leaders want to create an economically thriving region in the future.

The characteristics that had propelled Wichita forward through the mid-twentieth century were essentially rooted in mundane regularity. Looking forward to a future of stable (if not lavish) progress, historian Craig Miner predicted in 1988 that Wichita "would continue to be American: not too large, not too small, not too pretty or too ugly, not far ahead of things, nor far behind, neither typical nor unique." One year later, Jack DeBoer unveiled his audacious riverfront redevelopment proposal, with an ostentatious 299-foot *Keeper of the Plains* statue as its centerpiece, and he beseeched the city to elevate its expectations, proclaiming, "We're stepping up to the big table, Wichita." Although DeBoer's full redevelopment vision never became reality, the ambitious and competitive DeBoerist philosophy took root firmly in the city's business community, and it has not relented since. The persistent quest to make the city stand out, however, has generally manifested itself in efforts to catch up to and emulate regional peers in ways that are baldly evident to visitors who have traveled elsewhere. One young professional, a native Wichitan who returned temporarily to her parents' home to work her Washington, DC, job remotely during the pandemic, put it succinctly in an interview with *The Wichita Eagle*: "I think Wichita is successful when it realizes what is good about itself and its own identity, and it doesn't try to be Kansas City or Oklahoma City."[28]

Contrary to the claims of the boastful bumper sticker, Wichita is rather boring. For most of its history, that was acceptable—even valued—as the city grew, and much of its population prospered in spite of its unglamorous image. It should still be possible today to manage a small or medium-sized city in a way that supports the quality of life of its residents across the socioeconomic spectrum; makes residents want to live there, raise families, and expect their children will also be happy building lives there; and provides a reasonable environment for businesses to succeed and maintain a healthy level of profitability. What will it take to get there?

At the local level, city, county, and school district budgets, fortified by enhanced property tax collection practices, must be dedicated to funding the upkeep of the core social infrastructure that makes communities good places to live for poor, working-class, and middle-class people. Water and sewer upgrades; regular park and playground maintenance; widespread tree planting and routine mowing and weed control in public rights-of-way; investment in public library collections, technology, and programming; rebates to support residents' ability to invest in energy-efficient home upgrades; incubator funds to assist residents who want to start and grow small businesses; clean, efficient, and reliable public transportation networks that can compete with private automobile travel as a first choice for daily commuters; competitive compensation packages for public employees across all city departments (which will put upward pressure on private sector wages, as well)—these (and many others) are the boring line items in a city budget that make our places healthy, inviting to potential newcomers, and satisfying for the people who already live there.[29]

Perhaps most important of all, cities must make a sustained commitment to providing high-quality public elementary and secondary schools along with public postsecondary institutions. Investments in teacher salaries, new cutting-edge school facilities, educational resources, technology, and measures to enhance school safety are critical for improving the lived experience of the city for families of all class backgrounds. Such investments are the most effective way to generate a skilled and productive local workforce that can sustain the local economy and appeal to companies looking for a new home. Even for households without school-age children, good schools prop up home values and real estate markets in a way that convention centers, restaurants, and destination leisure venues cannot.

Local governments already make provisions for most of these items, but across many cities, significantly more investment is needed on these factors that undergird the quality of life of the majority of the population. Taken together, growing this civic and social infrastructure will entail substantial increases in local governmental expenditures, which are difficult to achieve amidst an environment of perennially tight budgets, anti-tax orthodoxy, and competing priorities. For municipal governments, which typically must maintain balanced budgets, making room for these expansions will require a combination of new revenues and reduced expenditures elsewhere.

On both ends of that budgetary equation, the clearest target is the corporate sector, which has benefited for decades from taxpayer-funded subsidies, incentives, and exemptions that have siphoned off revenues that could be put toward the types of human-oriented investments I have outlined. These maneuvers also exclude potential major sources of new revenue that could fortify such investments. Relocation incentives, property tax abatements, industrial revenue bonds, and workforce training initiatives are just some of the ways in which local governments subsidize the operations of the corporate sector, all in the hopes of creating new jobs (or out of fear of losing existing jobs). In Wichita, a particularly glaring example of this trend has prevailed for decades, as the city has delivered these and other gifts to major aircraft manufacturing firms that by design (as discussed in chapter 5) have deliberately excluded themselves altogether from incorporation into the city's territory through a series of non-annexation agreements. By seeking these accommodations and by threatening (both implicitly and explicitly) to relocate in search of more generous offers from competitor cities, major employers jeopardize the financial stability of local governments and impede the full realization of valuable human-scale investments.

Generating the revenue needed for these goals will require local governments to expect more from their corporate residents. Major political willpower from local officials will be needed to demand and extract greater tax revenue from commercial and industrial landholders, and significant ideological shifts will have to take place to invert the current valence of demands, concessions, and gratitude embedded within the relationships between companies and local governments. It should be CEOs, real estate developers, and chambers of commerce who supplicate themselves before mayors, city councils, and residential communities, not the other way around. Local governments' beneficence, supply of land and skilled labor, and tolerance of the negative externalities generated by commercial and industrial activities near their homes necessitate a reversal of this dynamic. The prevailing pattern, whereby government must tread carefully and cater to the demands of business, stems from the reality that other economically vulnerable cities run by politicians eager to produce job growth are willing to outbid and undercut one another to lure mobile firms. Given the uneven balance of power in these negotiations, these city leaders are not acting irrationally. Still, this competition over jobs and firm relocation is not healthy for communities, and higher authorities will have to step in to rectify the situation.

What is needed, above all else, is a détente among city and state leaders who mutually agree to cool interregional competition by declining to dangle costly incentive packages in front of companies in the hopes of poaching corporate operations and jobs from their peers. Unfortunately, there are few incentives for local and state governments to join together like this, and unilateral disarmament by just one virtuous leader would be ill advised and reckless. This is a situation in which the federal government should step in through a combination of corporate tax reform and regulatory reform to protect the finances of local governments.

Federal corporate income tax policies should be used to reward loyalty and penalize capricious relocation threats through new tax deductions and penalties. New federal legislation banning the solicitation or receipt of local relocation incentives and sharply curtailing local corporate property tax abatements is in order. As a final backstop, directing federal revenue-sharing into city coffers will help to promote urban equity. While the federal government provides billions of dollars per year in block grant programs and targeted grants awarded to localities that apply for them, direct, unrestricted federal aid to cities was mostly phased out decades ago. During the COVID-19 pandemic, which devastated many previously reliable funding streams for cities, the federal CARES Act and American Rescue Plan provided much-needed aid that helped to stabilize municipal budgets across the country. Making that model permanent, and supporting it through increased corporate taxes, capital gains taxes, and income taxes on high earners, would deliver a source of fiscal stability to local governments that would help to free them from the need to generate local revenue by appealing to strategies oriented toward business recruitment, real estate speculation, and gentrification.

In the near term, the likelihood of realizing any of these policy goals is rather low. Conservative anti-tax ideology and neoliberal dominance show no signs of abating, and reactionary antipathy toward the unhoused is on the rise. In its 2023–24 term, the US Supreme Court handed down several monumental decisions that will have broad long-term impacts upon urban governance and hinder the policy agenda laid out above. In *Loper Bright Enterprises v. Raimondo*, the court strongly curtailed the power of federal agencies to interpret and apply administrative law, which will likely limit the ability of federal departments to intervene directly with cities and to aid the vulnerable people who inhabit them. And in *City of Grants Pass v. Johnson*, the justices gave cities broad leeway to clear encampments and further criminalize the activities of the homeless. In chapter 3, I examined the long history of struggles in Wichita to oust the homeless from downtown spaces to clear the way for new gentrification. Prior judicial restrictions on encampment sweeps had stymied some efforts in Wichita (and cities across the US) to enact harsher restrictions on unhoused individuals. With the newfound freedom conferred on cities and police departments by *Grants Pass*, harsher treatment of the homeless—in service to the profitability of downtown businesses and property developers—has already begun.

Given these rulings, and a Supreme Court that appears poised to hold a strong conservative majority for decades to come, the policy agenda I have presented here may appear rather utopian. That is no reason to despair, though. As the great sociologist Erik Olin Wright explained,

> We simply do not know what the ultimate limits to the expansion of democratic egalitarian social empowerment might be. The best we can do, then, is treat the struggle to move on the pathways of social empowerment as an experimental process in which we continually test and retest the limits of possibility and try, as best as we can, to create new institutions which expand the limits themselves. In doing so we not only envision real utopias, but contribute to making utopias real.

Utopian thinking is thus necessary, powerful, and important, both in shaping culture and ideology and in laying the groundwork for future structural and institutional change.[30]

Under the model of urbanism that has been prevalent in the US for decades, it may seem ludicrous to promote a vision for a "boring" city and call that project "utopian," but in many ways the idea is quite radical. Cities, first and foremost, are the geographical backdrops to the lived experiences of people. Reprioritizing the mundane daily experiences of the millions of humans who inhabit Wichita and dozens of cities like it will require major policy reforms, many of which may be unattainable in the near term. Until sweeping national policy change becomes more feasible, work—both incremental and utopian—can proceed to influence prevailing cultural and ideological conceptions of what urbanism means.

ACKNOWLEDGMENTS

In the summer of 2013, I set foot in Naftzger Park for the first time. My wife Maya and I had just moved to Wichita from Boston, and we first settled in a loft apartment in the city's "Old Town" area, seeking as urban an experience as we could hope to find in our new home. Walking through the wrought iron gates into a space that was so different from the surrounding parking lots and underdeveloped downtown neighborhood, I was immediately perplexed. What was this park, why was it there, and why was it always nearly devoid of people?

My determination to find the answers to those questions was the origin of a decade of research that culminated in this book. Commencing the requisite Baudelairean flânerie that motivates every urban sociologist encountering a city for the first time, I immediately set out to see, feel, and begin to understand this strange new city. I absorbed (and gradually grew less startled by) the alarming sounds of the 4 a.m. freight train whistles, noontime tornado sirens, and sudden hailstorms that disrupted my days and nights. I tried to figure out why an old beat-up airplane with a flat tire surrounded by empty Quonset huts next to a junk yard nevertheless boasted a bold sign proudly proclaiming that it was "Air Force One, the First One" and why no one else in town seemed particularly impressed. I calibrated my nose like a weather vane until I felt confident in my ability to predict—based upon the prevailing wind direction—whether the whole city would smell like dog food on a given day. I learned how to pronounce the name of the Arkansas River. It took years, but I finally began to feel like I had a solid grasp on the place, its people, its factions, and its trajectory.

So, before I acknowledge any individuals, I have to thank the city. This is a book about Wichita, a city whose sprawling strip malls, trailer parks, highway interchanges, and gated subdivisions seem indistinguishable at first glance from the rest of America and whose singular characteristics—both its hard edges and its soft, subtle compassion—only become truly perceptible after years of living in their midst. Wichita can be a frustrating and challenging place to inhabit, and I am among the most vocal critics of the city and its leadership. But I do love this city and its people. Wichita is my home and the place where my family was started. My work, including this book, is designed to contribute to Wichita and make it a better place for its current inhabitants and future generations.

My colleagues at Wichita State University have been consistent sources of support. It has been a privilege to be a part of the friendly, collegial, and hardworking Department of Sociology for more than a decade, and I have been fortunate to work alongside Jodie Hertzog, Twyla Hill, LaDawna Hobkirk, Chuck Koeber, Alyssa Lynne-Joseph, Ron Matson, Jenny Pearson, Kathy Perez, Jodie Simon, Shirlene Small, Lisa Thrane, and Tisha Whitehead. Beyond the department, there are too many great scholars to name at WSU, but Neal Allen, George Dehner, John Dreifort, Ed Flentje, and Jens Kreinath stand out for the ways they have encouraged my research and enriched my thinking.

Gretchen Eick, Jay Price, Marti Smith, and Liv Vest read portions of this manuscript and provided helpful feedback, as well as encouragement, and so did the students in my Urban Sociology seminar in the fall semester of 2024. Russell Fox and Shelley Kimelberg read the whole thing. They came at it from different perspectives—Russell is a political scientist from Wichita who was able to give a much-needed reality check on some of my more controversial claims, while Shelley is an urban sociologist from Buffalo who provided an outsider's perspective that helped me put my findings in context. Both are trusted collaborators and friends; their insights, and their confidence in my work, helped to make this book possible. Jonathan Wynn and David Banks also read the full manuscript as peer reviewers for the publisher. Their detailed critiques forced me to clarify my arguments and helped me to identify weak spots in my claims. All these individuals have greatly improved the book; whatever errors remain are mine alone.

I maintain regular correspondence with a wide range of journalists, local officials, and current and former elected leaders. Many of them are named, quoted, and/or cited in the text, and I have shared excerpts from this book with some of them to gauge their reactions. To protect the confidentiality of our conversations, I won't name them here, but I hope they know how valuable their trust is to me and how important their work is to the daily life of the city and region.

At the University Press of Kansas, I thank David Congdon for guiding this project to completion. In addition to being a talented editor, David is himself an accomplished author and scholar, so he speaks from experience when he advises authors on the best way to craft their arguments within a cohesive narrative whole. I am grateful to him, as well as the rest of the staff at UPK, for all the labor they have put in to make this book a reality.

I began to collect ideas for this book during the COVID-19 pandemic. The pandemic reshaped so much of our society and occupied our attention nonstop; indeed, the impact of COVID on the city and its economy forms a key focus of this book's final chapter. Stay-at-home orders and pivots to remote work provided prolonged stretches of time with little else to do but sit and type—conditions that many writers had long dreamed of. Yet, as many writers found, productivity often proved elusive in the midst of pervasive anguish, dread, and tedium. Writing requires solitude, but it also requires a human energy that thrives on social connection. Like people throughout the world, during the most isolating stretches of the pandemic Maya and I found that much-needed social connection in a group of friends spread across the country, meeting remotely on a weekly basis to hang out, play games, and share stories of getting by during a dark time. Years later, that community persists. Charlie Acquista, Margaret Banker, Tim Banker, Crissi Bariatti, Justin Lasoff, and Chris Tripler: thank you. This would not have gotten done without you.

Zack Gingrich-Gaylord is a radical in the best sense of the word—radical in his compassion, his expansive view of human dignity, and his selflessness. He is also one of the keenest and most incisive social and political critics in Wichita, unrivaled in his ability to see the connections between the boring minutiae of city council meeting agendas and the broad sweep of global political economy. He has lifted me up, and brought me back down to earth, more times than I can count. His friendship is a gift to all who have had the privilege to experience it, and his influence on my thinking about cities, politics, and society courses throughout the text.

Finally, I owe my career, and my whole life, to the constant love and care of my family, especially Bruce and Cindy Billingham, Valerie Nelson Billingham, Dayna, Erik, William, and Evelyn Morton, Susan Field, and Karen, Sylvan, and Maxanne Menezes. Maya Menezes Billingham and Alistair Billingham are the core of my existence and the driving force behind everything I do. My experience of Wichita—and, by extension, every observation contained in this book—cannot be separated from the life I have built here with them. Ali has known no other home, and if this book contributes in any way toward making Wichita a better place for him and the rest of the city's children, it will have been a success.

NOTES

Preface

1. Kevin Draper, "How the D.C. Plane Crash Shattered Wichita's Big Dreams of Skating and Flight," *New York Times*, January 31, 2025, https://www.nytimes.com/2025/01/31/us/wichita-figure-skaters-plane-crash.html.

Introduction: Creating Authenticity Through Mimicry

1. The January 14, 2020, presentation can be viewed in its entirety at "Riverfront Legacy Master Plan January 14 Public Open House," YouTube, 30:38, https://youtu.be/unHjJhhmlFE.

2. "MAPS History," The City of Oklahoma City, accessed June 11, 2025, https://www.okc.gov/Infrastructure-Development/Current-Planning-Projects/MAPS-History.

3. "A Riverfront Destination," Gathering Place: Tulsa's Riverfront Park, accessed June 11, 2025, https://www.gatheringplace.org/our-story; "Our Story," Klyde Warren Park, accessed June 11, 2025, https://www.klydewarrenpark.org/our-story.

4. The renderings described here can be viewed at "Final Recommendations," Riverfront Legacy Master Plan, accessed June 11, 2025, https://www.riverfrontlegacywichita.org/final-recommendations.

5. The history of baseball in Wichita is chronicled in Bob Rives, *Baseball in Wichita* (Charleston, SC: Arcadia, 2004). See also Travis Larsen, "Baseball Can Survive: How Semi-Pro Baseball Thrived in Wichita during the 1930s and 1940s," *Heritage of the Great Plains* 40 (2007): 29–40; Brian Carroll, "Beating the Klan: Baseball Coverage in Wichita Before Integration, 1920–1930," *Baseball Research Journal*, https://sabr.org/journal/article/beating-the-klan-baseball-coverage-in-wichita-before-integration-1920-1930/; R. M. "Dick" Long, *Wichita Century: A Pictorial History of Wichita, Kansas, 1870–1970* (Wichita, KS: Wichita Historical Museum Association, 1969).

6. Dion Lefler, "Triple-A Baseball Team Plans Move to Wichita," *Wichita Eagle*, September 7, 2018, 1A.

7. Chance Swaim, "Before City Council Vote, Plan for Ballpark Is Full of Unknowns," *Wichita Eagle*, March 18, 2019, 1A; Carrie Rengers, "Mayor Longwell: If We're Not Growing, We're Moving Backwards," *Wichita Eagle*, March 18, 2019, 1A; Carrie Rengers, "Baby Cakes Owner Is Pitching His Baseball Dream to Wichita," *Wichita Eagle*, March 19, 2019, 1A; Chance Swaim and Jason Tidd, "City Council Votes to Sell 4 Acres for $4 as Part of Wichita Baseball Park Development," *Wichita Eagle*, March 21, 2019, 1A.

8. Stephen Buckman and Alex Pemberton, "Suicide Squeeze: How Minor League Cities Chase Economic Development with Big-League Stadium Schemes," *Journal of Urban Affairs* 45, no. 8 (2023): 1452–1468. For further details on Wichita's stadium project, see Kallie Kimble, "Searching for the 'Crown Jewel': A Qualitative Examination of the Utilization of Multi-Use Sports Venues for Downtown Redevelopment in Wichita, KS" (master's thesis, Wichita State University, 2019).

9. The groundbreaking event, including the remarks of Toland and Fluhr, can be viewed at "Baseball Stadium Groundbreaking," City of Wichita, February 13, 2019, YouTube, 19:23, https://youtu.be/6fYixLmXjko.

10. For insights from an observer of Knoxville, TN, on how the residents of different cities regularly tell themselves the same stories about their own cities' uniqueness, see Mike Cohen, "Every City Thinks It's Exceptional—in Exactly the Same Ways," *Knox News*, August 3, 2018, https://www.knoxnews.com/story/opinion/columnists/2018/08/03/every-city-thinks-its-exceptional-exactly-same-ways-opinion/850865002/.

11. Kyle Chayka, "Same Old, Same Old. How the Hipster Aesthetic Is Taking over the World," *Guardian*, August 6, 2016, https://www.theguardian.com/commentisfree/2016/aug/06/hipster-aesthetic-taking-over-world; Kyle Chayka, "Welcome to AirSpace: How Silicon Valley Helps Spread the Same Sterile Aesthetic Across the World," *Verge*, August 3, 2016, https://www.theverge.com/2016/8/3/12325104/airbnb-aesthetic-global-minimalism-startup-gentrification. British brand strategist Alex Murrell has described this phenomenon as part of a bigger trend toward homogenization in all elements of contemporary culture. See Alex Murrell, "The Age of Average," March 20, 2023, https://www.alexmurrell.co.uk/articles/the-age-of-average.

12. Abilene Convention and Visitors Bureau, *Official Visitors Guide*, 2023, https://www.abilenevisitors.com/newsletter-signup/visitors-guide/.

13. Travel Dubuque, *Travel Dubuque: The 2023 Edition*, https://issuu.com/traveldubuque/docs/2023_travel_dubuque_travel_guide_web.

14. Visit Bakersfield, *Bakersfield, California: Official Insiders' Guide*, accessed June 11, 2025, https://maddendigitalbooks.com/cavbovg23/.

15. James Trumm, "Study—and Everyday Toledoans—Say City's Economy Is on the Move," *Blade*, September 1, 2024, https://www.toledoblade.com/business/development/2024/09/01/study-and-everyday-toledoans-say-city-s-economy-is-on-the-move/stories/20240823120; Stefanie Monge, "Omaha and Lincoln Gain Ground in 2024 Best of the Midwest: Startup City Rankings," *Silicon Prairie News*, August 14, 2014, https://siliconprairienews.com/2024/08/omaha-and-lincoln-gain-ground-in-2024-best-of-the-midwest-startup-city-rankings/; Shelby Kellerman, "Wichita Breaks into Top 50 Best-Performing Cities

List from Milken Institute," *Wichita Business Journal*, January 14, 2025, https://www.bizjournals.com/wichita/news/2025/01/14/wichita-50-best-performing-cities-milken-institute.html.

16. On scooters in Duluth, see "About," Leaf Rides Duluth, accessed June 11, 2025, https://www.leafrides.com/about. For information about ChattaScooter, see "About ChattaScooter," Adventure Sports Innovation, LLC, accessed July 1, 2025, https://web.archive.org/web/20221129142652/https://chattascooter.com/about-us/. On Scoot Spokane, see Nicholas Deshais, "Visit Spokane, Lime Join Forces to Encourage 'Accidental Discoveries' in City Neighborhoods," *Spokesman-Review*, May 28, 2019, https://www.spokesman.com/stories/2019/may/28/visit-spokane-lime-join-forces-to-encourage-accide/.

17. Miriam Greenberg, *Branding New York: How a City in Crisis Was Sold to the World* (New York: Routledge, 2008); Kevin Fox Gotham, *Authentic New Orleans: Tourism, Culture, and Race in the Big Easy* (New York: New York University Press, 2007); Christopher Mele, *Race and the Politics of Deception: The Making of an American City* (New York: New York University Press, 2017); David A. Banks, *The City Authentic: How the Attention Economy Builds Urban America* (Berkeley: University of California Press, 2023). See also Christopher Mele, *Selling the Lower East Side: Culture, Real Estate, and Resistance in New York City* (Minneapolis: University of Minnesota Press, 2000).

18. John R. Logan and Harvey L. Molotch, *Urban Fortunes: The Political Economy of Place* (Berkeley: University of California Press, 1987).

19. Logan and Molotch, *Urban Fortunes*. This is certainly not the first research to examine the operation of the urban growth machine in small cities or in cities that struggle to grow. Earlier studies on similar topics include L. Owen Kirkpatrick and Michael Peter Smith, "The Infrastructural Limits to Growth: Rethinking the Urban Growth Machine in Times of Fiscal Crisis," *International Journal of Urban and Regional Research* 35, no. 3 (2011): 477–503; Alissa Mazar, "Growth Coalitions in Declining Cities: Casinos, Redevelopment, and Inter-Urban Competition," *Urban Geography* 39, no. 6 (2018): 822–843; Seth Schindler, "Detroit After Bankruptcy: A Case of *Degrowth Machine Politics*," *Urban Studies* 53, no. 4 (2016): 818–836.

1. Catalyzing Growth in Cow Town

1. In 2023, there were approximately 52.7 million people living within municipalities with a population between 100,000 and 500,000 (roughly 15.9 percent of the US population, which stood at approximately 331.5 million in that year). By comparison, there were approximately 44.8 million people living within municipalities with a population above 500,000 people (about 13.5

percent of the nation's population). See US Census Bureau, *Annual Estimates of the Resident Population for Incorporated Places of 20,000 or More, Ranked by July 1, 2023 Population: April 1, 2020 to July 1, 2023* (2023), https://www2.census.gov/programs-surveys/popest/tables/2020-2023/cities/totals/SUB-IP-EST2023-ANNRNK.xlsx.

2. Paige Ouimet, "Remote Work, High-Skill Migration and Our Changing Cities," Kenan Institute of Private Enterprise, October 14, 2022, https://kenaninstitute.unc.edu/commentary/remote-work-high-skill-migration-and-our-changing-cities/; Adam Ozimek and Connor O'Brien, "As Major Cities Struggle to Rebound, Remote Work Continues to Shift Population Growth," Economic Innovation Group, April 5, 2023, https://eig.org/2022-county-population-trends/. See also Chase M. Billingham, "Rethinking the City and the Community for a Post-Pandemic World," Perspectives on the Pandemic Lecture Series, Wichita State University, September 2, 2020, YouTube, 1:01:26, youtu.be/nwRqtd6Ep_0.

3. Deirdre Oakley, "Broadening Our Focus: Regional Cities as a New Frontier of Urban Sociology," *City & Community* 14, no. 3 (2015): 249–253; Richard E. Ocejo, Ervin B. Kosta, and Alexis Mann, "Centering Small Cities for Urban Sociology in the 21st Century," *City & Community* 19, no. 1 (2020): 3–15; Japonica Brown-Saracino, "Epilogue: Lessons from the Sociology of Small Cities and Other Understudied Locales," *City & Community* 19, no. 1 (2020): 217–222. See also Chase M. Billingham, "The Broadening Conception of Gentrification: Recent Developments and Avenues for Future Inquiry in the Sociological Study of Urban Change," *Michigan Sociological Review* 29 (2015): 75–102; Zhe Zhang, Shelley M. Kimelberg, and Robert M. Adelman, "Considering Small-City Gentrification," *Contexts* 23, no. 4 (2024): 57–59.

4. Japonica Brown-Saracino, "How Places Shape Identity: The Origins of Distinctive LBQ Identities in Four Small U.S. Cities," *American Journal of Sociology* 121, no. 1 (2015): 1–63; Japonica Brown-Saracino, *How Places Make Us: Novel LBQ Identities in Four Small Cities* (Chicago: University of Chicago Press, 2017); Richard E. Ocejo, "From Apple to Orange: Narratives of Small City Migration and Settlement Among the Urban Middle Class," *Sociological Perspectives* 62, no. 3 (2019): 402–425; Richard E. Ocejo, "The Precarious Project and the Wasted Opportunity: The Social and Cultural Dynamics of Conflict over Urban Development," *Urban Affairs Review* 57, no. 4 (2021): 952–983; Richard E. Ocejo, *Sixty Miles Upriver: Gentrification and Race in a Small American City* (Princeton, NJ: Princeton University Press, 2024), 9.

5. David Cuberes and Richard Ramsawak, "Understanding Recent Growth Dynamics in Small Urban Places: The Case of New England," *City & Community* 19, no. 1 (2020): 44–75; Leonard Nevarez and Joshua Simons, "Small-City

Dualism in the Metro Hinterland: The Racialized 'Brooklynization' of New York's Hudson Valley," *City & Community* 19, no. 1 (2020): 16–43; Christopher Mele, *Race and the Politics of Deception: The Making of an American City* (New York: New York University Press, 2017); Jon R. Norman, *Small Cities USA: Growth, Diversity, and Inequality* (New Brunswick, NJ: Rutgers University Press, 2013); Catherine Tumber, *Small, Gritty, and Green: The Promise of America's Smaller Industrial Cities in a Low-Carbon World* (Cambridge, MA: MIT Press, 2012); James J. Connolly, ed., *After the Factory: Reinventing America's Industrial Small Cities* (Lanham, MD: Lexington Books, 2010). See also John Joe Schlichtman, "Big City Problems: Private Equity Investment, Transnational Users, and Local Mobilization in the Small City," *City & Community* 19, no. 1 (2020): 98–131; Chase M. Billingham and Shelley McDonough Kimelberg, "Identifying the Urban: Resident Perceptions of Community Character and Local Institutions in Eight Metropolitan Areas," *City & Community* 17, no. 3 (2018): 858–882.

6. Jamie Peck, "Transatlantic City, Part 1: Conjunctural Urbanism," *Urban Studies* 54, no. 1 (2017): 4–30; Jamie Peck, "Transatlantic City, Part 2: Late Entrepreneurialism," *Urban Studies* 54, no. 2 (2017): 327–363.

7. Eric H. Monkkonen, *America Becomes Urban: The Development of U.S. Cities and Towns, 1780–1980* (Berkeley: University of California Press, 1988).

8. Sinclair Lewis, *Babbitt* (New York: Grosset & Dunlap, 1922), 181.

9. Craig Miner, *Kansas: The History of the Sunflower State, 1854–2000* (Lawrence: University Press of Kansas, 2002).

10. James R. Shortridge, *Cities on the Plains: The Evolution of Urban Kansas* (Lawrence: University Press of Kansas, 2004), 56.

11. Carl Fenn Dittemore, "This Man Murdock" (master's thesis, Wichita State University, 2012).

12. Marshall Murdock, "Born Booming," *Wichita Daily Eagle*, December 5, 1886, 4.

13. Dittemore, "This Man Murdock."

14. Shortridge, *Cities on the Plains*.

15. Shortridge, *Cities on the Plains*; H. Craig Miner, *Wichita: The Early Years, 1865–80* (Lincoln, University of Nebraska Press, 1982); Craig Miner, *Wichita: The Magic City* (Wichita, KS: Wichita-Sedgwick County Historical Museum Association, 1988), 34.

16. Miner, *Wichita: The Magic City*; R. M. "Dick" Long, *Wichita Century: A Pictorial History of Wichita, Kansas, 1870–1970* (Wichita, KS: Wichita Historical Museum Association, 1969).

17. Miner, *Wichita: The Magic City*; Long, *Wichita Century*; Miner, *Kansas*.

18. Miner, *Wichita: The Magic City*; Long, *Wichita Century*; Andrea Dawn

Wilson, "Building Boeing-Wichita: Julius Earl Schaefer, Wichita's Lost Aviation Leader" (master's thesis, Wichita State University, 2018).

19. Miner, *Wichita: The Magic City*; Wilson, "Building Boeing-Wichita"; Jay M. Price, *Wichita's Legacy of Flight* (Charleston, SC: Arcadia, 2003).

20. The richest and fullest account of African American migration to Wichita, the civil rights struggles of Wichita's Black community, and the ways in which Black activists fought against segregation in the community can be found in Gretchen Cassel Eick, *Dissent in Wichita: The Civil Rights Movement in the Midwest, 1954–72* (Urbana: University of Illinois Press, 2001). See also Brent M. S. Campney, "'Stamping Out Segregation in Kansas': Jim Crow Practices and the Postwar Black Freedom Struggle," *Great Plains Quarterly* 43, no. 4 (2023): 359–383.

21. Price, *Wichita's Legacy of Flight*; Office of History, 22d Air Refueling Wing, *Heritage and Legacy: A Brief History of the 22d Air Refueling Wing and McConnell Air Force Base* (KS: McConnell Air Force Base, 2017), https://www.mcconnell.af.mil/Portals/27/22%20ARW%20Heritage%20Pamphlet%20%28Jul%202019%29.pdf.

22. Jay M. Price, "'Peerless Princess of the Southwest': Boosterism and Regional Identity in Wichita, Kansas," *Kansas History: A Journal of the Central Plains* 38 (2015): 79–106.

23. "Wichita—'The Air Capital of America,'" *Wichita*, August 1927, 11.

24. "Will Advertise Wichita as Air Capital of U.S.," *Wichita Eagle*, August 13, 1927, 13; Miner, *Wichita: The Magic City*; Long, *Wichita Century*; Price, "'Peerless Princess of the Southwest'"; Jay M. Price, "Cowboy Boosterism: Old Cowtown Museum and the Image of Wichita, Kansas," *Kansas History: A Journal of the Central Plains* 24 (2001–2): 300–317.

25. Miner, *Wichita: The Magic City*; Price, "Cowboy Boosterism"; Price, "'Peerless Princess of the Southwest'"; Michael E. Porter, *Wichita: Clusters of Innovation Initiative* (Washington, DC: Council on Competitiveness, 2001), https://competepast.org/storage/images/uploads/File/PDF%20Files/CoC_wichita_cluster.pdf.

26. The employment location quotient for NAICS code 3364 (Aerospace Product and Parts Manufacturing) in the second quarter of 2024 was 29.85 in Sedgwick County, KS, and 35.14 in Snohomish County, WA. The location quotient measures the share of a region's employment in a specific sector relative to that sector's share in the national economy. In other words, Sedgwick County's rate of aerospace manufacturing employment is roughly thirty times higher than the rate of employment in that industry across counties nationwide. In terms of absolute employment figures, Sedgwick County ranked fourth out of all US counties in the second quarter of 2024 in aerospace employment, with 28,759, trailing three much more populous counties in major metropolitan

regions: Los Angeles County, CA; King County, WA; and Snohomish County, WA. Location quotient and employment data come from the "Quarterly Census of Employment and Wages," US Bureau of Labor Statistics, last modified September 7, 2022, https://data.bls.gov/cew/apps/table_maker/v4/table_maker.htm#type=1&year=2024&qtr=2&own=5&ind=3364&supp=0.

27. Glenn W. Miller, "The Labor Force and Labor Market of Wichita," in *Metropolitan Wichita: Past, Present, and Future*, ed. Glenn W. Miller and Jimmy M. Skaggs (Lawrence: Regents Press of Kansas, 1978), 58; Lawrence E. McKibbin, "Commerce and Industry in Metropolitan Wichita, 1960 to the Present," in *Metropolitan Wichita: Past, Present, and Future*, ed. Glenn W. Miller and Jimmy M. Skaggs (Lawrence: Regents Press of Kansas, 1978), 105.

28. Data on aircraft manufacturing employment are drawn from US Bureau of Labor Statistics and Federal Reserve Bank of St. Louis, All Employees: Manufacturing: Durable Goods: Aerospace Product and Parts Manufacturing in Wichita, KS (MSA), updated May 22, 2025, https://fred.stlouisfed.org/series/SMU20486203133640001SA.

29. Molly McMillin, "Cessna's Cuts to Total 4,600," *Wichita Eagle*, January 30, 2009, 1A.

30. Molly McMillin, "Boeing Bails on Wichita," *Wichita Eagle*, January 5, 2012, 1A; Bill Wilson and Jerry Siebenmark, "Economy to Hurt, at Least in Short Term," *Wichita Eagle*, January 5, 2012, 1A; Beccy Tanner, "Boeing's Wichita Roots Go to 1927," *Wichita Eagle*, January 5, 2012, 6A; Rhonda Holman, "Boeing Decision Stings," *Wichita Eagle*, January 5, 2012, 7A.

31. Price, "Cowboy Boosterism"; Price, "'Peerless Princess of the Southwest.'"

32. The seminal statement on deindustrialization and its impact on urban communities is found in Barry Bluestone and Bennett Harrison, *The Deindustrialization of America: Plant Closings, Community Abandonment, and the Dismantling of Basic Industry* (New York: Basic Books, 1982). On retooling, shrinking, and loft conversions, see Connolly, *After the Factory*, for a series of case studies on small US cities confronting similar dilemmas; see also Tumber, *Small, Gritty, and Green*. On the "Boston Renaissance," see Barry Bluestone and Mary Huff Stevenson, *The Boston Renaissance: Race, Space, and Economic Change in an American Metropolis* (New York: Russell Sage, 2000).

33. On "diversification" in the Wichita economy, see McKibbin, "Commerce and Industry in Metropolitan Wichita"; Porter, *Wichita*.

34. Georg Simmel, "The Metropolis and Modern Life," in *Georg Simmel on Individuality and Social Forms*, ed. Donald Levine (Chicago: University of Chicago Press, 1971), 324.

35. Louis Wirth, "Urbanism as a Way of Life," *American Journal of Sociology* 44, no. 1 (1938): 1–24, 7.

36. Herbert J. Gans, "Urbanism and Suburbanism as Ways of Life: A Reevaluation of Definitions," in *People, Plans, and Policies* (New York: Columbia University Press, 1991), 52.

37. Ernest W. Burgess, "The Growth of the City: An Introduction to a Research Project," in *The City*, by Robert E. Park, Ernest W. Burgess, and Roderick D. McKenzie (Chicago: University of Chicago Press, 1925), 47.

38. Chauncy D. Harris and Edward L. Ullman, "The Nature of Cities," *Annals of the American Academy of Political and Social Science* 242 (1945): 7–17, 7.

39. Brian J. L. Berry, "Cities as Systems Within Systems of Cities," *Papers in Regional Science* 13, no. 1 (1964): 147–163.

40. Walter J. Nicholls, "The Los Angeles School: Difference, Politics, City," *International Journal of Urban and Regional Research* 35, no. 1 (2011): 189–206.

41. Michael Dear, "Los Angeles and the Chicago School: Invitation to a Debate," *City & Community* 1, no. 1 (2002): 5–32, 16–17; emphasis in original.

42. The diffusion of patterns of development across cities presents a notable example of "institutional isomorphism." Introduced into the sociology of organizations by the leading proponent of the human ecology perspective, Amos Hawley, isomorphism refers to the tendency of organizational structures to take on similar forms when situated within similar sets of social and environmental constraints and pressures. It was the landmark 1983 article by Paul DiMaggio and Walter Powell, "The Iron Cage Revisited," that cemented the place of "institutional isomorphism" in the pantheon of sociological concepts. Noting that bureaucratic organizations have a tendency over time to increasingly resemble one another in terms of structural form, orientation, and actions, DiMaggio and Powell deployed the idea of institutional isomorphism to explain the processes through which this progressive similarity occurs. They identified three mechanisms furthering the process of isomorphism: *coercive* pressures brought to bear on organizations by other organizations upon which they depend for resources; *normative* pressures that stem from the increasingly homogenized professionalization norms adopted by the staff members of bureaucratic firms, many of whom are trained using similar curricula across the same set of professional schools within contemporary universities; and *mimetic* pressures, through which organizations attempt to deal with difficult or novel problems which they have never before encountered by modeling their responses on strategies undertaken by other organizations that they view as peers. In the face of ambiguity or uncertainty, *mimesis* (in other words, replicating "best practices") is often a rational response for an organization, even if the peer organizations that are copied have not demonstrated convincingly that they are any more adept at solving the problem in question: "Organizations tend to model themselves after similar organizations in their field that

they perceive to be more legitimate or successful," they wrote. "The ubiquity of certain kinds of structural arrangements can more likely be credited to the universality of mimetic processes than to any concrete evidence that the adopted models enhance efficiency." When replicated and aggregated, mimetic isomorphism leads to a growing sameness that diffuses across organizational fields—including, importantly for my purposes here, contemporary urban governance bureaucracies.

While the coercive and normative pressures that DiMaggio and Powell identified certainly affect the structure of urban governance and placemaking today, it is this process of mimesis—cities' tendency to turn (often uncritically) to the examples of peers in order to formulate their own development strategies—that best characterizes the organizational diffusion of trends of imitation across cities that I describe here. See Amos Hawley, "Human Ecology," in *International Encyclopedia of the Social Sciences*, ed. David L. Sills (New York: Macmillan, 1968), 328; Michael T. Hannan and John Freeman, "The Population Ecology of Organizations," *American Journal of Sociology* 82, no. 5 (1977): 929–964; Paul J. DiMaggio and Walter W. Powell, "The Iron Cage Revisited: Institutional Isomorphism and Collective Rationality in Organizational Fields," *American Sociological Review* 48, no. 2 (1983): 147–160. The quotation above can be found on p. 152.

43. Lewis Mumford, *The City in History: Its Transformations, and Its Prospects* (New York: Harcourt, Brace, 1961), 506.

44. See, among others, Jane Jacobs, *The Death and Life of Great American Cities* (New York: Random House, 1961); David Riesman, with Nathan Glazer and Reuel Denney, *The Lonely Crowd: A Study of the Changing American Character* (New Haven, CT: Yale University Press, 1961); C. Wright Mills, *White Collar: The American Middle Classes* (New York: Oxford University Press, 1951); Kenneth T. Jackson, *Crabgrass Frontier: The Suburbanization of the United States* (New York: Oxford University Press, 1985); but see Gans, "Urbanism and Suburbanism as Ways of Life" for an alternative approach that expresses skepticism toward the antisuburban stance of many twentieth century critics.

45. See Sharon Zukin, "Gentrification: Culture and Capital in the Urban Core," *Annual Review of Sociology* 13 (1987): 129–147; Chase M. Billingham, "The Broadening Conception of Gentrification: Recent Developments and Avenues for Future Inquiry in the Sociological Study of Urban Change," *Michigan Sociological Review* 29 (2015): 75–102.

46. Billingham, "Broadening Conception of Gentrification"; Loretta Lees, Tom Slater, and Elvin Wyly, *Gentrification* (New York: Routledge, 2008).

47. Japonica Brown-Saracino, ed., *The Gentrification Debates* (New York: Routledge, 2010). Indeed, a search for the term "gentrification" in the Google

Books Ngram Viewer (a crude source, admittedly, but a commonly cited one that provides at least a suggestive glance at current intellectual tendencies) demonstrates a plateauing of the usage of the term from the mid-1980s through the mid-1990s, followed by a steep and monotonic increase in the ensuing three decades, rising more than 600 percent in terms of the frequency of usage in books over the first two decades of the current century. This trend can be viewed at https://books.google.com/ngrams/graph?content=gentrification&year_start=1960&year_end=2022&corpus=en&smoothing=0.

48. Sharon Zukin, *Naked City: The Death and Life of Authentic Urban Places* (New York: Oxford University Press, 2010), xi.

49. Kenneth Frampton, "Towards a Critical Regionalism: Six Points for an Architecture of Resistance," in *Postmodern Culture*, ed. Hal Foster (London: Pluto, 1985), 16.

50. Li Wen, "Can Local Architecture Help Cure the Ills of Globalism?," *Metropolis*, October 12, 2022, https://metropolismag.com/viewpoints/can-local-architecture-help-cure-the-ills-of-globalism/.

51. Patrick Sisson, "Why Do All New Apartment Buildings Look the Same?," *Curbed*, December 4, 2018, https://archive.curbed.com/2018/12/4/18125536/real-estate-modern-apartment-architecture.

52. Kriston Capps, "The Problem With 'Fast-Casual Architecture,'" *Bloomberg*, October 17, 2017, https://www.bloomberg.com/news/articles/2017-10-17/washington-d-c-s-wharf-is-fast-casual-design-so; Anna Kodé, "America, the Bland," *New York Times*, January 20, 2023, https://www.nytimes.com/2023/01/20/realestate/housing-developments-city-architecture.html; Coby Lefkowitz, "Why Everywhere Looks the Same," *Medium*, April 28, 2021, https://marker.medium.com/why-everywhere-looks-the-same-248940f12c4. For a discussion of how this trend has manifested itself in one city, see David Ross Scheer, "Why Do All the New Apartment Buildings Look the Same (and Do They Have To)?," *Salt Lake Tribune,* April 5, 2020, https://www.sltrib.com/artsliving/2020/04/05/david-ross-scheer-why-do/.

53. Jason Hackworth, *The Neoliberal City: Governance, Ideology, and Development in American Urbanism* (Ithaca, NY: Cornell University Press, 2007); Jamie Peck and Adam Tickell, "Neoliberalizing Space," *Antipode* 34, no. 3 (2002): 380–404; Jamie Peck, "Austerity Urbanism: American Cities Under Extreme Economy," *City* 16, no. 6 (2012): 626–655; Kevin Fox Gotham, "Creating Liquidity out of Spatial Fixity: The Secondary Circuit of Capital and the Subprime Mortgage Crisis," *International Journal of Urban and Regional Research* 33, no. 2 (2009): 355–371.

54. Rachel Weber and Sara O'Neill-Kohl, "The Historical Roots of Tax Increment Financing, or How Real Estate Consultants Kept Urban Renewal Alive,"

Economic Development Quarterly 27, no. 3 (2013): 193–207; Rachel Weber, "Selling City Futures: The Financialization of Urban Redevelopment Policy, *Economic Geography*, 86, no. 3 (2010): 251–274; Craig L. Johnson and Kenneth A. Kriz, eds., *Tax Increment Financing and Economic Development: Uses, Structures, and Impact*, 2nd ed. (Albany: State University of New York Press, 2019).

55. Nicole P. Marwell, Delia Baldassari, and Erez Arahon Marantz, "The Microrelations of Urban Governance: Dynamics of Patronage and Partnership," *American Journal of Sociology* 125, no. 6 (2020): 1559–1601. See also Nicole P. Marwell and Shannon L. Morrissey, "Organizations and the Governance of Urban Poverty," *Annual Review of Sociology* 46 (2020): 233–250; Nicole P. Marwell, "Privatizing the Welfare State: Nonprofit Community-Based Organizations as Political Actors," *American Sociological Review* 69, no. 2 (2004): 265–291; Nicole P. Marwell, *Bargaining for Brooklyn: Community Organizations in the Entrepreneurial City* (Chicago: University of Chicago Press, 2007). For more on public-private partnerships, see Hackworth, *Neoliberal City*.

56. Josh Pacewicz, "Playing the Neoliberal Game: Why Community Leaders Left Party Politics to Partisan Activists," *American Journal of Sociology* 121, no. 3 (2015): 826–881; Josh Pacewicz, *Partisans and Partners: The Politics of the Post-Keynesian Society* (Chicago: University of Chicago Press, 2016).

57. Darran Anderson, "Why Every City Feels the Same Now," *Atlantic*, August 24, 2020, https://www.theatlantic.com/technology/archive/2020/08/why-every-city-feels-same-now/615556/.

58. Harvey L. Molotch, "Toward a More Human Human Ecology: An Urban Research Strategy," *Land Economics* 43, no. 3 (1967): 336–341.

59. Harvey Molotch, "The City as a Growth Machine: Toward a Political Economy of Place," *American Journal of Sociology* 82, no. 2 (1976): 309–332; see also John R. Logan and Harvey L. Molotch, *Urban Fortunes: The Political Economy of Place* (Berkeley: University of California Press, 1987).

60. David Harvey, "From Managerialism to Entrepreneurialism: The Transformation in Urban Governance in Late Capitalism," *Geografiska Annaler* 71, no. 1 (1989): 3–17.

61. Richard Florida, *The Rise of the Creative Class: And How It's Transforming Work, Leisure, Community and Everyday Life* (New York: Basic Books, 2003). See also Richard Florida, "Cities and the Creative Class," *City & Community* 2, no. 1 (2003): 3–19.

62. Florida, "Cities and the Creative Class," 10.

63. For a recent example of efforts along these lines in the Capital Region of upstate New York, see David A. Banks, *The City Authentic: How the Attention Economy Builds Urban America* (Berkeley: University of California Press, 2023). See also Connolly, *After the Factory*.

64. Terry Nichols Clark, with Richard Lloyd, Kenneth K. Wong, and Pushpam Jain, "Amenities Drive Urban Growth," *Journal of Urban Affairs* 24, no. 5 (2002): 493–515.

65. Edward Glaeser, *Triumph of the City: How Our Greatest Invention Makes Us Richer, Smarter, Greener, Healthier, and Happier* (New York: Penguin Books, 2011), 10.

66. Glaeser, *Triumph of the City*, 11.

67. Saskia Sassen, *The Global City: New York, London, Tokyo* (Princeton, NJ: Princeton University Press, 2002).

68. Peter Marcuse and Ronald van Kempen, "Conclusion: A Changed Spatial Order," in *Globalizing Cities: A New Spatial Order?*, ed. Peter Marcuse and Ronald van Kempen (Malden, MA: Blackwell, 2000), 249. Russell Arben Fox, a political scientist and urban theorist who provides regular commentaries on local affairs in Wichita, has introduced the term "mittelpolitanism" to refer to the struggles facing smaller and midsized metropolitan regions in the age of globalization. For his essays on mittelpolitanism, see Russell Arben Fox, *On Wichita, the Mittelpolitan, and More*, https://mittelpolitan.substack.com/.

2. Selling a Dream of Wichita's Future

1. One set of rankings which Wichita perennially tops is the annual assessment of the severity of allergens across US cities. The Asthma and Allergy Foundation of America has identified Wichita as the "#1 Allergy Capital" in the United States for three straight years. See Asthma and Allergy Foundation of America, *2025 Allergy Capitals: The Most Challenging Places to Live with Allergies* (2025), https://aafa.org/wp-content/uploads/2025/03/aafa-2025-allergy-capitals-report.pdf.

2. Willa Cather, *My Antonía* (New York: Houghton Mifflin, 1918), 1.

3. H. Craig Miner, *Wichita: The Early Years, 1865–80* (Lincoln: University of Nebraska Press, 1982), x. For an insightful evaluation of how geography, topography, and climate combined to set the stage for Kansas's development, see Craig Miner, *Kansas: The History of the Sunflower State, 1854–2000* (Lawrence: University Press of Kansas, 2002), 19–33.

4. I am indebted to Jay Price, one of the great chroniclers of Wichita's history, for raising this question and using it as a jumping-off point for profound ruminations on the city's past and its current identity during personal conversations over the past several years.

5. Stan Hoig, *Cowtown Wichita and the Wild, Wicked West* (Albuquerque: University of New Mexico Press, 2007). For an immersive journey along the upper Arkansas River, examining the settlements and cultures that it nourishes from

Leadville, Colorado, to Arkansas City, Kansas, see Max McCoy, *Elevations: A Personal Exploration of the Arkansas River* (Lawrence: University Press of Kansas, 2018).

6. Miner, *Wichita: The Early Years*; Hoig, *Cowtown Wichita.*

7. Miner, *Wichita: The Early Years*, 56.

8. Craig Miner, *Wichita: The Magic City* (Wichita, KS: Wichita-Sedgwick County Historical Museum Association, 1988); Jimmy M. Skaggs, "Wichita, Kansas: Economic Origins of Metropolitan Development, 1870–1960," in *Metropolitan Wichita: Past, Present, and Future*, ed. Glenn W. Miller and Jimmy M. Skaggs (Lawrence: Regents Press of Kansas, 1978), 4–21; Hugh G. Bevans, *Water Resources of Sedgwick County, Kansas* (Lawrence, KS: US Geological Survey, 1989). However, water from the Little Arkansas River has been used in the twenty-first century to recharge the depleted Equus Beds. Moreover, the city does use the Arkansas River as its main destination for releasing treated sewage. See Kansas Water Science Center, "Equus Beds Aquifer Storage and Recovery (ASR) Project," USGS, March 28, 2025, https://www.usgs.gov/centers/kansas-water-science-center/science/equus-beds-recharge-project; "How Wichita Runs Water," City of Wichita, accessed June 14, 2025, https://www.wichita.gov/DocumentCenter/View/11801/How-Our-Current-Water-Facility-Operates-PDF.

9. Skaggs, "Wichita, Kansas," 16.

10. If anything, the river served as a consistent threat and nuisance for the city. Destructive floods inundated Wichita in 1877, 1904, 1923, and 1944, finally prompting the execution of one of the most ambitious public works projects in the city's history. In collaboration with the US Army Corps of Engineers, the city constructed a floodway to divert flood waters from the Arkansas River, the Little Arkansas River, and Chisolm Creek. This new floodway began at a point north of Wichita, winding around the city's west side before emptying back into the Arkansas south of the city. Nicknamed the "Big Ditch," this canal has prevented major floods within the city since its completion in 1957. See David Guilliams, "The Big Ditch: The Wichita-Valley Center Flood Control Project," *Fairmount Folio: Journal of History* 2 (1998): 29–40.

11. Miner, *Wichita: The Magic City*, 201–204; Celeste Bogart Racette, "Century II Performing Arts and Convention Center," National Register of Historic Places Registration Form (Washington, DC: US Department of the Interior, 2019), https://www.kshs.org/resource/national_register/nominationsNRDB/KS_SedgwickCounty_CenturyIIPerformingArts&ConventionCenter_Listed_10022020.pdf.

12. M. Christine Boyer, "Cities for Sale: Merchandising History at South Street Seaport," in *Variations on a Theme Park: The New American City and the*

End of Public Space, ed. Michael Sorkin (New York: Hill and Wang, 1992), 198; Pierce F. Lewis, *New Orleans: The Making of an Urban Landscape* (Santa Fe, NM: Center for American Places, 2003); John Tierney, "How Green Riverfronts Transformed Pittsburgh," *Atlantic*, November 20, 2014, https://www.theatlantic.com/national/archive/2014/11/how-green-riverfronts-transformed-pittsburgh/382928/.

13. On the development of Old Town and Wichita's mid-century doldrums, see Chase M. Billingham, "Waiting for Bobos: Displacement and Impeded Gentrification in a Midwestern City," *City & Community* 16, no. 2 (2017): 145–168; Chase M. Billingham, "Urban Renewal, Homelessness, and the Birth and Death of Wichita's Naftzger Park," *Kansas History: A Journal of the Central Plains* 42, no. 4 (2019/2020): 270–291.

14. Forrest S. Gossett, "Grateful DeBoer Expresses Thanks with River Plans," *Wichita Eagle*, May 27, 1990, 1A.

15. PBS Kansas, "One on One with Victor Hogstrom," February 27, 2018, YouTube, 28:35, youtu.be/_04IH4F768s.

16. "Jack DeBoer," Conrad N. Hilton College of Global Hospitality Leadership, University of Houston, accessed June 14, 2025, https://www.uh.edu/hilton-college/About/Hospitality-Industry-Hall-of-Honor/Inductees/Jack-Deboer/; Carrie Rengers, "Wichita Hotel Pioneer with a Zest for Business and Adventure Dies at 90," *Wichita Eagle*, March 13, 2021, https://www.kansas.com/news/business/biz-columns-blogs/carrie-rengers/article249915968.html; Jack DeBoer, *Risk Only Money: Success in Business Without Risking Family, Friends, and Reputation* (Kansas City, MO: Rockhill Books, 2011).

17. RTKL Planning Team, *Development Plan for Downtown Wichita* (1989), 3, https://downtownwichita.org/user/file/DwntwnDevPlan1989linked.pdf.

18. RTKL Planning Team, *Downtown Plan*, 6–7; Alissa Rubin, "City Plan Focuses on River," *Wichita Eagle-Beacon*, May 25, 1988, 1A.

19. Rubin, "City Plan Focuses on River."

20. Susan Freinkel, "Leave West Bank Wide Open, Wichita Park Director Urges," *Wichita Eagle-Beacon*, May 26, 1988, 14D.

21. Jim Cross, "William Project Endorsed," *Wichita Eagle-Beacon*, May 5, 1989, 1D.

22. Bill Hirschman, "DeBoer New Chief of Downtown Group," *Wichita Eagle-Beacon*, March 29, 1989, 10A.

23. Jim Cross, "Master Plan for Revival," *Wichita Eagle*, October 25, 1989, 1A; Gossett, "Grateful DeBoer Expresses Thanks."

24. Cross, "Master Plan for Revival."

25. Jim Cross, "Let Voters Decide," *Wichita Eagle*, January 4, 1990, 1D; "Downtown Group Reports," *Wichita Eagle*, January 19, 1990, 3D; Jim Cross,

"Downtown Pooh-Bahs Ponder Agency to Buy, Raze," *Wichita Eagle*, February 27, 1990, 1A.

26. Ruffin, who scoffed at the idea of the riverfront hotel during the planning stages in the early 1990s, would end up buying the completed hotel at a bargain price a quarter century later.

27. Jim Cross, "WI/SE Intends to Put Up, Not Shut Up," *Wichita Eagle*, March 4, 1990, 1A.

28. Stan Finger, "City Gets Rollin' on the River," *Wichita Eagle*, March 28, 1990, 1A.

29. Jim Cross, "DeBoer Thinking Big for Downtown," *Wichita Eagle*, May 16, 1990, 1A; Jim Cross, "County Opposes New Arena," *Wichita Eagle*, May 22, 1990, 1D; Stan Finger, "WI/SE Seeks Assurances on Coliseum," *Wichita Eagle*, June 2, 1990, 1D.

30. For more on the history, construction, and cultural resonance of *The Keeper of the Plains*, see Loren Ryher, "Sculpture Portrays Heritage," *Wichita Beacon*, May 12, 1974, 5B; Bud Norman, "Keeper of the Plains," *Wichita Eagle*, May 27, 1990, 1B.

31. Cross, "DeBoer Thinking Big for Downtown"; Jim Cross, "Blackbear Bosin Would've Been Proud," *Wichita Eagle*, May 18, 1990, 1A.

32. Jim Cross, "DeBoer's Plan to Get Public Airing," *Wichita Eagle*, May 20, 1990, 3B; Jim Cross, "Ante Is High, Cards Are on the Table, DeBoer Says," *Wichita Eagle*, May 24, 1990, 1A.

33. Cross, "Ante Is High." (The Statue of Liberty is actually 305 feet tall, not 300.)

34. Judy Lundstrom Thomas, "Ambitious Plan Rises from Ashes of Lessons," *Wichita Eagle*, May 24, 1990, 8A; Al Polczinski, "State Looks Downtown for Offices," *Wichita Eagle*, June 5, 1990, 1A.

35. Judy Lundstrom Thomas, "Downtown Developers Take Show on the Road," *Wichita Eagle*, May 24, 1990, 14A.

36. Maurice Terrebonne, "Gilbert-Mosley Groundwater Contamination Site, City of Wichita, Kansas" (master's thesis, Wichita State University, 1990); Susan Rosegrant, "Wichita Confronts Contamination," in *Public Administration: Concepts and Cases*, 6th ed., ed. Richard J. Stillman II (Boston: Houghton Mifflin, 1996), 148–154; Jean Hays, "Bank Sues Coleman, Charging Pollution," *Wichita Eagle*, February 7, 1990, 3D.

37. Terrebonne, "Gilbert-Mosley Groundwater Contamination Site"; David R. Tripp, "Wichita Strikes Back at the Blob: Municipal Liability Under CERCLA and How One City Solved Ground Water Problems and Rejuvenated Its Declining Tax Base," *Toxics Law Reporter* 6 (1991): 130–136; Mark Glaser, "Economic and Environmental Repair in the Shadow of Superfund: Local Government

Leadership in Building Strategic Partnerships," *Economic Development Quarterly* 8, no. 4 (1994): 345–352.

38. Mark Glaser and Chris Cherches, "A Case for Aggressive Local Government Environmental Policy: Operating Under the Threat of Superfund," *National Civic Review* 80 (1991): 169–174; Tripp, "Wichita Strikes Back at the Blob"; Jean Hays, "Pollution Puzzle May Scuttle Downtown Development," *Wichita Eagle*, August 27, 1990, 1A.

39. Richard Briffault, "The Most Popular Tool: Tax Increment Financing and the Political Economy of Local Government," *University of Chicago Law Review* 77, no. 1 (2010): 66–95; Rachel Weber and Sara O'Neill-Kohl, "The Historical Roots of Tax Increment Financing, or How Real Estate Consultants Kept Urban Renewal Alive," *Economic Development Quarterly* 27, no. 3 (2013): 193–207.

40. Glaser and Cherches, "Case for Aggressive Local Government Environmental Policy."

41. The city's TIF plan was itself beset by delays, lawsuits, and cost overruns from the beginning, however. Although the TIF plan was approved in 1991, the cleanup did not actually begin for another decade, and while the TIF district was originally scheduled to operate through 2011 and then expire, it was renewed for another ten years to account for all of the delays and cost overruns; it did not expire until 2021. It is expected that the groundwater cleanup will take several more decades to complete.

42. Glaser and Cherches, "Case for Aggressive Local Government Environmental Policy," 171.

43. Jim Cross, "Downtown Plan Hits Turbulence," *Wichita Eagle*, June 6, 1990, 1A; Jim Cross, "Pollution Liability Scares off Investors," *Wichita Eagle*, June 6, 1990, 1A; Jean Hays, "Pollution Puzzle May Scuttle Downtown Development," *Wichita Eagle*, August 27, 1990, 1A; Jim Cross, "Plan Has Tax Board's Blessing," *Wichita Eagle*, September 16, 1990, 1B.

44. Jim Cross, "City Can't Afford to Pass This Buck, DeBoer Says," *Wichita Eagle*, June 8, 1990, 1D; Jim Cross, "Pressing on Public Support for Downtown Plan," *Wichita Eagle*, June 18, 1990, 1A; Jim Cross, "Optimistic DeBoer Stares Down the Skeptics," *Wichita Eagle*, June 21, 1990, 1D; Lauretta McMillen, "Committee's Task: Find Tenants," *Wichita Eagle*, July 2, 1990, 1A.

45. Jim Cross, "Feisty DeBoer Digs In," *Wichita Eagle*, June 22, 1990, 1D; Jim Cross, "DeBoer Must Shield Plan's Achilles Heel," *Wichita Eagle*, June 24, 1990, 1A.

46. Jim Cross, "Heat Is on DeBoer at Town Meeting," *Wichita Eagle*, June 26, 1990, 1D; Jim Cross, "Old, Poor Don't Understand Downtown 'Fantasy,' McCray Says," *Wichita Eagle*, July 3, 1990, 1D.

47. Jim Cross, "City to Study DeBoer Plan," *Wichita Eagle*, June 27, 1990, 1D;

Jim Cross, "City's Hope for Tax Cuts Killed by Financial Woes," *Wichita Eagle*, July 11, 1990, 1D; Jim Cross, "Downtown Plan Favored in Poll," *Wichita Eagle*, July 26, 1990, 1A.

48. John R. Engen, "Coleman Officials Trim List of Office Sites to 3," *Wichita Eagle*, June 27, 1990, 1A; Jim Cross, "Boy Scouts Prepared to Build Downtown Headquarters," *Wichita Eagle*, August 23, 1990, 1D. I return to the travails of the Epic Center in chapter 4.

49. Jim Cross, "Farmers Market Deal Near," *Wichita Eagle*, June 30, 1990, 1D; Al Polczinski, "County Approves Money for Downtown Market," *Wichita Eagle*, September 13, 1990, 1A.

50. Jim Cross, "All Aboard," *Wichita Eagle*, July 2, 1990, 1A; Jim Cross, "Call Goes Out for Agency to Lead Downtown Effort," *Wichita Eagle*, July 6, 1990, 1D.

51. Jim Cross, "Hotel Builder to Show Plans for Riverbank," *Wichita Eagle*, July 22, 1990, 1B.

52. Jim Cross, "It's Time to Check In," *Wichita Eagle*, August 1, 1990, 1A; Jim Cross, "DeBoer: New Hotel Needs No Freebies," *Wichita Eagle*, August 2, 1990, 1D; Jim Cross, "Downtown Plan Won't Supply Hotel's Needs," *Wichita Eagle*, August 3, 1990, 3D.

53. Jim Lynn, "Officials to Hatch Downtown Financing Plan," *Wichita Eagle*, November 15, 1990, 1D.

54. Jim Lynn, "One for Downtown," *Wichita Eagle*, November 17, 1990, 1A; Nickie Flynn, "Council Will Make Call on Downtown," *Wichita Eagle*, December 19, 1990, 1D.

55. Jim Lynn, "Downtown Looming Large over Coming City Elections," *Wichita Eagle*, November 18, 1990, 1A; Jim Lynn, "Legislators Balk at Downtown Tax," *Wichita Eagle*, December 20, 1990, 3D.

56. Jim Lynn, "Hotel Is Hotly Debated Piece of Wichita's Downtown," *Wichita Eagle*, November 24, 1990, 4D; Jim Cross, "Downtown Boosters Are Stalking Big Game," *Wichita Eagle*, January 30, 1991, 1D; Jim Cross, "Pledges to Help City Core," *Wichita Eagle*, February 1, 1991, 1D.

57. Jim Lynn, "In a Word, the Key to City Elections Is 'Downtown,'" *Wichita Eagle*, January 21, 1991, 1C; Jim Cross, "Downtown Dominates in Campaign for Mayor," *Wichita Eagle*, February 3, 1991, 1B; Jim Lynn, "Mayor Outdistances Challengers in Campaign Fund," *Wichita Eagle*, February 20, 1991, 3D.

58. Nickie Flynn, "Mayor Doesn't See Giant Keeper on Horizon," *Wichita Eagle*, March 8, 1991, 1A.

59. Jim Cross, "Martinez, Ferris Clash over Residency, Downtown," *Wichita Eagle*, March 12, 1991, 3D; Jim Cross, "Group Wants to Debate Downtown Reformers," *Wichita Eagle*, March 13, 1991, 3D; Jim Lynn, "Taxes Concern Many in the 2nd District," *Wichita Eagle*, March 25, 1991, 1C.

60. Bill Hirschman, "Kamen Retains 2nd District Seat," *Wichita Eagle*, April 3, 1991, 10A; Jim Lynn, "Downtown Debate Changes Course," *Wichita Eagle*, April 4, 1991, 1D.

61. "DeBoer, Weary of Naysaying, Pushes City," *Wichita Eagle*, May 1, 1991, 1A; Jim Lynn, "Politicians Point Fingers Back at DeBoer," *Wichita Eagle*, May 2, 1991, 1A; Bob Cox, "DeBoer: Move It or Lose It," *Wichita Eagle*, May 3, 1991, 1A.

62. Cox, "DeBoer: Move It or Lose It"; Jim Cross, "Rethinking Downtown," *Wichita Eagle*, May 23, 1991, 1A; Jim Lynn, "Give-and-Take Is in the Air," *Wichita Eagle*, May 4, 1991, 1D; Jim Lynn, "Downtown Debate Takes Turn," *Wichita Eagle*, May 14, 1991, 1D.

63. Jean Hays, "Gentry Limited Considers Bailing Out of Downtown," *Wichita Eagle*, May 31, 1991, 1A; Jim Lynn, "Mayor Wants Council to Reach Consensus on Downtown," *Wichita Eagle*, June 7, 1991, 1D; Jim Lynn, "Downtown Forum Vents Anger," *Wichita Eagle*, June 17, 1991, 1C.

64. Jim Lynn, "Knight Looking for a Showdown on Downtown," *Wichita Eagle*, June 24, 1991, 1A; Jim Lynn, "Knight Now Willing to Fix Downtown One Step at a Time," *Wichita Eagle*, June 25, 1991, 1A; Jim Lynn, "Council Knocks Downtown Revitalization," *Wichita Eagle*, June 26, 1991, 1A.

65. Jim Lynn, "City Has Less Money to Offer Downtown," *Wichita Eagle*, July 2, 1991, 1D; Jim Cross, "Council Gears Up for OT," *Wichita Eagle*, July 3, 1991, 1D; Jim Lynn, "Council Invites Public to Join Debate," *Wichita Eagle*, July 11, 1991, 1A; Jim Lynn, "Reluctant Taxpayers Weigh In on Downtown," *Wichita Eagle*, July 12, 1991, 1A; Jim Lynn, "Council Gives Signal to Start on Downtown," *Wichita Eagle*, July 17, 1991, 1A.

66. Jim Lynn, "Hotel Would Pay for Itself, Official Says," *Wichita Eagle*, July 19, 1991, 1A; Jim Lynn, "Council Endorses Bonds for Hotel," *Wichita Eagle*, July 24, 1991, 1A.

67. Bob Stratton, "Riverside Residents Oppose Park Plan," *Wichita Eagle*, September 20, 1990, 3N; Jim Lynn, "McLean Closing on Back Burner," *Wichita Eagle*, July 31, 1991, 1D.

68. Jim Lynn, "Museum Work Hinges on Endowment," *Wichita Eagle*, August 2, 1991, 1A.

69. Jim Lynn, "City Rejects Towering Keeper," *Wichita Eagle*, August 7, 1991, 1A.

70. Jim Lynn, "Arena, Ice Rink Proposals Stir Emotions," *Wichita Eagle*, August 9, 1991, 1A; Jim Lynn, "Council Detours McLean Issue, Backs Proposals," *Wichita Eagle*, August 14, 1991, 1D; Jim Lynn, "Trolleys May Roll, If Price Is Right," *Wichita Eagle*, August 16, 1991, 1A; Jim Lynn, "Money the Next Turn in Downtown Debate," *Wichita Eagle*, August 21, 1991, 3D.

71. Jim Lynn, "Compromise over McLean Wins Raves," *Wichita Eagle*, Au-

gust 23, 1991, 1A; Jim Lynn, "Council Clears the Path for Rerouting of McLean," *Wichita Eagle*, August 28, 1991, 1D.

72. Jim Lynn, "Downtown Off and Running," *Wichita Eagle*, September 5, 1991, 1A.

73. Jim Cross, "Downtown Cash, Strings Go Together," *Wichita Eagle*, October 8, 1991, 1A; Jim Cross, "Business Leaders Grow Wary," *Wichita Eagle*, October 13, 1991, 1A.

74. Suzanne Perez, "Full Steam Ahead," *Wichita Eagle*, February 9, 1992, 1B; Jim Cross, "Deadline Time for Business," *Wichita Eagle*, February 28, 1992, 1A; Suzanne Perez, "Wichita Mayor Welcomes Successes as They Come," *Wichita Eagle*, February 23, 1992, 7L.

75. Jim Cross, "Another Crossroads for Downtown," *Wichita Eagle*, March 30, 1992, 1A; Suzanne Perez, "Alford Rings WI/SE Alarm," *Wichita Eagle*, April 3, 1992, 1D.

76. Jim Cross, "WI/SE Moves to Reclaim Its Downtown Role," *Wichita Eagle*, May 8, 1992, 1D; Jim Cross, "Downtown Gets Down to Business," *Wichita Eagle*, November 16, 1992, 1A.

77. Suzanne Perez, "Downtown Hotel Returns for Debate," *Wichita Eagle*, June 23, 1992, 1A.

78. Perez, "Downtown Hotel Returns for Debate"; Suzanne Perez, "Downtown Casino Gets City Officials' Attention," *Wichita Eagle*, June 24, 1992, 1D.

79. Suzanne Perez, "Vision for a Bettor Downtown," *Wichita Eagle*, July 6, 1992, 1A; Suzanne Perez, "Is a Casino in the County a Sure Thing?," *Wichita Eagle*, July 20, 1992, 1A; Suzanne Perez, "Knight Doesn't Like Downtown Casino Plan," *Wichita Eagle*, July 21, 1992, 1D; Suzanne Perez, "68 Percent of Wichitans Back Hotel-Casino," *Wichita Eagle*, July 22, 1992, 1D; Jim Cross, "Kassebaum, Haines Say No to Casino," *Wichita Eagle*, August 4, 1992, 1A; Suzanne Perez, "Glickman Noncommittal on Casino," *Wichita Eagle*, August 15, 1992, 3D; Jim Cross, "Glickman, Yost Blast Casino Plan," *Wichita Eagle*, October 22, 1992, 1D.

80. Julie Wright, "WI/SE Group Will Study Downtown Hotel Options," *Wichita Eagle*, August 7, 1992, 1D; Suzanne Perez, "Casino Backers Threaten to Leave, Developers Say," *Wichita Eagle*, August 11, 1992, 1A; Suzanne Perez, "Casino—Opposition Says Put Issue to Public Vote," *Wichita Eagle*, August 25, 1992, 12D; Suzanne Perez, "Anti-Casino Group Gains Allies," *Wichita Eagle*, October 8, 1992, 1A; Suzanne Perez, "Race Is On for Betting Dollars," *Wichita Eagle*, September 28, 1992, 1A.

81. Suzanne Perez, "Kansas Tribe Opposes Casino," *Wichita Eagle*, August 14, 1992, 1A; Jim Cross, "Minnesota Indian Casinos Find Success," *Wichita Eagle*, September 6, 1992, 1A.

82. Suzanne Perez, "Casino Land Sale Decision Near," *Wichita Eagle*, October

31, 1992, 1D; Jennifer Comes, "Casino Foes Accuse Council of Rushing Deal," *Wichita Eagle*, November 2, 1992, 1C; Jim Cross, "Casino Opponents to Seek Injunction," *Wichita Eagle*, November 3, 1992, 1A.

83. Suzanne Perez, "Split Council Delays Vote on Sale of Land," *Wichita Eagle*, November 4, 1992, 1D; Suzanne Perez, "Newest Council Member Would Play Crucial Role," *Wichita Eagle*, November 5, 1992, 1A.

84. Suzanne Perez, "Aday Will Take Seat on Council," *Wichita Eagle*, November 11, 1992, 1A; Suzanne Perez, "Casino Foes Leave Nothing to Chance," *Wichita Eagle*, November 26, 1992, 1F.

85. Perez, "Casino Foes Leave Nothing to Chance"; Jim Cross, "Casino Developers Mulling Their Options," *Wichita Eagle*, January 7, 1993, 1A; Jim Cross, "Casino Foes Put Full-Court Press," *Wichita Eagle*, January 13, 1993, 1A; Jim Cross, "Downturn to Slow Downtown Revival," *Wichita Eagle*, February 21, 1993, 3J.

86. Jim Cross, "Endowment the Stumbling Block for Museums," *Wichita Eagle*, May 4, 1993, 1D.

87. Guy Bouton, "WI/SE a Part of History and a Guide for the Future," *Wichita Eagle*, September 29, 1996, 1B.

3. Removing Human Obstacles to Progress

1. Dion Lefler, "Naftzger Park to Close for Spaghetti Works Project," *Wichita Eagle*, May 11, 2018, 2A; "Naftzger Park Improvements Starting," KSN-TV, May 10, 2018, https://www.ksn.com/news/local/naftzger-park-improvements-starting/1171741523; Jacklyn Chappel, "Naftzger Park Set to Close at End of the Month," KAKE-TV, May 10, 2018, https://web.archive.org/web/20180514065220/http://www.kake.com/story/38165158/naftzger-park-set-to-close-at-end-of-the-month.

2. Chappel, "Naftzger Park Set to Close at End of the Month."

3. Neil Smith, *The New Urban Frontier: Gentrification and the Revanchist City* (New York: Routledge, 1996); Kevin Loughran, *Parks for Profit: Selling Nature in the City* (New York: Columbia University Press, 2022).

4. Dean Mosiman, "Madison Breaking Up Homeless Encampment at Reindahl Park," *Wisconsin State Journal*, December 8, 2021, https://madison.com/news/local/govt-and-politics/madison-breaking-up-homeless-encampment-at-reindahl-park/article_3da9eba2-f486-5545-866f-44a9951602a6.html; Aimee Hancock, "'Little Eden Park' Homeless Tent Camp Removed Near Wolf Creek in West Dayton," *Dayton Daily News*, July 19, 2024, https://www.daytondailynews.com/local/little-eden-park-homeless-tent-camp-removed-near-wolf-creek-in-west-dayton/EHQNM4J2PJHFRBPP5XL5PWPKOM/; Grace Benninghoff,

"Portland to Clear Homeless Encampment at Harbor View Memorial Park," *Portland Press Herald*, December 15, 2023, https://www.pressherald.com/2023/12/15/portland-to-clear-homeless-encampment-at-harbor-view-memorial-park/; Andres Gutierrez, "Kansas City, Missouri, Addresses Homeless Camp at Washington Square Park," KSHB, October 6, 2021, https://www.kshb.com/news/local-news/kansas-city-missouri-addresses-homeless-camp-at-washington-square-park.

5. For more information on the early history of Wichita, see H. Craig Miner, "Wichita in the Whirligig of Time, 1865–1910," in *Wichita: A Study in Preservation* (Oblinger-Smith Corporation, 1976), 1; H. Craig Miner, *Wichita: The Early Years* (Lincoln: University of Nebraska Press, 1982); O. H. Bentley, ed., *History of Wichita and Sedgwick County, Kansas*, vols. 1–2 (Chicago: C. F. Cooper, 1910); James R. Shortridge, *Cities on the Plains: The Evolution of Urban Kansas* (Lawrence: University Press of Kansas, 2004). For more information on Downtown Wichita's mid-century decline, see Craig Miner, *Wichita: The Magic City* (Wichita, KS: Wichita-Sedgwick County Historical Museum, 1988); Bob Hamrick, *Looking Back, Moving Forward: A Story of Wichita's Old Town* (Wichita, KS: Wichita Old Town Association, 2010).

6. Frank H. Backstrom, City Manager of Wichita, KS, memorandum to Wichita City Commission, February 13, 1958, City Commission Communication Series, CC 119, Ablah Library, Wichita State University; Jerry L. Cooper, *Urban Renewal* (Wichita, KS: Wichita Urban Renewal Agency, 1963); Robert Short, "Ken Kitchen's Vision Changed Face of City," *Wichita Eagle*, February 27, 1993, 4D.

7. Lew Townsend, "Douglas 'Blight' Appalls Agency," *Wichita Eagle*, January 9, 1967, 1A; "Redevelopment of East Douglas Sought by URA," *Wichita Eagle*, December 9, 1966, 1A.

8. Dale Daugherty, "East Douglas Top Problem," *Wichita Beacon*, September 23, 1968, 1A.

9. Lew Townsend, "Leader Is Key to Cleanup of East Douglas," *Wichita Eagle*, January 10, 1967, 1A; Townsend, "Douglas 'Blight' Appalls Agency"; Lew Townsend, "Blight-Area Improvements Dangle Until Landlords Know City Course," *Wichita Eagle*, January 12, 1967, 1A.

10. Townsend, "Leader Is Key."

11. Lew Townsend, "Healthy Boost for City's Treasury Seen in Renewal of East Douglas," *Wichita Eagle*, January 11, 1967, 1A; Townsend, "Blight-Area Improvements"; "Future of Douglas Area Questionable," *Wichita Beacon*, March 29, 1967, 4A; Lew Townsend, "Owners Worry, Few Offer Suggestions as Douglas Business Area Deteriorates," *Wichita Eagle*, January 13, 1967, 3A.

12. Townsend, "Douglas 'Blight' Appalls Agency"; Townsend, "Blight-Area Improvements."

13. "Wanted: Imagination for All of Downtown," *Wichita Beacon*, January 17, 1967, 8A.

14. "Owners on East Douglas to Discuss Rejuvenation," *Wichita Eagle*, March 23, 1967, 5A; "Future of Douglas Area Questionable," 4A.

15. "East Douglas Face-Lifting Bonus to City," *Wichita Sunday Eagle and The Wichita Beacon*, November 26, 1967, 1D; Daugherty, "East Douglas Top Problem."

16. Daugherty, "East Douglas Top Problem."

17. "Fourth National Hires Firm to Plan Hub Revitalization," *Wichita Eagle*, May 11, 1968, 1A; Jerry V. Williams, "Government Center Shift Unlikely," *Wichita Beacon*, July 18, 1968, 1A.

18. Daugherty, "East Douglas Top Problem"; Dale Daugherty, "E. Douglas Permanence Feeling Gone," *Wichita Beacon*, September 24, 1968, 1A.

19. Dale Daugherty, "Coleman Gains Time to Study Future," *Wichita Beacon*, September 25, 1968, 1A. After Coleman finally left its downtown location, the discovery of polluted groundwater beneath its abandoned factory triggered the Gilbert-Mosley groundwater crisis, which severely hampered downtown redevelopment efforts in the 1990s, as discussed in detail in chapter 2.

20. Dale Daugherty, "Way Opens to Skid Row's Renewal," *Wichita Beacon*, September 26, 1968, 1A; Pete Wittenberg, "Neighborhood Development Plan Is Approved over Bitter Protests," *Wichita Eagle*, January 1, 1969, 1A. For a concise history and assessment of Model Cities and other twentieth-century federal urban redevelopment initiatives, see Patrick Sharkey, *Stuck in Place: Urban Neighborhoods and the End of Progress Toward Racial Equality* (Chicago: University of Chicago Press, 2013).

21. Dolores Quinlisk, "Bid for Start on Midtown Renewal Set," *Wichita Eagle and Beacon*, April 4, 1970, 1A; Bruce Sankey, "Plan to Renew Center of City Gets New Push," *Wichita Eagle and Beacon*, May 30, 1971, 5A.

22. Bruce Sankey, "Commission Given Center City Plan," *Wichita Eagle*, August 23, 1972, 1A; Bruce Sankey, "Redevelopment of E. Douglas Urged," *Wichita Eagle*, April 27, 1972, 5A.

23. Sankey, "Commission Given Center City Plan"; "Center City," *Wichita Beacon*, August 24, 1972, 8A.

24. Charles Pearson, "Nearly Any Site Better Than the Parking Lot," *Wichita Eagle-Beacon*, March 31, 1974, 9C; "Shanahan Says E. Douglas Good Site for Art Museum," *Wichita Beacon*, March 14, 1974, 12C; Dorothy Belden, "It Hasn't Been Easy: Art Museum Has Grown into Refined Lady," *Wichita Eagle-Beacon*, October 23, 1977, 1E.

25. Don Wall and Betty Wells, "Do People Need a Skid Row?," *Wichita Beacon*, April 22, 1974, 1A.

26. Don Wall, "Shine Girls Better at Double-Talk, Sleight of Hand," *Wichita Beacon*, June 5, 1974, 1A.

27. Daugherty, "E. Douglas Permanence Feeling Gone"; Dorothy Belden, "The Last Rites for These Demised Premises," *Wichita Eagle*, October 2, 1977, 16D.

28. Craig Stock, "Proud 'Downtown Men' Aren't Drunks, Transients," *Wichita Beacon*, August 13, 1974, 1A.

29. Dale Daugherty, "URA Votes to Pursue E. Douglas Projects," *Wichita Eagle*, June 28, 1974, 1A; "Improving East Douglas," *Wichita Beacon*, July 3, 1974, 4A.

30. "Officials to Study Derelicts," *Wichita Eagle-Beacon*, May 31, 1975, 1A; "City Drunks Face Arrest," *Wichita Beacon*, June 10, 1975, 1A; "Facilities for Drunks Studied," *Wichita Beacon*, June 11, 1975, 8B; "It's Good News," *Wichita Beacon*, June 12, 1975, 4A.

31. "Some Good UR Goals," *Wichita Eagle-Beacon*, December 20, 1975, 2C; "Upgrading Downtown," *Wichita Beacon*, August 17, 1976, 4A; Terry Horne, "Wider Central Proposed," *Wichita Eagle*, December 24, 1976, 1C; Dolores Quinlisk, "Businesses Oppose Plan to Ban Parking," *Wichita Eagle*, December 23, 1976, 4D; "The Parking Problem," *Wichita Beacon*, December 27, 1976, 1C.

32. Gordon Atcheson, "New Old Look May Cost $800,000," *Wichita Eagle*, April 12, 1977, 16C.

33. Atcheson, "New Old Look May Cost $800,000," 16C; Dolores Quinlisk, "City Allocates $800,000 to Beautify E. Douglas," *Wichita Eagle*, April 27, 1977, 1C; Dolores Quinlisk, "URA Gives Go-Ahead for East Douglas Facelift," *Wichita Beacon*, May 13, 1977, 20B; "Capital Needed Now," *Wichita Beacon*, May 17, 1977, 4A.

34. Dolores Quinlisk, "East Douglas Renovation 'Beginning to Fall Together,'" *Wichita Beacon*, May 24, 1977, 1A.

35. Bob Getz, "On with the Face-Lift, Wichita," *Wichita Eagle*, October 28, 1977, 1B.

36. Terre Johnson, "Progress Upsets Lives of Skid Row Residents," *Wichita Eagle*, August 13, 1978, 1B.

37. Craig Stock, "URA Agrees to Fund Meetings on Transients," *Wichita Eagle*, October 13, 1978, 1C; Craig Stock, "Drifters Advertising Wichita's Improved E. Douglas," *Wichita Eagle*, June 29, 1979, 1C. For the results of the sociological study, see John W. Bardo, Jeffrey W. Riemer, Ronald R. Matson, and Robert K. Knapp, "The Social Ecology of Skid Row," *Sociological Spectrum* 1, no. 4 (1981): 415–428.

38. Stock, "Drifters Advertising Wichita's Improved E. Douglas"; Craig Stock, "Police: Skid Row Is Community's Problem," *Wichita Eagle*, July 13, 1979, 9A.

39. Ken Stephens, "Shops, Cops, Put Strings on 'Hanging Around,'" *Wichita Beacon*, March 9, 1979, 1A; Reg Fontenot, "East Douglas Ritual of Draggin' Cut in Half by Diverting Traffic," *Wichita Beacon*, May 15, 1979, 8C; Casey Scott, "Night Parking Ban on Douglas Cutting Crime, Officials Say," *Wichita Beacon*, May 22, 1979, 16B; Robbie Curry, "Graffiti Under the Overpass Spell Success for Big Board," *Wichita Beacon*, September 19, 1979, 8C.

40. "$100,000 Given for New Park" *Wichita Eagle-Beacon*, June 26, 1976, 1C. The Naftzgers were one of the oldest banking families in Wichita. L. S. Naftzger came to Wichita in 1886 after a previous banking career in Missouri. In 1892, L. S. Naftzger (along with J. M. Moore) purchased the Fourth National Bank of Wichita. Moore left the bank in 1908, and Naftzger served as president of the bank. In that year, his son, a young M. C. Naftzger, known as "Clif," was listed as an "assistant cashier" of the bank. After selling their interest in the Fourth National Bank (which would eventually be bought by Bank of America), the Naftzgers created a new one, the Southwest State Bank, which eventually became Southwest National Bank. Following the Great Depression and the death of L. S. Naftzger, M. C. Naftzger became president of the bank, a title he would hold for several decades. By the 1960s, M. C. Naftzger's son, John Naftzger, was the president of the Southwest National Bank. John Naftzger had been the key leader in the earliest discussions about East Douglas redevelopment in 1967. See L. S. Naftzger, "The Banks of Wichita," in *History of Wichita and Sedgwick County, Kansas*, vol. 1, ed. O. H. Bentley (Chicago: C. F. Cooper, 1910), 95–104; "History of Southwest National Bank," Southwest National Bank, https://www.southwestnb.com/our-history; "Owners on East Douglas to Discuss Rejuvenation," *Wichita Eagle*, March 23, 1967, 5A.

41. "Appropriate Tribute," *Wichita Beacon*, June 29, 1976, 12B; Dorothy Belden, "The Last Rites for These Demised Premises," *Wichita Eagle and Beacon*, October 2, 1977, 16D; Dolores Quinlisk, "URA Sets Aside Funds for East Douglas Park," *Wichita Eagle*, June 11, 1976, 1A.

42. Dolores Quinlisk, 1977, "URA Oks Razing of 'Army' Building," *Wichita Eagle*, November 11, 1977, 1C; "Victory Theater—The End," *Wichita Eagle*, December 7, 1977, 2D.

43. "Naftzger Park Plans OK'd," *Wichita Beacon*, June 27, 1978, 16B; Craig Stock, "URA Votes to Demolish Old Salvation Army Building," *Wichita Eagle*, April 27, 1979, 1D.

44. Bob Curtright, "Gift to All: Naftzger Park Honors a Giving Man," *Wichita Eagle-Beacon*, May 13, 1979, 5D; "Naftzger Park One Step Closer to Opening after Inspection," *Wichita Beacon*, June 13, 1979, 10A; Grant Overstake, "Problems Delay Naftzger Park Opening," *Wichita Eagle*, June 13, 1979, 12A.

45. Grant Overstake, "Naftzger Park to Be Unlocked Next Week," *Wichita Beacon*, June 6, 1979, 8C.

46. Bob Getz, "Looking for Depravity and Decay in Naftzger Park," *Wichita Eagle-Beacon*, August 26, 1979, 1E.

47. Frank Garofalo and Jack McNeely, "URA Probably Is Doomed as Independent City Agency," *Wichita Eagle*, February 29, 1980, 1A; Frank Garofalo, "City Gives URA Reins to Denton," *Wichita Eagle*, March 5, 1980, 1A; Short, "Ken Kitchen's Vision Changed Face of City." Kitchen retired shortly thereafter in 1982.

48. Elaine Vitt, "Developer Files Bankruptcy Plea," *Wichita Eagle-Beacon*, January 1, 1981, 1A; "Feds Reject Bid for Grant," *Wichita Eagle-Beacon*, January 1, 1981, 1A; "Downtown Revitalization Set Back," *Wichita Eagle-Beacon*, January 1, 1981, 1A; Angela Herrin, "Salvation Army Building Destroyed," *Wichita Eagle-Beacon*, January 1, 1981, 1A.

49. Elaine Vitt, "Old Town: 'Urban Pioneers' Are Trying to Give the Area New Life," *Wichita Eagle-Beacon*, February 2, 1981, 1A.

50. Vitt, "Old Town: 'Urban Pioneers.'"

51. On the history of the early Old Town pioneers, see Hamrick, *Looking Back, Moving Forward.*

52. "Market to Open Saturday," *Wichita Eagle*, August 25, 1976, 8A; "No 'Farm and Art' Market?," *Wichita Beacon*, April 27, 1979, 4A; Gordon M. Henry, "Successes Enhance Old Town's Dream," *Wichita Eagle-Beacon*, July 26, 1983, 4Z; Anne Valentine, "Old Warehouse to Get Facelift," *Wichita Eagle-Beacon*, June 9, 1984, 1D.

53. Jim Cross, "After Arresting Muggers, Police Jailed Victim, Too," *Wichita Eagle-Beacon*, October 6, 1982, 1A.

54. Michael Ginsberg, "Naftzger Park: Broken Dream," *Wichita Eagle-Beacon*, July 4, 1983, 1A.

55. Ginsberg, "Naftzger Park: Broken Dream."

56. Gordon Henry, "Park's Dreams Are Unfulfilled," *Wichita Eagle-Beacon*, October 8, 1983, 10Z; Ginsberg, "Naftzger Park: Broken Dream."

57. Michael Ginsberg, "Experiment with Earlier Lockup Upsets Naftzger Park Regulars," *Wichita Eagle-Beacon*, August 16, 1983, 1C.

58. Henry, "Park's Dreams Are Unfulfilled."

59. Henry, "Park's Dreams Are Unfulfilled." The stalemate between Kassebaum and OTA leaders is explained in detail in Chase M. Billingham, "Waiting for Bobos: Displacement and Impeded Gentrification in a Midwestern City," *City & Community* 16, no. 2 (2017): 145–168.

60. Billingham, "Waiting for Bobos."

61. "Two Held in Charges of Joining in Attack," *Wichita Eagle*, April 3, 1990, 3D; Eric Gorski, "Attacked Shopkeeper Finds Strength to Go On," *Wichita Eagle*, July 22, 1992, 1D; Bud Norman, "Among the Down and Out," *Wichita Eagle*, December 12, 1993, 1A; Anita Schrodt, "In Their Own Hands," *Wichita Eagle*, March 12, 1996, 9A.

62. Robert Short, "Police, City Working to Change Park Image," *Wichita Eagle*, May 13, 1998, 15A.

63. Reforms to the structure of city government in the 1980s led to the elimination of the former city commission and the creation of a new city council body with an elected mayor.

64. Lois Lessner, "Officers Want to Change Public Drinking Law," *Wichita Eagle*, December 12, 1996, 18A; Jennifer Comes Roy, "A Battle over Naftzger Park," *Wichita Eagle*, November 14, 1999, 17A; Short, "Police, City Working to Change Park Image"; Jennifer Comes Roy, "'Where Would They Be Without Us?'" *Wichita Eagle*, December 20, 1999, 9A.

65. Roy, "A Battle over Naftzger Park"; Roy, "'Where Would They Be Without Us?'"

66. Roy, "A Battle over Naftzger Park"; Chris Cooper, "Opening Up Naftsger [*sic*] Park to the Public," *Wichita Old Town Gazette*, November 1999, 7. The Union Rescue Mission would eventually relocate to the outskirts of Wichita in 2004.

67. Roy, "A Battle over Naftzger Park"; Jennifer Comes Roy, "Fee-to-Feed Doesn't Deter Group," *Wichita Eagle*, November 21, 1999, 19A.

68. Roy, "'Where Would They Be Without Us?'"

69. Lillian Zier Martell, "City Council Lifts Fee on Feeding Homeless in Park," *Wichita Eagle*, December 22, 1999, 1A; Rhonda Holman, "Homeless Problem Bigger Than Naftzger Park," *Wichita Eagle*, March 19, 2000, 15A; Lillian Zier Martel, "State Cuts Funding for Homeless," *Wichita Eagle*, January 13, 2000, 1A.

70. Kristin Strole, "Naftzger Park Getting Renovation," *Wichita Old Town Gazette*, November, 2000, 6; Cyndi Saxon, "Naftzger Park the New Hot Place for Lunch," *Wichita Old Town Gazette*, May, 2001, 7; Lillian Zier Martell, "Downtown's Needy Displaced," *Wichita Eagle*, January 15, 2001, 9A; Stan Finger, "The Mean Streets," *Wichita Eagle*, July 18, 2005, 1A. See also Billingham, "Waiting for Bobos."

71. Stan Finger, "Record Highs Claim Lives," *Wichita Eagle*, July 21, 2006, 1A; Hurst Laviana, "Homeless Advocates Hold Memorial Service," *Wichita Eagle*, July 28, 2006, 1B.

72. Daniel McCoy, "Pastor Arrested at Gay Pride Festival," *Wichita Eagle*, June 30, 2008, 1B; Beccy Tanner, "Rally, Parade, Festival Cap Wichita Pride Week," *Wichita Eagle*, June 29, 2009, 3A; Denise Neil, "Trashing Tradition," *Wichita Eagle*, August 16, 2007, 10E; Tim Potter and Deb Gruver, "City Weighs

Spending $108 Million Near Arena," *Wichita Eagle*, March 27, 2007, 1A. The construction of the arena is discussed in detail in chapter 4.

73. Goody Clancy, *Project Downtown: The Master Plan for Wichita* (2010), http://www.downtownwichita.org/user/file/ProjectD_public_100928.pdf; Bill Wilson, "First Look at City's Future," *Wichita Eagle*, September 29, 2010, 1A. I discuss *Project Downtown* in more detail in chapter 4.

74. Wichita Downtown Development Corporation, *Wichita Metropolitan Studio* (2013), http://www.downtownwichita.org/user/file/WDDC%20Final%20Book%20Digital.pdf.

75. Dan Voorhis and Amy Renee Leiker, "Man Found Dead in Naftzger Park," *Wichita Eagle*, April 28, 2013, 1B; Matt Riedl, "Man, 52, Loses $100, Cellphone, Two Teeth," *Wichita Eagle*, July 3, 2013, 3B; Denise Neil, "Man, 19, Stabbed Friday Afternoon at Naftzger Park," *Wichita Eagle*, September 28, 2013; Stan Finger, "Man Stabbed in Fight Near Downtown Park," *Wichita Eagle*, April 16, 2014, 1B.

76. Kelsey Ryan, "11 Things Wichita Promised to Land the 2018 NCAA Men's Basketball Tournament," *Wichita Eagle*, November 29, 2014, https://www.kansas.com/news/local/article4188702.html.

77. Vitt, "Old Town: 'Urban Pioneers'"; Valentine, "Old Warehouse to Get Facelift"; Jean Hays, "Plenty of Pasta: Spaghetti Warehouse Franchisee Buys Building," *Wichita Eagle*, October 15, 1992, 6B; Deb Gruver, "Downtown Restaurant Calls It a Day," *Wichita Eagle*, January 15, 2004, 4B; Nora Pat Small, "Wichita Wholesale Grocery Company," National Registry of Historic Places Inventory—Nomination Form (Washington, DC: US Department of the Interior, 1983), https://www.kshs.org/resource/national_register/nominationsNRDB/Sedgwick_WichitaWholesaleGroceryCompanyNR.pdf; "Wichita Wholesale Grocery Company," Kansas Historic Resources Inventory, 173-5880-00180, Kansas Historical Society, 2009, https://khri.kansasgis.org/index.cfm?in=173-5880-00180.

78. Bill Wilson, "Hotelier to Sell Building: Former Spaghetti Works on Market," *Wichita Eagle*, July 16, 2008, 6B.

79. Carrie Rengers, "Spaghetti Works Building to Be a 'Live, Play, Work' Concept," *Wichita Eagle*, April 5, 2016, 6A.

80. Dion Lefler, "March Madness Spurs Park Improvement Plan That May Include Artificial Turf," *Wichita Eagle*, May 16, 2017, https://www.kansas.com/news/politics-government/article150801177.html.

81. Bob Weeks, "Naftzger Park Contract: Who Is in Control?," *Voice for Liberty*, August 7, 2017, https://wichitaliberty.org/wichita-government/naftzger-park-wichita-contract-who-controls/.

82. In addition to my own notes recorded during public forums regarding the

Naftzger Park redevelopment, this section draws upon the following resources: Stan Finger, "Crowd Gathers to Talk About Naftzger Park's Future, Redesign," *Wichita Eagle*, July 29, 2017, 2A; Kirk Seminoff, "Trying to Please Everyone with Naftzger Park," *Wichita Eagle*, July 30, 2017, 4B; Katherine Burgess, "Homeless in Naftzger Park: 'This Is Our World,'" *Wichita Eagle*, August 10, 2017, 1A; Dion Lefler, "Naftzger Park Plans Call for No Walls, Restrooms," *Wichita Eagle*, August 11, 2017, 1A.

83. Dion Lefler, "Funds to Reconstruct Naftzger Park Win Council's Approval," *Wichita Eagle*, August 16, 2017, 2A; Janet Miller, "Serving City's Most Vulnerable," *Wichita Eagle*, August 20, 2017, 7B.

84. Dion Lefler, "Design Council Not Wowed by Naftzger Plans," *Wichita Eagle*, August 29, 2017, 2A; Dion Lefler, "Naftzger Park May Not Be Ready for March Madness," *Wichita Eagle*, September 1, 2017, 1A.

85. Dion Lefler, "Naftzger Park Won't Be Torn Down, Rebuilt After Developer Nixes Proposal," *Wichita Eagle*, November 18, 2017, 1A.

86. Carrie Rengers, "$23 Million Development Envisioned Downtown," *Wichita Eagle*, December 15, 2017, 1A.

87. Minutes of the Meeting of the Wichita City Council, January 9, 2018, http://wichitaks.granicus.com/MediaPlayer.php?view_id=2&clip_id=3703&meta_id=197667.

88. Meeting Agenda of the Wichita City Council, December 12, 2017, https://www.wichita.gov/DocumentCenter/View/14094/12–12–2017-Final-City-Council-Agenda-Packet-PDF.

89. Minutes of the Meeting of the Wichita City Council, December 12, 2017, http://wichitaks.granicus.com/MediaPlayer.php?view_id=2&clip_id=3697.

90. In addition to my own fieldnotes recorded during the "Fan Fest," this section draws upon the following sources: Rengers, "New $23 Million Downtown Development"; Dion Lefler, "Wichita's NCAA Fanfest: B-ball, Big Screens, Beer and Bathrooms," *Wichita Eagle*, March 4, 2018, 2A; Dion Lefler, "Local Improvement Projects Set Table for NCAA March Madness," *Wichita Eagle*, March 4, 2018, 1A.

91. In addition to my own fieldnotes, this section draws upon the following sources: Dion Lefler, "Naftzger Park Re-envisioned as Flexible, 'Vibrant Open Space,'" *Wichita Eagle*, March 22, 2018, 1A; *Wichita Eagle* Editorial Board, "Feedback What City Needed on Naftzger," *Wichita Eagle*, March 23, 2018, 9A.

92. I was among the last people to set foot in the old Naftzger Park before it was locked up and demolition began in May 2018. In addition to my fieldnotes, this section draws upon the following source: Lefler, "Naftzger Park to Close."

93. The Carry Nation monument, which included a drinking fountain, was donated to the city by the Women's Christian Temperance Union in 1918, and

for decades it stood in front of Union Station until (according to local folklore) it was purportedly knocked over by a beer truck. Following the closing of Union Station, the fountain was placed in storage. It later found a home in Wichita's Old Cowtown Museum until the late 1980s, when it was moved to Naftzger Park (in the shadow of the Eaton Hotel, whose bar Nation had famously ransacked in 1900). See Beccy Tanner, "Nation Clubbed Wichita Bar," *Wichita Eagle*, September 14, 1989, 2N; "Carry Nation Memorial Drinking Fountain," Roadside-America.com, accessed June 18, 2025, https://www.roadsideamerica.com/story/15471.

94. For several years, as a moderator of a social media community dedicated to these topics, I have tracked the history of Naftzger Park, ongoing debates about its future, and policymaking regarding its redevelopment. This group of over nine hundred people, which includes a large number of the region's most notable figures in politics, government, and the media, has served as a key site of debate and argument over Downtown Wichita's future since its creation in 2017. I have used the community as a repository for photographs, government documents, and my own reporting on Naftzger Park and the surrounding area. These documents and conversations provide empirical support for much of the material in this section and throughout the entire chapter. They are open to the public and may be accessed at "Naftzger Park," public Facebook group, https://www.facebook.com/groups/NaftzgerPark.

4. Promoting the Potemkin City

1. "Expect More out of Life," Greater Wichita Partnership, accessed June 19, 2025, https://choosewichita.com/live/overview.

2. "Epic Center Opens a New Era," *Wichita Eagle*, November 12, 1987, 2D; Jean Hays, "Epic Center Is Sold Again," *Wichita Eagle*, April 18, 1998, 16A.

3. John R. Logan and Harvey L. Molotch, *Urban Fortunes: The Political Economy of Place* (Berkeley: University of California Press, 1987), 50–51.

4. A useful review of this literature and an incisive investigation into the motivations and attitudes of growth actors that poses an empirical challenge to the idea of a cohesive, monolithic growth coalition can be found in Shelley McDonough Kimelberg, "Inside the Growth Machine: Real Estate Professionals on the Perceived Challenges of Urban Development," *City & Community* 10, no. 1 (2011): 76–99.

5. Harvey Molotch, "The City as a Growth Machine: Toward a Political Economy of Place," *American Journal of Sociology* 82, no. 2 (1976): 315. See also Logan and Molotch, *Urban Fortunes*, 70–73.

6. Jim Cross, "WI/SE Names VP to Work Full Time on Downtown Area,"

Wichita Eagle, September 19, 1992, 1A; Jim Cross, "On the Trail of a 'Hip' Downtown," *Wichita Eagle*, March 26, 1997, 13A.

7. Jim Cross, "The Science of Redevelopment," *Wichita Eagle*, May 31, 1997, 1A.

8. Colleen McCain, "Downtown Business Asked to Pay Fee," *Wichita Eagle*, July 28, 1997, 1A; Jim Cross, "Knight Wary of Tax District," *Wichita Eagle*, December 13, 1997, 13A; Jim Cross, "Hearing Is Set on Downtown Tax Authority," *Wichita Eagle*, December 17, 1997, 13A.

9. Jim Cross, "Downtown Vote Too Close to Call," *Wichita Eagle*, January 26, 1998, 9A; Jim Cross, "City Council Divided over Tax," *Wichita Eagle*, January 28, 1998, 13A; Bill Bartel, "Downtown Tax Faces Large Hurdle," *Wichita Eagle*, February 28, 1998, 11A; Jim Cross, "Downtown Group Cut Loose by City," *Wichita Eagle*, March 25, 1998, 11A.

10. Alan Bjerga, "Businesses to Consider Downtown Tax District," *Wichita Eagle*, November 15, 2000, 1A; Alan Bjerga, "Plan for Downtown Tax District Is Detailed," *Wichita Eagle*, November 17, 2000, 1A; Lillian Zier Martell, "Central Wichita Gets Tax Increase," *Wichita Eagle*, March 21, 2001, 1A; Lillian Zier Martell, "Downtown Tax District Working Out Its Agenda," *Wichita Eagle*, May 27, 2001, 1B.

11. Molly McMillin, "Chamber Exec to Leave Development Post," *Wichita Eagle*, December 2, 1997, 13A.

12. Dan Voorhis, "Downtown Czar Sees Ways to Lure Firms to City's Core," *Wichita Eagle*, February 7, 2002, 4B; Rhonda Holman, "Optimistic," *Wichita Eagle*, February 10, 2002, 14A.

13. The history of the DynaPlex and INTRUST Bank Arena, as well as other attempts to utilize sports facilities to generate economic development in Downtown Wichita, is detailed in Kallie Kimble, "Searching for the 'Crown Jewel': A Qualitative Examination of the Utilization of Multi-Use Sports Venues for Downtown Redevelopment in Wichita, KS" (master's thesis, Wichita State University, 2019).

14. Jerry Siebenmark and Dan Voorhis, "Leader of Downtown Coalition Resigns," *Wichita Eagle*, October 12, 2007, 1A.

15. Bill Wilson, "Downtown Group's Leader Ready to Build Partnerships," *Wichita Eagle*, August 29, 2008, 6B; Bill Wilson, "Winning Wichita: WDDC's New President Impresses Right off the Bat," *Wichita Eagle*, September 25, 2008, 1C; Bill Wilson, "Downtown's Development Direction Will Soon Be Clear," *Wichita Eagle*, September 26, 2010, 1A. The complete *Project Wichita* master plan, along with supporting materials and all other WDDC research and promotional material since that time, can be viewed at https://downtownwichita.org/.

16. Carrie Rengers, "Let's Make a Deal," *Wichita Eagle*, March 17, 2005, 4B; Dan Voorhis, "Bargain Buildings," *Wichita Eagle*, February 9, 2005, 1A.

17. Voorhis, "Bargain Buildings."

18. Dan Voorhis, "Downtown Group Wins Big Lease," *Wichita Eagle*, April 8, 2005, 6B; Fred Mann, "Unanimous Vote," *Wichita Eagle*, November 10, 2005, 1A; Dan Voorhis, "Downtown's Makeover," *Wichita Eagle*, May 11, 2005, 6B; Carrie Rengers, "Minnesotans Nab Another Building," *Wichita Eagle*, July 17, 2005, 1C.

19. Dan Voorhis, "Downtown Lineup," *Wichita Eagle*, January 29, 2006, 1A; Dan Voorhis, "Exchange Place Space Trades Up," *Wichita Eagle*, January 29, 2006, 1C; Randy Scholfield, "Exciting—Downtown Wichita Is on Its Way Back," *Wichita Eagle*, January 29, 2006, 10A.

20. Phyllis Jacobs Griekspoor, "Developer Wants Firms Downtown," *Wichita Eagle*, March 15, 2006, 6B; Dan Voorhis, "Two Downtown Properties Sold," *Wichita Eagle*, June 3, 2006, 6B; Dan Voorhis, "Downtown Biz Space with High-Tech Perks," *Wichita Eagle*, August 3, 2006, 6B; Carrie Rengers, "Downtown Tree House," *Wichita Eagle*, August 15, 2006, 4B; Carrie Rengers, "Minnesota Developers Reveal Their Next Steps," *Wichita Eagle*, September 7, 2006, 1C; Dan Voorhis, "Real Development Closes on 2 More Downtown Sites," *Wichita Eagle*, September 28, 2006, 2C.

21. Real Development, advertising circular, February 19, 2006. This multipage circular featured glowing quotations endorsing the Minnesota Guys' work from Wolverton and city council member Sharon Fearey, whose district included Downtown Wichita.

22. Michael Elzufon, "Wichita Can Turn Its Downtown Around," *Wichita Eagle*, October 12, 2006, 9C.

23. Dan Voorhis, "Parole Operations to Merge Downtown," *Wichita Eagle*, January 11, 2007, 1C; Bill Wilson, "Downtown Goal," *Wichita Eagle*, March 1, 2007, 1C; Dan Voorhis, "Law Firm at SC Telcom to Move to Epic Center," *Wichita Eagle*, March 7, 2007, 6B.

24. Randy Scholfield, "Downtown Arena Is Already a Success," *Wichita Eagle*, March 9, 2007, 7A.

25. Dan Voorhis, "Developers Ask City to Help Finance Condos," *Wichita Eagle*, March 27, 2007, 4B; Dan Voorhis, "Revenue into Residences," *Wichita Eagle*, May 1, 2007, 4B; Dan Voorhis, "Agent Claims He Was Cut Out of Sale," *Wichita Eagle*, April 5, 2007, 3C; Bill Wilson, "Developers Close on SC Telcom Site," *Wichita Eagle*, May 22, 2007, 4B.

26. Dan Voorhis, "Downtown Condos on the Rise," *Wichita Eagle*, October 28, 2007, 1C; Dan Voorhis, "$284,000 in Taxes Due on Exchange Place," *Wichita Eagle*, January 31, 2008, 3C; Dan Voorhis, "Façade Loans Near Approval," *Wichita*

Eagle, March 4, 2008, 6B; Fred Mann, "$3 Million from City to Help Fix Up Sutton," *Wichita Eagle*, September 10, 2008, 6B.

27. Dan Voorhis, "Downtown Appraisals Under Fire," *Wichita Eagle*, March 6, 2008, 1C; Carrie Rengers, "Real Development Won't Buy Building," *Wichita Eagle*, November 13, 2008, 2C; Dan Voorhis, "Realtor Files Suit over Condo Project," *Wichita Eagle*, December 25, 2008, 1C.

28. Dan Voorhis, "Two Downtown Buildings," *Wichita Eagle*, January 7, 2009, 1C; Dan Voorhis, "Parking Garage Proposed," *Wichita Eagle*, January 24, 2009, 5B.

29. Dan Voorhis, "Developing Momentum Downtown," *Wichita Eagle*, January 25, 2009, 5B; Bill Wilson, "Downtown Buildings' Face-Lifts Set to Start," *Wichita Eagle*, March 19, 2009, 1C; Bill Wilson, "Shopping Center near Kellogg, Tyler for Sale," *Wichita Eagle*, April 18, 2009, 6B.

30. Bill Wilson, "Development Faces Threats," *Wichita Eagle*, June 5, 2009, 6B; Dan Voorhis, "Minnesota Guys File $7 Million Suit," *Wichita Eagle*, July 9, 2009, 3C.

31. Bill Wilson, "Minnesota Guys Need to Raise $8 Million," *Wichita Eagle*, September 3, 2009, 1C; Dan Voorhis, "Bank Forecloses on Condos with Minn. Ties," *Wichita Eagle*, October 11, 2009, 1A; Bill Wilson, "Consultant: Patience Key to Downtown Plan," *Wichita Eagle*, November 19, 2009, 1C.

32. Bill Wilson, "Exchange Place to Seek TIF Boost," *Wichita Eagle*, March 18, 2010, 1C; Bill Wilson, "Hearing Set for Exchange Place TIF," *Wichita Eagle*, March 24, 2010, 1C; Bill Wilson, "Real Development Hopes for April Loan," *Wichita Eagle*, March 18, 2010, 6C.

33. Brent Wistrom and Bill Wilson, "Denial May Force Out Developers, City Told," *Wichita Eagle*, April 14, 2010, 1A; Brent D. Wistrom, "Developers Hope to Retool Condo Project," *Wichita Eagle*, April 20, 2010, 1A; Rhonda Holman, "No More Money for Exchange Place," *Wichita Eagle*, April 20, 2010, 13A.

34. Brent D. Wistrom and Bill Wilson, "City OKs $10.3 Million for Condo Project," *Wichita Eagle*, April 21, 2010, 1A; Brent D. Wistrom, "Real Development's Exchange Place," *Wichita Eagle*, April 24, 2010, 1A; Brent D. Wistrom, "Downtown Project Gets Final OK," *Wichita Eagle*, April 28, 2010, 1B.

35. Bill Wilson, "Minn Guys: Loan Issues Won't Delay Condo Plan," *Wichita Eagle*, May 20, 2010, 1A; Dan Voorhis, "Real Development Creditors Sue," *Wichita Eagle*, June 10, 2010, 3C; Bill Wilson, "Exchange Place's Refinance Set for Fall," *Wichita Eagle*, August 19, 2010, 1C; Bill Wilson, "Officials Waver on Plans for Grocery," *Wichita Eagle*, August 24, 2010, 1A.

36. Dan Voorhis, "Downtown Developers: 'We Are Back in Business,'" *Wichita Eagle*, April 30, 2011, 1A; Carrie Rengers, "Tax Firm Sues over Developers'

2-Year Debt," *Wichita Eagle*, May 11, 2011, 1C; Carrie Rengers, "Minnesota Developers Face $28,000 Judgment," *Wichita Eagle*, September 1, 2011, 1C; Bill Wilson, "Leasing Agent Resigns at Real Development," *Wichita Eagle*, September 2, 2011, 7B.

37. Bill Wilson, "Downtown Is on a Roll," *Wichita Eagle*, September 8, 2011, 1C; Bill Wilson, "Conflict Alleged in Fiancee's Ties to Bond Project," *Wichita Eagle*, January 13, 2012, 1A.

38. Bill Wilson, "Minnesota Guys Eyeing Resort in Georgia," *Wichita Eagle*, November 1, 2012, 1A; Bill Wilson, "Developers Say They Are Victims in Case," *Wichita Eagle*, November 13, 2012, 1A.

39. Bill Wilson and Dan Voorhis, "Downtown Projects at Risk," *Wichita Eagle*, November 9, 2012, 1A; Bill Wilson, "Developers Could Face Criminal Charges," *Wichita Eagle*, November 10, 2012, 1A; Wilson, "Developers Say They Are Victims"; Bill Wilson, "Minnesota Guys: We're Victims," *Wichita Eagle*, November 20, 2012, 3A.

40. Dan Voorhis, "Real Development to Sell 3 Buildings," *Wichita Eagle*, December 6, 2012, 1A; Rick Plumlee, "Building's Auction Could Mean Homeless Shelter Will Close," *Wichita Eagle*, December 6, 2012, 1A; Bill Wilson, "Acquisition Breathes Life into Project Downtown," *Wichita Eagle*, December 17, 2012, 1A.

41. Dan Voorhis, "Bank of Kansas Seeking to Foreclose on Kaufman Building," *Wichita Eagle*, June 13, 2013, 3C; Dan Voorhis, "Owners of Building's Land Seek to Own Building," *Wichita Eagle*, July 5, 2013, 5B; Dan Voorhis, "Lender Takes Ownership of Wichita Executive Centre," *Wichita Eagle*, July 30, 2013, 1C.

42. Bill Wilson and Dan Voorhis, "Petition Alleges Developers Broke Securities Law," *Wichita Eagle*, December 25, 2013, 1B; Bill Wilson, "Developer Calls Wichita Experience a 'Nightmare,'" *Wichita Eagle*, December 27, 2013, 1A; Dan Voorhis, "Partners to Take Control of Most of Sutton Place," *Wichita Eagle*, April 1, 2014, 7C; Dan Voorhis, "Building's Investors Are Eager to Bid Minnesota Guys Farewell," *Wichita Eagle*, May 15, 2014, 1C.

43. Dan Voorhis, "Kansas Official Files Fraud Charges Against Developers," *Wichita Eagle*, February 24, 2015, 1A; Matt Riedl, "'Minnesota Guy' Dave Lundberg Jailed in Wichita," *Wichita Eagle*, February 27, 2015, 6A; Amy Renee Leiker, "Elzufon Appears in Court in Fraud Case," *Wichita Eagle*, March 15, 2015, 4A; Dan Voorhis, Affidavit Details Case vs. Developers," *Wichita Eagle*, April 25, 2015, 10A; Carrie Rengers, "Construction, Architecture Firms Sue Developers," *Wichita Eagle*, June 4, 2015, 1B.

44. Bryan Horwath, "Most Charges Dismissed Against Minn. Developers," *Wichita Eagle*, November 13, 2015, 2A; Dan Voorhis, "Court Reinstates Fraud

Charges Against 'Minnesota Guys,'" *Wichita Eagle*, March 4, 2017, 2A; Dion Lefler and Amy Renee Leiker, "Court Drops Fraud Charges Against 'Minnesota Guys,'" *Wichita Eagle*, July 20, 2019, 1A.

45. Carrie Rengers, "What Progress Looks Like: Clouds of Dust," *Wichita Eagle*, March 23, 2006, 6B; Brent D. Wistrom, "Council Oks Downtown Hotel," *Wichita Eagle*, March 21, 2007, 6B; Carrie Rengers, "Stirrings on Downtown Hotel," *Wichita Eagle*, October 26, 2008, 5B.

46. Carrie Rengers, "Developers Add a Site to Projects Downtown," *Wichita Eagle*, July 8, 2011, 6B; Carrie Rengers, "Pop-Up Park to Fill 'Pit,'" *Wichita Eagle*, November 25, 2014, 1C; Denise Neil, "New Pop-Up Urban Park Draws Big Downtown Crowds on Douglas," *Wichita Eagle*, September 25, 2015, https://www.kansas.com/entertainment/restaurants/dining-with-denise-neil/article36600567.html.

47. On "tactical urbanism," including examples from cities across the US, see Josh Mahar, "Tactical Urbanism: Applying a Big City Placemaking Technique to Smaller Communities," Municipal Research and Services Center, February 4, 2016, https://mrsc.org/stay-informed/mrsc-insight/february-2016/tactical-urbanism-in-smaller-communities; Mike Lydon, ed., *Tactical Urbanism*, vol. 1 (Next Generation of New Urbanists, 2011), https://issuu.com/streetplanscollaborative/docs/tactical_urbanism_vol.1. The definitive sociological statement on "DIY Urbanism" comes from Gordon Douglas, who takes a critical approach to studying these urban design phenomena, noting not just the ways that they can revitalize urban communities but also how they reflect "hubris and elitism" among the affluent gentrifiers who tend to be their most active proponents and practitioners. See Gordon C. C. Douglas, *The Help-Yourself City: Legitimacy and Inequality in DIY Urbanism* (New York: Oxford University Press, 2018), 13.

48. Neil, "New Pop-Up Urban Park Draws Big Downtown Crowds on Douglas."

49. In addition to my own fieldnotes, this section is informed by the following sources: Carrie Rengers, "Summer Pop-Up," *Wichita Eagle*, May 21, 2015, 4B; Shelby Reynolds, "With Dirt in Place, Downtown's Appearance Is Hole-Lot Better," *Wichita Eagle*, August 14, 2015, 4A; Neil, "New Pop-Up Urban Park Draws Big Downtown Crowds on Douglas." For a video of highlights of the grand opening, see "Pop-Up Urban Park Opens at What Used to Be a Hole on Douglas (+video)," *Wichita Eagle*, September 25, 2015, https://www.kansas.com/news/local/article36602814.html.

50. Matt Riedl, "Free Downtown Music Festival Will Rock Pop-Up Park in March," *Wichita Eagle*, February 23, 2018, 6C; Rod Pocowatchit, "Tallgrass Film Festival: Lucky 13," *Wichita Eagle*, October 11, 2015, 1C; Matt Riedl, "New Movie Venue Is Not a Theater—It's a Shipping Container," *Wichita Eagle*, October 7,

2017, 2A; Denise Neil, "Spinning Globe of Fun Appears in Downtown Park," *Wichita Eagle*, March 18, 2017, 2A; Matt Riedl, "Downtown Wichita Lacked a Beach, So It Made One," *Wichita Eagle*, July 14, 2017, 19C; Denise Neil, "Wichita Food Trucks Will Keep Running, Even as Cold Sets In," *Wichita Eagle*, December 6, 2015, 7C.

51. Chase M. Billingham, "Presence and Absence in the Gentrifying Urban Core," paper presented at the annual meeting of the Midwest Sociological Society, Chicago, April 20, 2019. This presentation is available from the author upon request. The findings reported here were also supported by the results of ethnographic research projects undertaken by students in my Urban Sociology course at Wichita State University in the spring semester of 2017.

52. Oliver Morrison, "Should City Makes [*sic*] the Homeless Leave Downtown Wichita Park?," *Wichita Eagle*, June 25, 2017, 1B; Jeff Fluhr, "Downtown Wichita Being Transformed," *Wichita Eagle*, September 4, 2016, 5B. Annual *State of Downtown* reports can be accessed at https://downtownwichita.org/development/state-of-downtown.

53. Neil, "Spinning Globe of Fun"; Daniel Salazar, "Downtown Wichita's Bike-Share Program Starts Up," *Wichita Eagle*, May 5, 2017, 1A; Katherine Burgess and Daniel Salazar, "Get Your Glasses Now, and Make Sure They're Safe," *Wichita Eagle*, August 15, 2017, 1A.

54. Michael Stavola, "Wichita Protestors' Arrests Include Using Sidewalk Chalk," *Wichita Eagle*, August 20, 2020, 2A; Carrie Rengers, "Pop-Up Park in Downtown Wichita Will Get a New Look, New Uses," *Wichita Eagle*, August 21, 2020, 1A.

55. Torin Anderson, "First a Pit, Now an Art Gallery. But Wichita's Pop-Up Park Has an Uncertain Future," *KMUW*, February 5, 2021, https://www.kmuw.org/arts/2021-02-05/first-a-pit-now-an-art-gallery-but-wichitas-pop-up-park-has-an-uncertain-future.

56. Belinda Luscombe, "Workplace Salaries: At Last, Women on Top," *Time*, September 1, 2010, https://content.time.com/time/business/article/0,8599,2015274,00.html; Hanna Rosin, *The End of Men: And the Rise of Women* (New York: Riverhead Books, 2012); Hanna Rosin, "New Data on the Rise of Women," TED Talk, December 2010, 15:55, https://www.ted.com/talks/hanna_rosin_new_data_on_the_rise_of_women.

57. Philip N. Cohen, "Time Check," *Family Inequality Blog*, September 27, 2010, https://familyinequality.wordpress.com/2010/09/27/time-check/; "Fact Check: Do Young, Childless Women Earn More Than Men?," ABC News, September 9, 2014, https://www.abc.net.au/news/2014-09-10/young-childless-women-earn-more-than-men-fact-check/5712770.

58. Bill Wilson, "City View for $1 Million Prize," *Wichita Eagle*, March 5,

2011, 6B; Dennis I. Clary, "Why Superman Landed in Kansas," *Wichita Eagle*, March 3, 2013, 8G.

59. "Speaker Series to Focus on Retaining Talent," *Wichita Eagle*, August 7, 2014, 1C; Jennifer Allen, "Arts Make Wichita Vibrant," *Wichita Eagle*, November 6, 2014, 9A; Jon Rosell, "Move Us Forward," *Wichita Eagle*, September 21, 2014, 22A; John Allison, "Education Is Vital to the Community's Economic Success," *Wichita Eagle*, March 1, 2015, 3H. Chung's "Fuel the Fire" presentation can be viewed at "Fuel the Fire - James Chung," Downtown Wichita, September 24, 2014, YouTube, 1:16:58, youtu.be/1aPGjuEFrf4.

60. Kelsey Ryan, "Koch Company Primary Donor to Opponents of Sales Tax," *Wichita Eagle*, December 24, 2014, 1A.

61. Roy Wenzl, "Analyst Presents Sobering View of Wichita Economy, Community," *Wichita Eagle*, September 23, 2015, 1A.

62. Roy Wenzl, "Is One of City's Best-Known Traits Now Old History?," *Wichita Eagle*, September 27, 2015, 1A.

63. Rhonda Holman, "Change City's Trajectory," *Wichita Eagle*, September 27, 2015, 14A; Rhonda Holman, "Fix Perception Problem," *Wichita Eagle*, October 4, 2015, 14A. The website for The Chung Report can be viewed at https://thechungreport.com/.

64. Roy Wenzl, "Wichita Entrepreneurs to Have Incubator," *Wichita Eagle*, October 11, 2015, 1B; Robert Litan, "Develop New Generation of Entrepreneurs," *Wichita Eagle*, December 20, 2015, 7B; John Bardo, "Region Must Collaborate, Innovate," *Wichita Eagle*, February 7, 2016, 7B.

65. On urban branding campaigns and their role in economic development across the world, see Keith Dinnie, ed., *City Branding: Theory and Cases* (New York: Palgrave MacMillan, 2011). One of the most insightful texts on branding and its impact on the economic trajectories of one city can be found in Miriam Greenberg, *Branding New York: How a City in Crisis Was Sold to the World* (New York: Routledge, 2008). The specific branding examples mentioned in this paragraph are drawn from the convention and visitors' bureau websites of those specific cities, as accessed on February 13, 2025.

66. John M. Purcell, "Wichita, Kansas," *Raven: A Journal of Vexillology* 9/10, no. 1 (2002/2003): 371–373; Frank Good, "Wichita Has a City Flag," *Wichita Eagle and Beacon*, February 28, 1965, 10D; Delores Quinlisk, "Flag Day '71 Significant for Wichita," *Wichita Eagle and Beacon*, June 13, 1971, 10A.

67. Edward B. Kaye, "The American City Flag Survey of 2004," *Raven: A Journal of Vexillology* 12, no. 1 (2005): 27–61; "Wichita Flag Flunks Public Loyalty Test," *Wichita Beacon*, May 22, 1970, 12B.

68. Rhonda Holman, "When It Waves, Few Wave Back," *Wichita Eagle*, June 14, 1997, 13A.

69. Beccy Tanner, "Flag Fans Love City Flag—Ever Seen It?," *Wichita Eagle*, October 6, 2004, 1A.

70. Angie Elliott, "Wave the Wichita Flag to Show Pride in Our City," *Wichita Eagle*, July 16, 2015, 4B.

71. Denise Neil, "Gift Guide: Stuff Their Stockings with 'Wichitawesome,'" *Wichita Eagle*, December 6, 2015, 1C; Carrie Rengers, "Workroom's Flag Swag Pop-Ups to Debut Next Week," *Wichita Eagle*, September 5, 2015, 12A; Bryan Horwath, "Not All Fun and Games at Exposure," *Wichita Eagle*, September 25, 2015, 12A.

72. Kaitlyn Alanis, "Your Car Could Sport a City of Wichita Flag License Plate in 2019," *Wichita Eagle*, October 13, 2017, 3A; Matt Riedl, "Wichitans and Their Eye-Catching Crazy Suits: Who Wore It Best?," *Wichita Eagle*, December 25, 2018, 3A; Denise Neil, "USS Wichita Crest Incorporates City Flag, Heritage," *Wichita Eagle*, July 3, 2016, 2A; Taylor Eldridge, "Semipro FC Wichita Envisions Pro Future," *Wichita Eagle*, July 8, 2017, 1B; Denise Neil, "Riverfest Reveals Art for 'Party for ICT,'" *Wichita Eagle*, January 30, 2016, 2A; Bryan Horwath, "Popularity of Wichita Flag Firmly Planted in City, Inscribed on Skin," *Wichita Eagle*, June 14, 2017, 1A.

73. Carrie Rengers, "Nonchalant Nabbing," *Wichita Eagle*, July 21, 2016, 5B; Supriya Sidhar, "#WichitaFlagTravelContest Carries City Pride Far Afield," *Wichita Eagle*, July 22, 2017, 4A; Kaitlyn Alanis, "Wichita Flag Finds Itself on Pumpkins and Skulls This Halloween," *Wichita Eagle*, October 31, 2017, https://www.kansas.com/entertainment/holidays/article181901496.html; Suzanne Perez Tobias, "You're About to See Even More Wichita Flags Flying," *Wichita Eagle*, June 15, 2018, 1A; Denise Neil, "That Flag You See Everywhere? It's a Sign of Wichita Pride," *Wichita Eagle*, March 14, 2018, 18D.

74. "Wichita Is Moving Forward," *Wichita Eagle*, March 1, 2017, 11A; Janelle King, "Put Douglas Design District Improvements on Fast Track," *Wichita Eagle*, March 2, 2018, 9A; Melinda Schnyder, "Pride-in-Place Aims to Shape Perceptions of Wichita," *Wichita Eagle*, February 26, 2017, 9J.

75. Liby explained in an interview on a local podcast that he deliberately selected music to convey various emotions associated with Wichita's failures and successes. The podcast can be accessed at *Wheat State Creates*, "Stax of Wax Ep 6—Local Wichita Filmmaker, Julian Liby," February 3, 2021, https://open.spotify.com/episode/7HG7zvIxOpcy0YHVvyxtNR.

76. The full film can be viewed at *Welcome Home, Wichita*, Julian Liby, December 4, 2020, YouTube, 34:09, youtu.be/rnIHNLBptZM. After premiering the film in late 2020, the filmmaker moved out of Kansas the following year.

77. In addition to my own fieldnotes recorded during Chung's 2018 presentation, this section is informed by the following sources: Stan Finger, "Wichita at 'a Really Interesting Point' in Its Long History," *Wichita Eagle*, June 11, 2018,

1A; Stan Finger, "Analyst Offers Ideas to Reverse Wichita's Decline," *Wichita Eagle*, June 12, 2018, 1A. To view the Wichita Community Foundation's "Truth *and* Dare" cards, see "Truth & Dare Campaign," Visual Fusion Graphic Design, accessed June 22, 2025, https://visualfusiongraphicdesign.com/portfolio/case-studies/truth-dare-wichita-community-foundation/.

78. "Wichita Got Its Wake-Up Call. Time to Get Up," *Wichita Eagle*, June 17, 2018, 4B; Stan Finger, "Economic Leaders Frame Response to 'Wake-Up Call,'" *Wichita Eagle*, June 17, 2018, 1A.

79. City of Wichita, "Coronavirus Update March 12, 2020," Facebook video, 1:29, https://www.facebook.com/watch/live/?ref=watch_permalink&v=843015662830972.

5. Building a Legacy in the Post-Pandemic City

1. Rhonda Holman, "Douglas Dream," *Wichita Eagle*, August 11, 1996, 1D; Rhonda Holman, "Street Art Sweetens Plans for Douglas," *Wichita Eagle*, October 14, 1996, 1A; Beccy Tanner and Jenny Upchurch, "Art Hits the Streets," *Wichita Eagle*, May 2, 2000, 9A.

2. Thomas Frank, *What's the Matter with Kansas? How Conservatives Won the Heart of America* (New York: Henry Holt, 2004), 58–59. My own fieldnotes recorded in Downtown Wichita in the 2010s regularly confirmed this pattern of emptiness noted by Frank. The number of people that I encountered during ethnographic observation downtown was generally small enough (ten to thirty people per hour, on average) that I would frequently pick out specific individuals whose path I crossed and describe them in detail. The absence of people and activity emerged as a key theme throughout my fieldnotes. One brief example illustrates the mundane activity that pervades my fieldnotes:

> Two young white men in shorts and tee-shirts were putting up umbrellas and chairs at the Funky Monkey Shaved Ice store. Otherwise, there was little pedestrian action. Lots of car traffic, though, as usual. I walked back under the bridge, dust blowing in my eyes from the Naftzger site. I passed two men, both Black and middle-aged, walking the other direction. I continued down Douglas, encountering few other pedestrians, even at this hour. One white man with a beard left the juice place. . . . I walked up from the park and walked to the central library. Tomorrow is the opening day for the new library across the river, and there is going to be a celebratory march from the old library to the new one. Today, though, it's quiet here. There was one bike leaning against one exterior wall. There was one bedroll on the southeast corner of the library, and some shoes under a bench and a collection of

belongings on the Main Street sidewalk, but I didn't see any people. (June 15, 2018)

3. Matt Riedl and Dion Lefler, "Groups Designing 'Riverfront Master Plan' for Next Century of Downtown," *Wichita Eagle*, April 19, 2019, 1A.

4. Chance Swaim, "Century II or Something New? Group Seeks Answers to Wichita's Riverfront Questions," *Wichita Eagle*, July 3, 2019, 2A; Dion Lefler, "Sedgwick County Gives $100,000 for Riverfront Planning Process," *Wichita Eagle*, July 11, 2019, 2A.

5. Dion Lefler, "Century II May Not Fit into Bold Vision for Riverfront," *Wichita Eagle*, August 1, 2019, 1A.

6. Project Wichita, *Project Wichita: A Report to the Community* (2019), https://www.projectwichita.org/share; Project Wichita, "Riverfront Legacy Master Plan to Create Comprehensive Vision and Plan and Connect Projects for Both Banks of Arkansas River," April 18, 2019, https://www.projectwichita.org/press-releases.

7. "Planning Principles," Riverfront Legacy Master Plan, accessed June 23, 2025, https://www.riverfrontlegacywichita.org/planning-principles; Riverfront Legacy Master Plan, "In 1993, Oklahoma City made a conscious decision," Facebook, February 26, 2020, https://www.facebook.com/share/p/1M9GUTkDet/.

8. Riverfront Legacy Master Plan, "Recently, the Gathering Place, a 66-acre park, opened in Tulsa," Facebook, March 9, 2020, https://www.facebook.com/share/p/1B3ZgKS1NG/.

9. Riverfront Legacy Master Plan, Facebook posts, February 26, March 4, and March 17, 2020, https://www.facebook.com/RiverfrontLegacyWichita; Matthew Kelly and Chance Swaim, "Riverfront Possibilities Abound," *Wichita Eagle*, October 3, 2021, 3A.

10. Lefler, "Century II May Not Fit into Bold Vision for Riverfront"; Dion Lefler, "Wichita Century II Supporters Fight Back Against Master Plan," *Wichita Eagle*, September 15, 2019, 2A.

11. Michael Monteferrante, "Riverfront Planning Is Public—and About More Than Century II," *Wichita Eagle*, September 19, 2019, 11A; Jason Tidd, "Group Fighting to Protect Century II Calls It the 'Most Iconic Structure in Wichita," *Wichita Eagle*, September 18, 2019, 3A.

12. Dion Lefler, "Tour Displays Downtown River Access, C-II Issues," *Wichita Eagle*, September 25, 2019, 1A.

13. Dion Lefler, "5 Riverfront Proposals; Only 1 Saves Century II," *Wichita Eagle*, November 15, 2019, 1A; Dion Lefler and Chance Swaim, "O'Donnell Says Wichita Riverfront Plan a Farce in Order to Raze Century II," *Wichita Eagle*, December 8, 2019, 1A.

14. Chance Swaim, "Century II Faces Demolition in Latest Riverfront Plans," *Wichita Eagle*, December 18, 2019, 1A; Dion Lefler and Chance Swaim, "Upscale Building at WaterWalk Will Have 80,000 Square Feet," *Wichita Eagle*, December 19, 2019, 5A.

15. Dion Lefler and Chance Swaim, "Petition Drive Aimed at Saving Century II Starts Monday," *Wichita Eagle*, January 8, 2020, 1A; Dion Lefler, "Fans of Century II Launch Petition Drive, Need 12,554 to Sign," *Wichita Eagle*, January 14, 2020, 1A.

16. Carrie Rengers, "Spirit Layoffs Will Hurt, but Experts Say There's Hope," *Wichita Eagle*, January 12, 2020, 1A; Chance Swaim, "Sales Tax Could Fund Half of Huge Riverfront Legacy Plan," *Wichita Eagle*, January 15, 2020, 1A.

17. Chance Swaim, "Is Century II Building Historic or Just Old?," *Wichita Eagle*, January 19, 2020, 1A.

18. Swaim, "Is Century II Building Historic or Just Old?"; Darryl Kelly, "A Letter to Wichita from the Future," *Wichita Eagle*, February 6, 2020, https://www.kansas.com/opinion/guest-commentary/article240014543.html; Matt Riedl, "Wichita Is the Only Major City in the Region Not to Get 'Hamilton' Tour. Here's Why," *Wichita Eagle*, March 31, 2019, https://www.kansas.com/entertainment/ent-columns-blogs/keeper-of-the-plans/article227785309.html.

19. Dion Lefler, "Broadway Hit Musical 'Hamilton' Coming," *Wichita Eagle*, March 4, 2020, 1A; Suzanne Perez Tobias, "Will the 'Hamilton' Announcement Save Wichita's Century II?," *Wichita Eagle*, March 6, 2020, 9A; Dion Lefler, "A Play Might Change Wichita Skyline," *Wichita Eagle*, March 9, 2020, 1A.

20. Chance Swaim, "Challenger Larkin Slams Dennis on Shutdown, Support for Cruse," *Wichita Eagle*, June 21, 2020, 2A.

21. The statement from the official RLMP Twitter account is available at Riverfront Legacy Master Plan (@RiverfrontICT), "Once we come out from this unprecedented time," Twitter, March 20, 2022, https://twitter.com/RiverfrontICT/status/1241114829814992898.

22. In a public presentation delivered remotely early in the pandemic, I addressed the virus's potential impact upon urban growth and made projections about its likely effects on economic development in Wichita, touching on many of the themes discussed in this chapter. See Chase M. Billingham, "Rethinking the City and the Community for a Post-Pandemic World," Perspectives on the Pandemic Lecture Series, Wichita State University, September 2, 2020, YouTube, 1:01:26, youtu.be/nwRqtd6Ep_0.

23. Chance Swaim, "Wichita Looking for Ways to Offset $50 Million Shortfall," *Wichita Eagle*, June 25, 2020, 1A.

24. Dion Lefler and Chance Swaim, "Wichita Endorses Historic Status for

Buildings," *Wichita Eagle*, July 14, 2020, 1A; Chance Swaim, "Save Century II Petition Has Nearly 17,000 Petitions," *Wichita Eagle*, July 10, 2020, 1A; Dion Lefler, "Wichita in Court to Preserve Right to Demolish Century II," *Wichita Eagle*, July 30, 2020, 1A; Chance Swaim, "City Council OKs Legal Challenge to Save Century II Petition," *Wichita Eagle*, August 5, 2020, 1A.

25. Dion Lefler and Chance Swaim, "Save Century II Petition Is Not Valid, Court Rules," *Wichita Eagle*, August 29, 2020, 1A; John Todd, "Residents Should Decide the Fate of Century II," *Wichita Eagle*, September 13, 2020, 15A; Matthew Kelly, "Appeals Court Rejects Save Century II Petition; Mayor Says C2 Not in Danger," *Wichita Eagle*, January 3, 2023, 3A.

26. Chance Swaim, "Century II Privatization Could Eliminate Need for Tax Subsidy, City Manager Says," *Wichita Eagle*, January 3, 2021, 1A; Dion Lefler, "Privatization Debated as City Preps to Outsource Century II," *Wichita Eagle*, September 20, 2021, 1A; Brandon Johnson and Bryan Frye, "After COVID-19 Pause, It's Time Again to Talk About Wichita's Riverfront," *Wichita Eagle*, March 23, 2021, 6A.

27. City of Wichita, "Century II Options Workshop February 28, 2023," YouTube, 1:48:00, youtu.be/aOlYsyyni2s. The revised Populous plan for the Wichita riverfront can be viewed at Populous, *Wichita Century II and Bob Brown Convention Center: District & Visioning* (2023), https://www.wichita.gov/DocumentCenter/View/17633/02-28-2023-Century-II-Presentation-PDF.

28. City of Wichita, "Century II Options Workshop."

29. Chance Swaim, "City Unveils $400m Plan That Saves Century II, Former Library," *Wichita Eagle*, March 1, 2023, 1A.

30. Celeste Racette frequently recruited volunteers to maintain the flowerbeds around the abandoned library, and she reported regularly on the vandalism affecting the structure on her Save Century II social media page. This work can be viewed at "Wichita Century II," public Facebook page, https://www.facebook.com/wichitac2. See also Joe Stumpe, "Save Century II Founder Expands Watchdog Role," *Active Age*, January 1, 2023, https://theactiveage.com/century-ii-founder-expands-watchdog-role/. Building on the notoriety that she received in the fights over Century II and RLMP, Racette ran for mayor of Wichita in 2023, receiving nearly 7,000 votes, placing fourth in the primary election, and contributing to the defeat of incumbent Mayor Brandon Whipple.

31. Jon Ostrower, "It's Complicated: The Strained Union of Boeing and Spirit AeroSystems," *Air Current*, May 3, 2023, https://theaircurrent.com/industry-strategy/boeing-spirit-reintegration-ramp-up-special-report/. Spirit also established itself as a key supplier for Airbus, thereby expanding its portfolio and allowing it to grow its workforce.

32. Ostrower, "It's Complicated"; "Alaska Airlines to Offer Nonstop Flight from Wichita to Seattle," KWCH, August 3, 2016, https://www.kwch.com/content/news/Alaska-Airlines-Offers-Nonstop-to-Seattle-389063612.html.

33. Larry Fish, "Cessna Seeks Buffer Against Annexation," *Wichita Beacon*, February 2, 1979, 18B; Frank Garofalo, "City Expected to OK Pact on Annexing," *Wichita Eagle*, May 14, 1979, 1C; Frank Garofalo, "Boeing May Ask Wichita for Bonds," *Wichita Eagle*, October 16, 1979, 1B; City of Wichita, Legal Publication, Ordinance No 44–829. This ordinance can be read in *The Wichita Eagle*, December 23, 2000, 15A. See also City of Wichita, Minutes of the Meeting of the Wichita City Council, December 12, 2000, https://web.archive.org/web/20020513201513/http://wichita.gov/Minutes&Agendas/Councilmin00/text_files/12-12-2000Council_Minutes.txt.

34. Most people in Wichita are not familiar with the non-annexation agreements. When I raised the issue on social media in anticipation of the renewal of the non-annexation agreement with Spirit in 2021, it provoked immense debate about the benefits and costs of these agreements. See Chase Billingham, "Have you ever looked at a map of the City of Wichita," Facebook, December 4, 2021, https://www.facebook.com/chase.billingham/posts/pfbid02hqtQPtdpSM4gnGmA44Wei7VHdh81C8jv3MUyyuZQReASceUT51L5vBTx5dkTenFnl.

35. City of Wichita, Minutes of the Meeting of the Wichita City Council, December 9, 1997, https://web.archive.org/web/20020515075634/http://wichita.gov/Minutes&Agendas/Councilmin97/text_files/12-09-1997Council_Minutes.txt; employment data come from US Bureau of Labor Statistics and Federal Reserve Bank of St. Louis, All Employees: Manufacturing: Durable Goods: Aerospace Product and Parts Manufacturing in Wichita, KS (MSA), accessed July 7, 2025, https://fred.stlouisfed.org/series/SMU20486203133640001.

36. City of Wichita, Minutes of the Meeting of the Wichita City Council, December 7, 2021, https://www.wichita.gov/AgendaCenter/ViewFile/Minutes/_12072021-1949; Matthew Kelly, "Renewal Deal Means Spirit Won't Pay Property Taxes," *Wichita Eagle*, December 8, 2021, 1A.

37. City of Wichita, Non-annexation agreement with the Aerospace Industrial District of Sedgwick County, Kansas, December 7, 2021, https://legistarweb-production.s3.amazonaws.com/uploads/attachment/pdf/1161470/Aerospace_Industrial_District_2021_Non-Annexation_Agreement_with_Legals_Descriptions.pdf; Kelly, "Renewal Deal."

38. Ostrower, "It's Complicated."

39. Ostrower, "It's Complicated"; Chance Swaim, "CEO: Spirit AeroSystems to Add 1,400 Jobs in Wichita," *Wichita Eagle*, December 20, 2018, 1A.

40. Jeff Wise, "6 Minutes of Terror: What Passengers and Crew Experienced

Aboard Ethiopian Airlines Flight 302," *New York*, April 9, 2019, https://nymag.com/intelligencer/2019/04/what-passengers-experienced-on-the-ethiopian-airlines-flight.html.

41. For more information on the MCAS, its role in the MAX disasters, and the troubling lapse in FAA oversight in its implementation, see Jack Nicas, Natalie Kitroeff, David Gelles, and James Glanz, "Boeing Built Deadly Assumptions Into 737 Max, Blind to a Late Design Change," *New York Times*, June 1, 2019, https://www.nytimes.com/2019/06/01/business/boeing-737-max-crash.html; Natalie Kitroeff, David Gelles, and Jack Nicas, "The Roots of Boeing's 737 Max Crisis: A Regulator Relaxes Its Oversight," *New York Times*, July 27, 2019, https://www.nytimes.com/2019/07/27/business/boeing-737-max-faa.html.

42. Zeke Miller, Rob Gillies, and Amy Renee Leiker, "US Grounds Boeing 737 Max Aircraft After Ethiopia Crash," *Wichita Eagle*, March 14, 2019, 1A; Amy Renee Leiker and Associated Press, "Boeing Slows Production of 737 to Fix Flight Software," *Wichita Eagle*, April 6, 2019, 1A; Amy Renee Leiker, "737 Max Supplier Spirit Plans Belt-Tightening, Not Layoffs," *Wichita Eagle*, May 2, 2019, 1B.

43. Chance Swaim and Amy Renee Leiker, "Spirit AeroSystems Workers Face Reduced Hours, Pay After 737 Max Grounding," *Wichita Eagle*, June 8, 2019, 1A; Amy Renee Leiker, "Spirit: Revenue Up, 737 Max Production Steady," *Wichita Eagle*, August 1, 2019, 5A; Dion Lefler, "Tarp-Shrouded Planes Line Up at Spirit as 737 Max Stays Grounded," *Wichita Eagle*, October 4, 2019, 1A; David Gelles and Natalie Kitroeff, "Boeing to Temporarily Shut Down 737 Max Production," *New York Times*, December 16, 2019, https://www.nytimes.com/2019/12/16/business/boeing-737-max.html; Amy Renee Leiker and Dion Lefler, "Spirit AeroSystems Will Suspend Production of 737 Max Jets on Jan. 1," *Wichita Eagle*, December 21, 2019, 1A.

44. Chance Swaim, "Spirit Offering Buyouts amid Boeing 737 Max Problems," *Wichita Eagle*, January 7, 2020, 1A; Chance Swaim, "Spirit Will Lay Off 2,800 After Boeing 737 Max Work Halted," *Wichita Eagle*, January 11, 2020, 1A; Michael Stavola, "Textron Aviation Announces Layoffs, Mainly at Headquarters in Wichita," *Wichita Eagle*, December 6, 2019, 1A; *Wichita Eagle* Editorial Board, "737 Max Grounding Means Major Problems for Wichita Economy," *Wichita Eagle*, December 24, 2019, 7A; Jason Tidd, "Boeing 737 Max Production Halt in Wichita 'Was Not Our Fault,' County Commissioner Says," *Wichita Eagle*, January 16, 2020, https://www.kansas.com/news/business/aviation/article239331638.html.

45. Michael Stavola, "Free Classes Available for Laid-Off Aviation Employees," *Wichita Eagle*, February 8, 2020, 1A; Chance Swaim, "Report: 737 Crisis Will Hit Economy of Wichita Hard," *Wichita Eagle*, February 9, 2020, 2A. The

"Air Capital Commitment" resources website was still live in 2025, years after most of the offers to laid off employees had expired; it can be viewed at https://www.aircapitaloftheworld.com/commitment. The Wells Fargo report can be viewed at Mark Vitner, Charlie Dougherty, and Matthew Honnold, *The Regional Impact of the Boeing 737 Max Grounding* (Wells Fargo Securities, 2020), https://externalcontent.blob.core.windows.net/pdfs/boeing-regional-20200205.pdf.

46. Chance Swaim, "Spirit AeroSystems to Resume Work on Boeing Max in March," *Wichita Eagle*, February 29, 2020, 1A.

47. "CDC Museum COVID-19 Timeline," Centers for Disease Control, accessed June 24, 2025, https://www.cdc.gov/museum/timeline/covid19.html.

48. "COVID-19 Timeline of Events," Sedgwick County, Kansas, updated January 13, 2023, https://web.archive.org/web/20230607192445/https://www.sedgwickcounty.org/covid-19/covid-19-timeline-of-events/; Jason Tidd and Chance Swaim, "First Sedgwick County Presumptive-Positive Coronavirus Patient Is in Home Isolation," *Wichita Eagle*, https://www.kansas.com/news/coronavirus/article241357566.html; Dion Lefler, "Spirit Suspends Boeing Wichita Work Due to Coronavirus," *Wichita Eagle*, March 25, 2020, 10A; Dion Lefler and Chance Swaim, "Sedgwick County Placed Under Stay-at-Home Order," *Wichita Eagle*, March 25, 2020, 1A; Chance Swaim, "Spirit AeroSystems Plans Massive Furloughs, Shortened Work Weeks," *Wichita Eagle*, April 6, 2020, https://www.kansas.com/news/business/aviation/article241820116.html; Dion Lefler, "Textron Announces Furloughs for 7,000 Workers," *Wichita Eagle*, March 19, 2020, 1A.

49. Dion Lefler and Chance Swaim, "Spirit Recalls Some Workers Idled by Coronavirus, 737 Max," *Wichita Eagle*, April 17, 2020, 1A.

50. Chance Swaim, "Spirit AeroSystems Offering Voluntary Layoffs During Pandemic," *Wichita Eagle*, May 1, 2020, 8A; Michael Stavola, "Spirit AeroSystems in Wichita to Lay Off 1,450 Employees," *Wichita Eagle*, May 2, 2020, 4A; Chance Swaim, "Spirit, Vyaire Partner to Make Ventilators for Virus Patients," *Wichita Eagle*, May 5, 2020, 1A; Megan Stringer, "Spirit AeroSystems to Furlough About 900," *Wichita Eagle*, June 11, 2020, 4A; Megan Stringer, "Spirit AeroSystems Will Lay Off 450 More Wichita Workers," *Wichita Eagle*, July 31, 2020, https://www.kansas.com/news/business/aviation/article244646757.html.

51. Megan Stringer, "Is Diverse Economy Better for Laid-Off Workers?," *Wichita Eagle*, July 26, 2020, 1A; Tidd, "Boeing 737 Max Production Halt in Wichita 'Was Not Our Fault'"; Carrie Rengers, "Spirit Layoffs Will Hurt, but Experts Say There's Hope," *Wichita Eagle*, January 12, 2020, 1A.

52. Dominic Gates, "Boeing 737 MAX Can Return to the Skies, FAA Says," *Seattle Times*, November 18, 2020, https://www.seattletimes.com/business/boeing-aerospace/boeing-737-max-can-return-to-the-skies-says-faa/;

Megan Stringer, "Some Jobs in Wichita Could Rebound Faster Than Expected," *Wichita Eagle*, May 5, 2021, 1A; Matthew Kelly, "Spirit AeroSystems Reports 16% Drop in Revenue in First Quarter," *Wichita Eagle*, May 6, 2021, 4A; Megan Stringer, "Spirit Expects to Hire More than 4,600 Workers Through 2024 and Expand Facilities," *Wichita Eagle*, July 21, 2021, 10A; Matthew Kelly, "Rising Narrowbody Deliveries Drive Spirit's Q2 Revenue," *Wichita Eagle*, August 6, 2021, 7A; Megan Stringer, "Wichita-Area Aviation Manufacturers Get Federal Relief to Save Jobs," *Wichita Eagle*, September 15, 2021, 3A.

53. Michael Stavola, "Spirit AeroSystems Reports Q2 Losses, Hopes Wichita Mass Hiring Will Help with Production," *Wichita Eagle*, August 5, 2022, 5A; Matthew Kelly, "Spirit Reports Losses in 4th Quarter, Plans to Scale Back Positions," *Wichita Eagle*, February 8, 2023, 8A; Matthew Kelly, "Spirit AeroSystems Machinists Vote to Sanction Strike Option," *Wichita Eagle*, March 31, 2023, 7A.

54. Matthew Kelly, "Machinists Will Vote on New Spirit Contract Next Week," *Wichita Eagle*, June 18, 2023, 4A; Matthew Kelly, "Machinists Union Members Reject Contract, Vote to Strike," *Wichita Eagle*, June 23, 2023, 1A.

55. Matthew Kelly, "Mesh Fences, Mobile Headquarters Go Up as Machinists, Spirit AeroSystems Prep for Strike," *Wichita Eagle*, June 22, 2023, https://www.kansas.com/news/business/aviation/article276669941.html; Matthew Kelly, Michael Stavola, and Casey Loving, "WSU Economic Expert Weighs In on Strike," *Wichita Eagle*, June 25, 2023, 1A.

56. Matthew Kelly, "Striking Machinists to Vote on a New Contract Proposal from Spirit AeroSystems," *Wichita Eagle*, June 29, 2023, 2A; Matthew Kelly, "Machinists Approve Spirit AeroSystems Contract, End Strike," *Wichita Eagle*, July 1, 2023, 1A.

57. Ostrower, "It's Complicated"; Dominic Gates, "Boeing 737 Max Production Hit by a New Defect in Supplier Part," *Seattle Times*, April 13, 2023, https://www.seattletimes.com/business/boeing-aerospace/boeing-737-max-production-hit-by-a-new-defect-in-supplier-part/; Matthew Kelly, "Spirit AeroSystems Reports $281 Million in Q1 Losses," *Wichita Eagle*, May 4, 2023, 1A; Matthew Kelly, "What the Machinists Strike Means for Spirit AeroSystems' Finances, 737 MAX Deliveries," *Wichita Eagle*, August 3, 2023, 4A.

58. Stock quotes and other financial data for Spirit AeroSystems are drawn from the company's annual reports and other data available on its "Investor Relations" web page, accessed June 24, 2025, https://investor.spiritaero.com/corporate-profile/default.aspx, as well as from "Spirit AeroSystems Holdings, Inc. (SPR)," Yahoo! Finance, accessed June 24, 2025, https://finance.yahoo.com/quote/SPR/. For more information on Gentile's resignation, see Matthew Kelly, "Tom Gentile Resigns as CEO of Spirit AeroSystems," *Wichita Eagle*, October 3, 2023, 1A.

59. Dominic Gates, "Boeing Pumps Cash into Spirit AeroSystems to Shore Up Troubled Supplier," *Seattle Times*, October 18, 2023, https://www.seattletimes.com/business/boeing-aerospace/boeing-pumps-cash-into-spirit-aerosystems-to-shore-up-troubled-supplier/; Matthew Kelly, "Spirit AeroSystems Reports $204 Million Loss in Q3," *Wichita Eagle*, November 3, 2023, 1A.

60. John Yoon, Victoria Kim, Orlando Mayorquin, Niraj Chokshi, and Mark Walker, "F.A.A. Orders Airlines to Ground Some Boeing 737 Max 9 Jets After Midair 'Incident,'" *New York Times*, January 5, 2024, https://www.nytimes.com/2024/01/05/business/alaska-airlines-flight-portland-landing.html.

61. Patrick Malone, "With Boeing in Hot Seat, Claims Against Supplier Spirit AeroSystems Take Shape," *Seattle Times*, February 21, 2024, https://www.seattletimes.com/business/with-boeing-in-hot-seat-claims-against-supplier-spirit-aerosystems-take-shape/; Sydney Ember and Mark Walker, "Alaska Airlines 737 May Have Left Boeing Factory Missing Bolts, N.T.S.B. Says," *New York Times*, February 6, 2024, https://www.nytimes.com/2024/02/06/business/ntsb-boeing-alaska-airlines-report.html; Mark Walker, "F.A.A. Audit Finds Quality-Control Lapses at Boeing and Spirit AeroSystems," *New York Times*, March 4, 2024, https://www.nytimes.com/2024/03/04/us/politics/faa-boeing-737-max-audit.html; Matthew Kelly, "Federal Suit Clams Spirit AeroSystems Concealed Serious Defects," *Wichita Eagle*, January 16, 2024, 4A; Dominic Gates, "Boeing, Not Spirit, Mis-installed Piece That Blew Off Alaska Max 9 Jet, Industry Source Says," *Seattle Times*, January 24, 2024, https://www.seattletimes.com/business/boeing-aerospace/boeing-not-spirit-mis-installed-piece-that-blew-off-alaska-max-9-jet/; Dominic Gates, "Key Bolts Missing When Boeing Delivered Alaska Blowout Jet, NTSB Report Says," *Seattle Times*, February 6, 2024, https://www.seattletimes.com/business/boeing-aerospace/ntsb-report-on-alaska-flight-1282-says-key-bolts-missing-when-boeing-delivered-jet/.

62. Ostrower, "It's Complicated."

63. Niraj Chokshi and Sydney Ember, "Boeing in Talks to Buy Spirit AeroSystems, a Struggling Supplier," *New York Times*, March 1, 2024, https://www.nytimes.com/2024/03/01/business/boeing-spirit-aerosystems.html; John Hemmerdinger, "Boeing Might Still Finalise Spirit AeroSystems Acquisition by Mid-Year," *FlightGlobal*, May 23, 2024, https://www.flightglobal.com/airframers/boeing-might-still-finalise-spirit-aerosystems-acquisition-by-mid-year/158433.article.

64. Matthew Kelly, "Spirit AeroSystems Plans to Lay Off as Many as 450 Wichita Employees," *Wichita Eagle*, May 19, 2024, 4A.

65. Lily Wu, "Spirit AeroSystems, workers are essential to our city," Facebook, May 16, 2024, https://www.facebook.com/MayorLilyWu/posts/pfbid02c

hfBC3Z9kmPRKyg1XfSzfyB4qh6giJTRNr9TRLvqvdMx4y5tdQWuJ12XP1XMC2FNl.

66. City of Wichita, "Today council members attended the ribbon cutting for Air Capital Blvd," Facebook, May 22, 2024, https://www.facebook.com/cityofwichita/posts/pfbid02fR2jp68PY4vHvBS7cr1KQptRetEzKDY3TNzcyEvs9Erpa2bRA4A5SY5eRgDowMMtl.

Conclusion

1. *Vincennes Commercial*, March 11, 1887, 2.

2. Craig Miner, *Uncloistered Halls: The Centennial History of Wichita State University* (Wichita, KS: Wichita State University Endowment Association, 1995), 9.

3. Mike Davis, *City of Quartz: Excavating the Future in Los Angeles* (New York: Verso, 1990), 3, 84.

4. "#ILoveWichita," Wichita Regional Chamber of Commerce, accessed June 25, 2025, https://www.wichitachamber.org/main/welcome-to-wichita/. The All-America City Award is conferred upon a collection of US cities each year by the National Civic League, honoring "communities that leverage civic engagement, collaboration, inclusiveness and innovation to successfully address local issues." Wichita has won the award five times, though its first win came in 1961, not 1962, according to the National Civic League. See "All-America City Winners," National Civic League, accessed June 25, 2025, https://www.nationalcivicleague.org/america-city-award/past-winners/.

5. Jamie Peck, "Transatlantic City, Part 1: Conjunctural Urbanism," *Urban Studies* 54, no. 1 (2017): 12.

6. United States Conference of Mayors Business Council, *2024 Best Practices Report: Mayors and Business Driving Economic Growth* (Washington, DC: United States Conference of Mayors, 2024).

7. Gabriel Tarde, *The Laws of Imitation* (New York: Henry Holt, 1903), 323; Kyle Chayka, *Filterworld: How Algorithms Flattened Culture* (New York: Doubleday, 2024). The Tarde quotation is drawn from Chayka's book, where it appears on p. 90.

8. Chayka, *Filterworld*, 89.

9. Sarah Barns, "Smart Cities and Urban Data Platforms: Designing Interfaces for Smart Governance," *City, Culture and Society* 12 (2018): 5–12; Sarah Barns, *Platform Urbanism: Negotiating Platform Ecosystems in Connected Cities* (Singapore: Palgrave Macmillan, 2018); Matt Patterson, "Scoreboard Urbanism: Theorizing Mental Life in the Digitally Mediated Metropolis," *City & Community* 23, no. 1 (2024): 26–46. See also David A. Banks, *The City Authentic: How*

the Attention Economy Builds Urban American (Berkeley: University of California Press, 2023).

10. Roy Wenzl, "Analyst Presents Sobering View of Wichita Economy, Community," *Wichita Eagle*, September 23, 2015, 1A. Details on Chung's "four challenges" can be found at "The Four Challenges," The Chung Report, July 28, 2016, https://thechungreport.com/the-four-challenges/.

11. Corie Brown, "A Tale of 2 Cities in the Midwest," *Los Angeles Times*, July 5, 2020, A1; Wichita Foundation, "Focus Forward 2018," YouTube, 1:16:34, youtu.be./dP9A0NtKzqo.

12. Brent D. Wistrom and Dion Lefler, "Tax Cuts, No Talks," *Wichita Eagle*, May 10, 2012, 1A; Daniel R. Alvord, "What Matters to Kansas: Small Business and the Defeat of the Kansas Tax Experiment," *Politics & Society* 48, no. 1 (2020): 27–66.

13. The city boasts of its property tax rate consistency in the annual budget, writing in the 2024–25 adopted city budget, for instance, that "for the past thirty years, the City of Wichita mill levy rate has not increased when each budget was adopted." See City of Wichita, *2024–2025 Adopted Budget* (Wichita, KS: 2025), https://www.wichita.gov/DocumentCenter/View/22598/2024–2025-Adopted-Budget-PDF. I have written and spoken extensively about the poor quality of public transportation in Wichita and its consequences for social and racial equity. In 2021, as part of the "Rethinking Wichita" colloquium held at Friends University with the noted urban planner Charles Marohn, I delivered a lecture titled "Rethinking Wichita's Mobility Paradigm." This presentation can be viewed at Chase M. Billingham, "Rethinking Wichita's Mobility Paradigm," Friends University IT Media Services, YouTube, 1:38:22, youtu.be/hYm6GEfHDh8. See also my four-part series of columns published in *The Wichita Eagle* in 2019 about public transportation in Wichita. Chase M. Billingham, "Can Wichita's Public Transportation System Be Saved?," *Wichita Eagle*, September 10, 2019, 7A; Chase M. Billingham, "Wichita Needs to Take Its Transit Reform Cues from the Q," *Wichita Eagle*, September 11, 2019, 9A; Chase M. Billingham, "Wichita Spends Far Less on Public Transportation Than Its Peers—That Has to Change," *Wichita Eagle*, September 12, 2019, 9A; Chase M. Billingham, "Fix for Wichita's Transit Issues Will Not Be Politically Popular," *Wichita Eagle*, September 13, 2019, 9A.

14. Wichita created the office of city manager in 1917. As in many other regions of the US, Kansas municipalities embraced professional city administration in the early twentieth century in an effort to root out corruption and promote "good government" during a period in which urban centers were growing and becoming more ethnically diverse with influxes of new immigrant

populations. For decades, the office of mayor was a temporary ceremonial position rotated among the various elected members of the city commission. Following reforms to the city government, the office of mayor was strengthened somewhat in the 1980s, as the mayor became a separate position elected citywide. Still, the mayor remains simply the first among equals of the members of the city council, with few unique powers and privileges and virtually no executive authority. See H. Edward Flentje and Chase M. Billingham, "The Political Roots of City Managers in Kansas," *Kansas History: A Journal of the Central Plains* 47, no. 3 (2024): 178–201; Craig Miner, *Wichita: The Magic City* (Wichita, KS: Wichita-Sedgwick County Historical Museum Association, 1988).

15. On the arena sales tax referendum and other major sports-related development projects in Wichita, see Kallie Kimble, "Searching for the 'Crown Jewel': A Qualitative Examination of the Utilization of Multi-Use Sports Venues for Downtown Redevelopment in Wichita, KS" (master's thesis, Wichita State University, 2019).

16. On the power of conservative politics in the region, see Thomas Frank, *What's the Matter with Kansas? How Conservatives Won the Heart of America* (New York: Henry Holt, 2004); Alvord, "What Matters to Kansas." For more information on the specific contributions of the Koch family to the region, see Daniel Schulman, *Sons of Wichita: How the Koch Brothers Became America's Most Powerful and Private Dynasty* (New York: Grand Central, 2014); Jane Mayer, *Dark Money: The Hidden History of the Billionaires Behind the Rise of the Radical Right* (New York: Doubleday, 2016); Brown, "A Tale of 2 Cities in the Midwest." The mission statement of the Kansas Policy Institute can be found at "Vision, Mission and History," Kansas Policy Institute, accessed June 26, 2025, https://kansaspolicy.org/about/.

17. On the debates over the driving forces behind gentrification, see Sharon Zukin, "Gentrification: Culture and Capital in the Urban Core," *Annual Review of Sociology* 13 (1987): 129–147; Japonica Brown-Saracino, ed., *The Gentrification Debates* (New York: Routledge, 2010); Japonica Brown-Saracino, "Explicating Divided Approaches to Gentrification and Growing Income Inequality," *Annual Review of Sociology* 43 (2017): 515–539; Chase M. Billingham and Shelley McDonough Kimelberg, "Middle-Class Parents, Urban Schooling, and the Shift from Consumption to Production of Urban Space," *Sociological Forum* 28, no. 1 (2013): 85–108; Chase M. Billingham, "The Broadening Conception of Gentrification: Recent Developments and Avenues for Future Inquiry in the Sociological Study of Urban Change," *Michigan Sociological Review* 29 (2015): 75–102.

18. Megan Stringer, "Computer Security Company Opening, Hiring," *Wichita*

Eagle, February 26, 2021, 1A; Chance Swaim and Katie Bernard, "$1.8B Integra Investment Means 2,000 Jobs, Needs CHIP Funding," *Wichita Eagle*, February 5, 2023, 1A.

19. Megan Stringer, "Permanent Remote Work May Help Wichita Keep, Attract Population," *Wichita Eagle*, March 28, 2021, 1A. Ocejo's work on Newburgh has been published in a series of journal articles in recent years and brought together in his insightful book examining the motivations of gentrifiers in that city, most of whom relocated after being priced out of or generally exhausted with life in New York City. See Richard E. Ocejo, *Sixty Miles Upriver: Gentrification and Race in a Small American City* (Princeton, NJ: Princeton University Press, 2024).

20. Jean Barnes, "Koch Engineering Will Build Manufacturing Plant and Office Complex," *Wichita Eagle*, June 25, 1967, 1C; Lew Townsend, "URA to Pay $461,000 for Koch Office Building," *Wichita Eagle*, March 29, 1968, 1A; Michael E. Porter, *Wichita: Clusters of Innovation Initiative* (Washington, DC: Council on Competitiveness, 2001); Dolores Quinlisk, "Downtown or Suburbs?," *Wichita Eagle and Beacon*, December 7, 1975, 1D; Jennifer Comes, "McCray Seeks Visible Support from Business for Downtown," *Wichita Eagle*, March 12, 1992, 1D.

21. On the "three T's" (talent, technology, and tolerance), which I previously discussed in chapter 1, see Richard Florida, *The Rise of the Creative Class: And How It's Transforming Work, Leisure, Community and Everyday Life* (New York: Basic Books, 2003); Richard Florida, "Cities and the Creative Class," *City & Community* 2, no. 1 (2003): 3–19. Downtown population data are drawn from the US Census Bureau, American Community Survey, five-year estimates between 2014 and 2024. Zip code 67202 is the geographic area utilized by Downtown Wichita to approximate the boundaries of the city core, accessed June 26, 2025, https://data.census.gov/table?q=population%2067202.

22. Chase M. Billingham, "Waiting for Bobos: Displacement and Impeded Gentrification in a Midwestern City," *City & Community* 16, no. 2 (2017): 145–168; Chase M. Billingham, "The State, the School, and the Family in the Gentrification of the American City" (PhD diss., Northeastern University, 2013); Billingham, "Broadening Conception of Gentrification."

23. Matthew Kelly, "Free Public Parking? You'll See a Lot Fewer Spots in Downtown Wichita Next Year," *Wichita Eagle*, June 22, 2024, https://www.kansas.com/news/politics-government/article289269895.html. For more details on automotive culture in Wichita, see Rami Toubia Stucky, "'Join the Parade to the Future': Automatic Car Washes in Wichita, 1920–1970," *Kansas History: A Journal of the Central Plains* 45, no. 4 (2022–23): 246–263.

24. Carrie Rengers, "Wichita Isn't Boring, but How About That Bumper Sticker?," *Wichita Eagle*, December 7, 2016, https://www.kansas.com/news/bu

siness/biz-columns-blogs/carrie-rengers/article119252998.html. Political scientist and urban theorist Russell Fox, who has written extensively about the dilemmas facing Wichita, makes a similar point when he draws attention to a billboard erected early in the century that bluntly informed local motorists, "Face it. You're in Wichita." See Russell Arben Fox, "Mid-Sized Meditations #3: Seeing Our (Non-Cosmopolitan) Selves," September 29, 2014, https://mittelpolitan.substack.com/p/mid-sized-meditations-3-seeing-our-non.

25. In Wichita, to take just one example, dispelling those inferiority concerns was a critical motivator for the city and state governments in offering millions of dollars in public incentives to secure the construction of a branch of the Topgolf recreation destination outlet. Accessing this chain of destination golf driving ranges, they surmised, had come to be an expectation of business travelers, and boasting a Topgolf location created "an opportunity for us to expose Wichita to individuals who may have never been to Wichita, or may have had a certain idea about Wichita," according to the city's assistant city manager and economic development chief. See Matthew Kelly, "Wichita's Proposed $25.9 million Topgolf Would Get $10.2 Million in State Incentives," *Wichita Eagle*, May 29, 2021, https://www.kansas.com/news/business/article251738958.html.

26. Florida, "Cities and the Creative Class." The classic statement on the rise of entrepreneurialism in urban governance is David Harvey, "From Managerialism to Entrepreneurialism: The Transformation in Urban Governance in Late Capitalism," *Geografiska Annaler* 71, no. 1 (1989): 3–17. See also Jason Hackworth, *The Neoliberal City: Governance, Ideology, and Development in American Urbanism* (Ithaca, NY: Cornell University Press, 2007).

27. Porter, *Wichita*, 116–121.

28. Miner, *Wichita: The Magic City*, 213; Jim Cross, "Ante Is High, Cards Are on the Table, DeBoer Says," *Wichita Eagle*, May 24, 1990, 1A; Stringer, "Permanent Remote Work."

29. My arguments here echo points made by many other sociologists, urban analysts, and activists. See especially Eric Klinenberg, *Palaces for the People: How Social Infrastructure Can Help Fight Inequality, Polarization, and the Decline of Civic Life* (New York: Crown, 2018), from which I have drawn the term "social infrastructure."

30. Erik Olin Wright, *Envisioning Real Utopias* (2008), 268, https://web.archive.org/web/20210414114403/https://www.ssc.wisc.edu/~wright/ERU.htm.

INDEX

Page numbers in italics refer to images.

www.ingramcontent.com/pod-product-compliance
Lightning Source LLC
Chambersburg PA
CBHW020502270326
41926CB00008B/704

* 9 7 8 0 7 0 0 6 4 0 9 2 8 *